A Shearwater Book

Scorched Earth

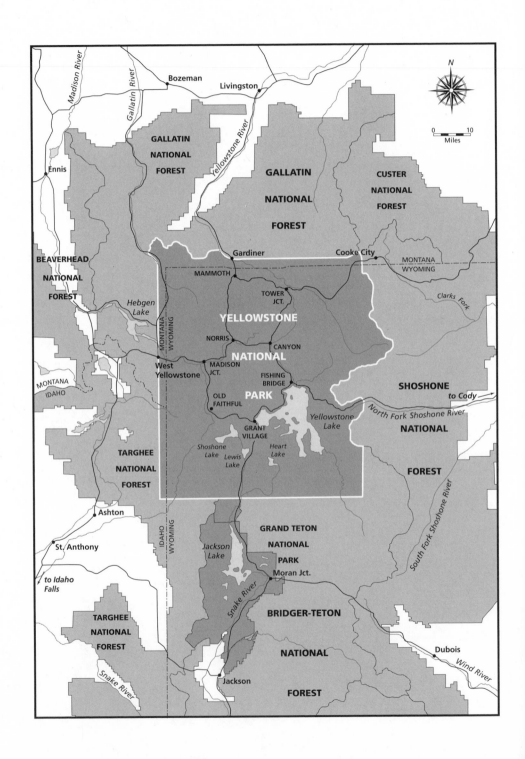

Scorched Earth

How the Fires of Yellowstone Changed America

Rocky Barker

ISLANDPRESS

Island Press / Shearwater Books
Washington • Covelo • London

A Shearwater Book
Published by Island Press

Shearwater Books is a trademark of
The Center for Resource Economics.

Library of Congress Cataloging-in-Publication data.

Barker, Rocky.

Scorched earth : how the fires of Yellowstone changed America / Rocky Barker.

    p. cm.

Includes bibliographical references and index.

ISBN 1-55963-735-8 (cloth : alk. paper)

1. Forest fires—Yellowstone National Park—Prevention and control. 2. Forest fires—Government policy—Yellowstone National Park. 3. Fire ecology—Yellowstone National Park. 4. Environmental policy—United States. 5. Yellowstone National Park. I. Title.

SD421.32.Y45B37 2005

634.9'618'0978752—dc22

2005017199

British Cataloguing-in-Publication data available.

Printed on recycled, acid-free paper

Design by Joyce C. Weston

Manufactured in the United States of America

10 9 8 7 6 5 4 3 2 1

This book is dedicated to J. Robb Brady.
His dedication to earth and humanity is second to none.

~ • ~

Contents

Prologue: September 7, 1988

All welcome the show with enthusiasm, and shout "Oh, how wonderful, beautiful, splendid, majestic!"

—John Muir, after a trip to Old Faithful in 1901

IT WAS STILL DARK when the first sleepy-eyed guests appeared in the cathedral lobby of the Old Faithful Inn. They lined up for coffee from two large silver cylinders. Next to the stone fireplace, a sign shaped like a clock with magnetic numbers read: "Next eruption: 6:20 a.m., plus or minus 10 minutes." Chatting in French, German, and various accents of English, these early risers migrated from the inn onto the deserted boardwalk, which snaked south a hundred yards and circled the smoking crater. They were hoping to catch sight of the famous geyser in its most natural state, with the colorful sunrise as backdrop. A few wisps of smoke hung at eye level, but the sky was denim blue.

Old Faithful is one of the nation's most popular natural attractions. Twenty-five percent of Americans will visit the area sometime in their lives, and every year nearly three million people witness its column of superheated water rise 180 feet into the air. Old Faithful is the iconic symbol of Yellowstone, the world's first national park, established in 1872. For most people, a trip to Yellowstone is a pilgrimage wrapped in memories of family vacations, going back generations. The geyser is surrounded by boardwalks, camera shops, ice cream stands, general stores, two hotels, and acres of paved parking lots. Across a barren landscape of white volcanic crust sits the venerable Old Faithful Inn. Completed in 1904 and copied throughout the National Park system, it is one of the world's largest log structures, at 79 feet high, 800 feet long, and with nearly 400 rooms. Its tapestry of lodgepole pine beams, native rhyolite rock, and gnarled wood railings fits perfectly into Yellowstone's natural setting.

September 7, 1988, was not a typical morning in paradise, however. Shortly after 7 a.m., a dozen bellmen fanned out across the inn, knocking on doors and telling the guests who were still in their rooms that they had to leave immediately. Less than five miles to the west, the North Fork fire, named for the little creek near where a logger's cigarette started it, was stirring again. The blaze had already consumed more than 200,000 acres of the 2.2-million-acre park and had threatened Old Faithful once before, in July. But now, with a patchwork of fire covering an area larger than the state of Delaware in and around the park, firefighters could no longer hold the line. As the humidity dropped through the morning, the blaze would grow from a series of smoldering ground fires into a racing crown fire bearing down on Old Faithful. Tour buses were lining up to evacuate not only guests but the Old Faithful village's seasonal workers as well.

This was just the scene that park managers had been dreading all summer as dozens of fires burned through sections of the park. The fires that lightning had started in June had been allowed to burn until mid-July. By then high winds had spread the blazes across the park, forcing officials to move tourists out of visitor villages on Yellowstone Lake and adjacent to its famous grand canyon thirty miles northeast of Old Faithful. On what later would be called "Black Saturday," 165,000 acres had burned in the park within a twenty-four-hour period. Giant mushroom-shaped clouds rose into the atmosphere, making it seem as if the area were under nuclear attack. National Park Service officials had called in more than 9,400 firefighters, the largest firefighting force ever assembled to date in one place. And now, on September 7, Old Faithful, the crown jewel of Yellowstone and the national park system, lay directly in the path of the inferno.

The orange sunset from the night before had been reminiscent of one of the great nineteenth-century paintings of Thomas Moran, the Hudson River School painter whose work depicting the region influenced Congress to declare Yellowstone a national treasure. Smoke mingling with the geyser's steam created a scene that was both eerie and beautiful. But the clear blue morning was unexpected. It was as if the visitors, the workers, and the firefighters were caught in the eye of a storm.

A herd of television satellite trucks moved into the parking lot that morning beginning at 9 a.m., preparing to send images of the fire out live for the evening news. Since late July the national media had swarmed to the park to report on a forest fire like none seen for generations. Not since 1910 had forest fires threatened such a large swath of the American West. Now the American public was being haltingly introduced to an important and long-standing debate within the science and conservation community over the role of fire in forests. In the years immediately running up to 1988 this debate had expanded into a larger discussion about the need to protect and restore natural processes over large landscapes worldwide. Yellowstone had become the focus of this debate, returning it to the center of conservation policy as it had been at the dawn of the movement in the late nineteenth century. But the complexities and long-term importance of the issue were lost in the disturbing video of the nation's sacred national park burning up.

More than 1,000 workers and guests were evacuated by noon. But, incredibly, no sooner did they leave than 1,200 new visitors were allowed to stream in to watch Old Faithful. Under pressure from senators Alan Simpson and Malcolm Wallop of Wyoming, Yellowstone Superintendent Robert Barbee had kept the park open. The senators and Barbee were hoping that the rain and cooler weather that usually arrived in early September would moderate the fires. Instead, the fires were generating their own weather, sucking the oxygen from the air and producing gale-force winds. Giant convection clouds would collapse into the fire cores, creating furnaces that would blow over the landscape.

Firefighters were already setting up hoses around the inn and digging fire lines along the area's perimeter. They were aided by 120 U.S. Army troops who had spent several days clearing away natural kindling near offices, cabins, shops, and dormitories to reduce their flammability when the fire came.

THIS WASN'T the first time the army had come galloping to the park's rescue. In fact, the army had played a pivotal role in the initial preservation of Yellowstone and, more surprisingly, in the evolution of the nation's conservation policies. The force behind the army's little-known formative role was Civil War General Phil Sheridan. This unlikely conservation pioneer was best known for his daring and brutal leadership of Union troops during the bloody last days of the war. After the war he used the same fierce tactics to bring American Indian tribes to heel, nearly sending the bison on which they depended into extinction. Yet a chance meeting in 1870 with a mountain man familiar with the wonders of Yellowstone turned the hunter and former ornithologist into one of the park's leading advocates.

Sheridan sent army escorts on the explorations that led Congress to protect the region from development. Later, he fought the Northern Pacific Railroad's effort to monopolize the park. He called for expansion of its boundaries to include the entire habitat of the park's big game, leading a movement for what was then called "Greater Yellowstone." When Congress cut off all Yellowstone funding and was prepared to end its preservation, Sheridan sent in the cavalry. On August 20, 1886, Moses Harris—awarded a Medal of Honor for his role in Sheridan's Civil War campaign—led troops into the park where forest fires had been raging for months. Captain Harris ordered his men to battle the flames, beginning the federal government's role in forest fire control.

It was Harris and his successors at Yellowstone who developed the firefighting strategies and tactics that were used September 7 and are still used today. The army system called for coordinated fire prevention efforts, a series of fire lookouts, and lightning-quick response to fire outbreaks. Army rangers also introduced the idea of public campgrounds to control visitors' campfires. The army's early success in firefighting convinced a National Academy of Sciences panel in 1897 to recommend expanding the role of the federal government in preservation of public lands. Thanks in no small part to the army's success, more than 600 million acres of wildlands remain today in the public domain. Conservation of land and federal control of it became one and the same in the minds of many reformers. But the soldiers' example also convinced managers they could control fire by eliminating it from the forest. On September 7 Park Superintendent Barbee and other fire managers knew the fire that time, however, was no longer in their control. All they could hope to do was protect the public and save places like the inn.

At noon, three giant clouds of smoke could be seen rising above the tree line as a finger of the North Fork fire churned itself into action. For the first time that day, dark smoke drifted over the geyser basin. Though they had taken the precaution of evacuating the inn, fire officials had at first been confident they would have another day before an assault on Old Faithful took place, but now they knew the fire was soon upon them.

Shortly after 3 p.m. a sparse crowd began filling the benches around the geyser. Steam puffed out of the geyser hole, the familiar smell of rotten eggs in the air. With a dull roar, the column of water rose intermittently until it reached its full height at exactly 3:30 p.m. It spread into a cloud of droplets and steam, forming a brief rainbow, and then splashed to the ground. As the geyser's waters trickled over the white crust, ash began to rain down from the sky. Off to the west, an air tanker came in low and dropped a slurry of magenta retardant on a hillside less than a mile west of the geyser. Sharp tongues of flame appeared out of the black smoke as the North Fork fire crested the western ridge.

In the parking lot, the last of the seasonal employees were sitting on the roof of a bus that was going to take them to safety. Most were shaggy-haired college kids in t-shirts and shorts, guzzling beer as if they were at a Grateful Dead concert. When the flames shot above the southwestern tree line, they cheered wildly, and the fire roared back like a tornado.

Dennis Bungarz, the U.S. Forest Service fire boss reacted quite differently to the sight. He was in charge of the 1,200 firefighters battling fires in the area from Old Faithful to West Yellowstone. He opened the trunk of his car, pulled out a protective fire shelter, and clipped it on his belt. The shelter was a metallic tent he could hide under in the event the fire overran him. Bungarz knew his team wasn't winning. He wanted to be prepared for the worst.

At the moment, it seemed the fire might skirt the southern edge of the geyser basin and miss all of Old Faithful's 400 buildings. Fire crews began watering down the historic Hamilton General Store and the gas station on the southern edge of the resort. A newly installed sprinkler system shot water over the inn's cedar shake roof. In the distance, firefighters moved up the southern ridge to start a backfire. But they abandoned the idea when it became clear that a wind shift would trap them between the main fire and their back burn.

Then the wind did shift and pick up speed, the smoky head of the fire advancing straight for the geyser. Wind gusts of eighty miles per hour began pulling leaves and pine needles into the fire's core, sucking all the oxygen out of the air. Anyone close to the fire began to choke. The firestorm struck terror into everyone in its path. It was only 4:15 p.m., but a smoky darkness had descended on the basin, and embers the size of bowling balls tumbled through the parking lots.

Jack Ward Thomas, an elk biologist with the U.S. Forest Service, had come to Old Faithful to witness preparations for fighting the fire. The gruff Texan was often the lone advocate for wildlife conservation in a room full of foresters, working in an agency focused on cutting timber instead of managing nature. Over the next four years he would lead a team of scientists whose reports on the endangered northern spotted owl would all but end the harvest of old-growth trees in national forests. In 1993, President Bill Clinton tapped him for the job of U.S. Forest Service chief, where, as its leader, he would put into place a management plan expanding on Sheridan's notion of a Greater Yellowstone. His plan would make preserving habitat, water quality, and the relationships among soil, plants, and animals as important as meeting human needs.

When it came to fighting forest fires, though, Thomas was out of his element. He'd dug a few fire lines in his career, but his experience with fire was limited. Little did he know that fires and fire policy would steer his future as he would reshape the future of public land management. Yellowstone's 1988 fires would be only the first of more than a decade of giant fires that would force the nation to rethink its ideas about controlling nature and people. Six years later, Thomas would find himself standing at the base of Storm King Mountain in Glenwood Springs, Colorado, waiting for word on fourteen dead firefighters, several under his command, wondering if putting men and women in front of such blazes made any sense. When the firestorm hit Old Faithful, however, he was flat on his stomach trying to survive.

At park headquarters in Mammoth Hot Springs, thirty-five miles north of Old Faithful, Yellowstone's managers and scientists were facing a different kind of firestorm. Ecologist Don Despain, the man most responsible for creating Yellowstone's natural fire policy, was evacuating his family. The policy encouraged managers to allow fires to burn when started by lightning and was at the heart of the National Park Service's twenty-year-old policy for restoring natural processes to the parks. Earlier that summer Despain had predicted that the fires would grow no larger than 40,000 acres. Now they approached 1 million. The nation's top fire behaviorists had thought that any fire in Yellowstone would either run out of fuel or be extinguished by rain by the end of August, and they had based their forecasts on Despain's research.

In the weeks leading up to September 7, Despain, Yellowstone Superintendent Robert Barbee, and National Park Service Director William Penn Mott endured the harshest criticism of their lives. They were accused of not doing enough to stop the fires because they had allowed the fires to burn, as recommended by Despain. Despain's words, "Burn, baby, burn," taken out of context, were plastered across the front page of the *Denver Post* in August as evidence that park officials favored burning down all of Yellowstone's forests. Residents of West Yellowstone had raised a banner calling the fire a "Barbee-que," and the *Billings Gazette* ran a cartoon with burning teddy bears called "Barbee Dolls."

Barbee, a former army officer, never took the criticism personally. In full gray and green uniform, he personified the National Park Service image of professionalism. Even if he couldn't control the fires, the press, or the public's reaction, he had learned how to keep his critics at bay, as long as he could protect Old Faithful.

He knew that Yellowstone's forests, rangelands, and animals had all evolved in the context of periodic fires. Restoring fire to the park would thus help restore and protect its ecological health. This idea had been gaining ground in recent decades, inspired in part by the work of Aldo Leopold, himself a reformed product of the fire control fraternity and who earlier in the century had developed an overarching ecological view of the land and what was needed for its long-term health. Barbee and others began experimenting with controlled burning in the 1960s to restore periodic fire to western forests, where it had been largely eliminated by the national policy of suppression first instituted by the army in this very location. Barbee and the scientists who supported the natural-fire view found themselves fighting a long, and still strong, tradition of fire suppression policy, however. Smokey Bear, perhaps the most effective advertising symbol ever created, had been emphasizing the need to stop forest fires for nearly fifty years. Meanwhile, the modern environmental movement, born in the late 1960s, was transforming the very idea of conservation. The new movement was in part inspired by Aldo Leopold, who advocated a land ethic based on the idea that we are all ultimately part of a larger community—not just of each other but of plants, animals, and even soil—and by others who argued that human attempts to dominate nature could well have a dark underside.

By the 1980s, the effects and limits of human control over nature were becoming ever more apparent. Dams were killing off entire runs of salmon. Rivers diverted into channels were destroying wetlands' ability to absorb floodwaters. Despite discussion of these consequences, the public still viewed forest fires as different. Managers clung to the belief that these destructive events could be controlled if enough people and materiel were brought to bear. Battling forest fires was like going into an all-out war against a foreign invader.

Nowhere were these clashes of values over the control of nature more apparent than in Yellowstone, perhaps the best-known international symbol of preservation values. Barbee and Despain were implementing a new philosophy to preserve the natural ecological processes with as little human interference as possible. Yet they discovered that the desire to protect scenic nature was so strong that few people were willing to let go.

The fires of 1988 tested America's ideas about wilderness, about fire, and about our relationship to nature. The sweep of environmental history had returned to the place where federal land preservation was born out of fire. Now, with millions of Americans watching live as Old

Faithful burned, the fate of a century of nature protection dating back to the days of Phil Sheridan was on the line. The fate of the inn and Robert Barbee's values had become inexorably tied.

The remarkable journey that led from the Civil War to Old Faithful in 1988 and on to today began on the stage road to Helena, Montana, with the chance meeting of Phil Sheridan and a crusty old mountain man. Conservation's series of events, achievements, and grassroots movements would lead in and out of Yellowstone for more than one hundred years, tempered by fires and shaped by the conflicts of both friends and foes.

CHAPTER 1

The General

With foam and with dust the black charger was gray;
By the flash of his eye, and his red nostril's play,
He seemed to the whole great army to say:
"I have brought you Sheridan all the way
From Winchester down to save the day."
—Thomas Buchanan Read, 1871

THE GILMER AND SALISBURY stage rolled north out of the shanty and tent town of Corrine, Utah, on May 13, 1870. It was carrying cargo more valuable than the mail and payrolls for Montana miners that were its usual fare. General Philip H. Sheridan, the feisty former cavalry commander, known as "Little Phil," was aboard after a long trip west on the Union Pacific Railroad. In the five years following the Civil War, Sheridan had already become an American legend. Along with William Tecumseh Sherman and Ulysses S. Grant, now the nation's president, he was one of the war's top three hero generals. He won the last major battle of the war, defeated cavalry genius Jeb Stuart, and led the Union's successful Shenandoah Valley campaign. His famous ride from Winchester, Virginia, to rally his troops to victory at Cedar Creek in 1864 would become the subject of a popular poem, recited by schoolchildren. He was honored and feted in the North, hated in the South because of his harsh policies during Reconstruction, and feared by American Indians in the West for his brutal winter attacks on women and children.

In 1870, Sheridan was in the midst of the federal government's war to subjugate western American Indian tribes and tame the frontier for settlement. He had ridden west to tour the forts in his vast command that stretched from the Rio Grande to Canada and west from Chicago. Corrine was a wide-open gentile shantytown amidst Brigham Young's Mormon-controlled Utah. The Golden Spike had been sunk only a year before, linking America's eastern and western shores by railroad. Corrine was the junction between the railroad and the Montana Road, which ran to the mining boomtowns of Bannack, Virginia City, and Helena, Montana. Sheridan's ride west had been by rail and in relative comfort up to now. He even got hold of a newspaper from back east that reported the outbreak of the Franco-Prussian War. The old warrior reacted to the news like a Dalmatian hearing a fire alarm. He started making plans for a trip to Europe to observe the first big war since his own glory days. But first he had commitments in Montana that could not be ignored.

Sheridan's five-hundred-mile journey carried him over the Cache Mountains, through Idaho's sagebrush desert, atop the high mountain passes of the Continental Divide, and finally through deep river canyons to Helena. Scenic as it was, a trip by stage in 1870 was arduous beyond any traveler's experience today. The six-horse teams pulled the two-seated, springless carriages ten to twelve miles per hour at top speed over rough, rocky roads. In the spring the dust turned to mud, and tiny stream crossings turned into mud wallows.

Sheridan stopped late in the second day at the Pleasant Valley stage station—as it would turn out, just thirty miles west of today's Yellowstone National Park. His party stayed only long enough for the driver to change the horses and check out the wheels and harnesses. Normally the stage drove straight through, a sixty-six-hour journey that could bust the strongest of kidneys. Sheridan wanted none of that. The bachelor general knew he would have full days and nights when he arrived in Helena, and he wanted a good night's sleep before his arrival. His staff negotiated a deal that allowed them to commandeer the stage for Sheridan and his entourage so he could insist on an overnight stop.

Late on the third day, the stage stopped for the night at a station near Parsons Bridge on the Jefferson River in Montana. There Sheridan and his road-weary crew met "an old mountaineer" named Atkinson, who had traveled widely through the Rocky Mountains. This chance frontier meeting would have a profound effect on the future of public land management and, later, the environmental movement. The mountain man regaled Sheridan with tales of a place of almost supernatural sensation where hot spouting springs gushed straight out of the ground a hundred feet in the air. Atkinson described boiling mud pots cooking red and yellow clays and volcanoes that sputtered mud and boiling water as they roared out of the side of mountains. This mysterious high-mountain locale, it was said, had fields of lime surrounded by meadows of wildflowers enveloping prismatic springs of sapphire and robin-egg-blue bubbling ponds. There were black glass mountains and petrified forests of solid quartz too. Such tales had been passed regularly among the trappers and explorers of the West for nearly sixty years. But the stories, often exaggerated, had yet to reach eastern circles as anything more than folk tales and rumors.

You can almost see Sheridan, an avid hunter and former ornithologist, leaning closer as Atkinson told of large game herds in that place protected from the settlers who were moving West by its high elevation and hard winters. The stories were so fascinating to Sheridan that he forgot the Franco-Prussian War for the moment and yearned to learn more. "His information was very indefinite, mostly second-hand," Sheridan would report in his memoirs.[1]

From that night to his death, Sheridan was to devote himself to the exploration and then preservation of the region that would soon become Yellowstone National Park. When historians talk about the great conservation figures in the nineteenth century, they talk about John Muir, who championed Yosemite National Park; Gifford Pinchot, who created the U.S. Forest Service; and perhaps George Bird Grinnell, a friend and protégé of Sheridan's who fought for Yellowstone and Glacier national parks and started the Audubon Society. Almost never mentioned is Sheridan.

Sheridan made his name in the Civil War with a scorched-earth campaign through Virginia's Shenandoah Valley to wipe out the Confederacy's last hope. And he's known for his leading role in the war against western American Indian tribes, encouraging the near-extinction of the bison to bring the tribes to heel. Yet, though rarely recognized today, he also became one of the most effective voices for protecting Yellowstone National Park's geologic wonders and wildlife. Sheridan's campaign against monopoly control of the park's resources by the Northern Pacific Railroad would save the park and help to inspire the budding preservation movement. His crusade was one of the precursors to the twentieth century's progressive movement. And Sheridan's view that a strong federal government was necessary to carry on preservation and conservation grew into the model that dominated thinking on the subject for a century. It was, in fact, Sheridan who first created a vision of a Greater Yellowstone, the idea of including important wildlife habitat beyond its borders. This was the seed upon which landscape or ecosystem management was developed, a concept that inspires environmental thought today worldwide.[2]

Sheridan stood five feet five inches tall and had a thick neck, long arms, short legs, and dark, shining hair. American Indians who negotiated with him in Kansas said he looked like an angry bear. To his troopers in the Civil War he was a beloved leader, a small town everyman whose Irish grit pushed him, and them, through every obstacle. His own motivations for saving Yellowstone would be many and by no means simply altruistic. Sheridan's worldview was shaped in the rural Irish Catholic immigrant home of his parents and tempered on the battlefield. He was born the third of six children on March 6, 1831, but no one knows for sure where. His parents, John and Mary Sheridan, came to the United States from Ireland around that time, and Sheridan eventually claimed Albany, New York, as his birthplace, though his mother said he was born on the ship from Ireland. His parents settled in Somerset, Ohio, then a town of one thousand people. His father became a building contractor, first on the Cumberland Road, and then on canals and roads throughout Ohio, which kept him away for much of Phil's childhood.

His mother, a strong quiet woman, taught Sheridan the virtues of honesty and hard work and raised him in the values of the Catholic Church. Sheridan himself became deeply patriotic at an early age. A boyhood friend recalled Sheridan watching an old Revolutionary War veteran in a Fourth of July celebration filled with cannon blasts, cheering crowds, and high oratory. "I never saw Phil's brown eyes open so wide or gaze with such interest," he said.3 Yet Sheridan's patriotism was tempered by a deep sense of partisanship. When Democratic vice presidential candidate Richard M. Johnson, a famous American Indian fighter, campaigned in Somerset in 1840, young Phil, a Whig, refused to shake his hand. This demonstration of loyalty and partisanship would later express itself in his view toward rebel enemies and in his support of those who fought under him. As Sheridan saw it, you were either for him or against him.

His first teacher regularly employed the rod and switch. He left his own indelible mark on Sheridan's character with the brand of justice he meted out in the one-room schoolhouse. "If unable to detect the real culprit when any offense had been committed, [he] would consistently apply the switch to the whole school without discrimination," Sheridan wrote in his memoirs. "It must be conceded that by this means he never failed to catch the guilty mischief-maker."4

At fourteen, Sheridan took a job in a country store in Somerset with a salary of $24 per year. After twelve months he left to earn more pay, finally in a dry goods shop where he earned $160 a year as a bookkeeper. In 1848, Sheridan obtained an appointment to West Point from an influential friend of his father Congressman Thomas Ritchie whom he had gotten to know. He left Ohio for the first time, traveling on steamboat into a world unfamiliar to his sparse rural upbringing. He found the pomp and pageantry of the academy pretentious, and he especially disliked the aristocratic manners of the southern cadets and upperclassmen who hazed and lorded over him, he said in his memoirs.5 He struggled academically, depending heavily on tutoring and hard work to pass his exams. Socially, he found it even more difficult to adjust.

His quick temper nearly cut short his military career before it really began. Sheridan was given a drill-field order from a cadet sergeant from Virginia that he "considered an improper tone."6 Sheridan charged at the Virginian with his bayonet, stopping just short of sticking his superior. Officials expelled him from West Point for a year, during which he returned to bookkeeping in Somerset, seething and brooding over his treatment. The academy allowed him to return only because of his previous good conduct. Despite this reprieve Sheridan remained bitter about the incident until years later.

When Sheridan returned to the academy, he stayed in line but remained a mediocre student. He graduated thirty-fourth out of a class of fifty-two, not high enough to win an immediate commission. He thus entered the army as a brevet second lieutenant and was assigned to the First Infantry in Fort Duncan, Texas. The Mexican border fort was considered among the most primitive and least desirable posts in the army. But Sheridan found in the creek bottoms and dry prairies of West Texas what became his lifelong love of the outdoors and the sport of hunting. Under the tutelage of a soldier named Frankman, Sheridan learned to stalk and kill deer, antelope, and wild turkeys. A butcher by trade, Frankman also showed the former bookkeeper how to field dress and prepare the meats. Eventually, Sheridan would revel in his ability to feed the marching columns of the command while on patrol in the grasslands and riparian oases of cottonwoods along West Texas streams. During this happy time Sheridan also took up ornithology, collecting specimens of the many colored birds that wintered in the Rio Grande area. Though Sheridan eventually gave up his active practice of ornithology, he remained a dedicated hunter the rest of his life. From these natural pursuits he developed an interest in science that eventually laid the foundation for his conservation efforts.

From Texas, Sheridan, now a lieutenant, moved to posts in California and the Pacific Northwest, participating in various American Indian wars and police duties on reservations. In these posts in the late 1850s, Sheridan came to know many American Indians, for whom he held little respect. He abhorred their religious practices and superstitions and viewed them as barbarous savages. Sheridan did make several friends, however, based primarily on their loyalty to him. He also took an American Indian mistress and learned the Chinook language. His early approach to American Indian affairs he would carry into his Reconstruction duties and his later command of the American Indian wars.

"I found abundant confirmation of my early opinion that the most effectual measures for lifting them from a state of barbarism would be a practical supervision at the outset, coupled with a firm control and mild discipline," Sheridan wrote about American Indians.7

Throughout his career the nation's leaders would turn to him when they needed "firm control." From the rebel farms of the Shenandoah Valley to the power politics of reconstructed New Orleans to the villages of the Plains Indians, Sheridan reinforced his belief that only the strong hand of the federal government could ensure a civilization of justice and efficiency.

On April 4, 1861, posted on the Grande Ronde Indian Reservation on the windswept high desert of eastern Oregon, First Lieutenant Philip Sheridan had built a mild reputation for his competency in administering American Indian policy but had yet to exceed the low expectations he carried from West Point. With events of this day, however, his fortunes would begin to change.

Across the country in Charleston, South Carolina, Confederate forces fired on Fort Sumter, starting the southern rebellion, a breach of loyalty the young officer could never reconcile with his own sense of honor. Sheridan was promoted to captain and in September was called east to St. Louis, where he was assigned as chief quartermaster for General Samuel Curtis, placing him behind the lines in charge of supplies. Here, it wasn't his temper but his honesty that got the former bookkeeper into trouble. His refusal to pay officers for horses they stole from rebel farmers caused Curtis to court martial him for disobeying orders and Sheridan was transferred. His case never went to trial; to his good fortune on May 25, 1862, he instead went to the front when offered command of the Second Michigan Cavalry.

His leadership as a warrior became apparent immediately. Sheridan, now elevated to the ranks of colonel, led his troops in a series of successful skirmishes, including a daring 180-mile raid into enemy territory and finally a brilliant defense of a forward outpost of 827 troopers near Booneville, Missouri, in July 1862. Outnumbered by more than 4,000 troops, Sheridan loaded up soldiers on train cars and sent them up the tracks to Booneville, where they conspicuously emptied out. Then surreptitiously, his troops marched back through the woods up the tracks and reloaded the train over and over, fooling the Confederates into believing he was getting reinforcements. They routed the Confederates, and Sheridan was promoted to brigadier general.

Sheridan rode into Union army legend on November 25, 1863, at the battle of Chattanooga. The Rebels had nearly 30,000 men dug in on a ripple of Georgia land three miles east of the Tennessee River called Missionary Ridge. Grant himself considered the position invulnerable to frontal attack. Sheridan's division and others were to attack the front only to prevent the Rebels from shoring up their flanks, but Sheridan's men didn't stop at the base of the ridge. They kept advancing, seeking safer ground closer to the Rebel ramparts. Sheridan saw the opportunity and asked for orders to attack. He was denied. "There the boys are, and they seem to be getting along; I can't stop them until they get to the top," he told his aide. Then with sword in one hand and his hat waving in the other, he rode up the ridge. "Forward boys, forward, we can get to the top," he cried. "Come on boys, give 'em Hell."[8]

Sheridan's division overran the Rebel line and the defenders took off in a panic. He chased them three miles, all the way to Chickamauga Station. Grant, the battle's commander, attributed the victory to Sheridan's quick, aggressive action. "Sheridan showed his genius in that battle," Grant later wrote. "Although commanding a division only, he saw in the crisis of that engagement that it was necessary to advance beyond the point indicated by his orders."[9]

When Grant went east to become general-in-chief of the Union armies, he called Sheridan to join him as chief of cavalry of the Army of the Potomac. Up to then the cavalry had been used primarily in defensive arrangements. The horsemen were used to protect supply trains and the army's flanks from attacks by Confederate cavalry commanded by the legendary General J.E.B. (Jeb) Stuart. But Sheridan had other ideas, and he didn't keep them to himself. General George Meade, commander of the Army of the Potomac, and Sheridan got into a huge argument over a mix-up in the placement of the cavalry. Sheridan lost his temper and said that if Meade didn't like Sheridan's approach he could give the cavalry orders—a clear act of insubordination. As he left in a huff, Sheridan told Meade if it was up to him he'd take his cavalry and go out and whip Stuart himself. Meade stomped off to complain to Grant, who listened to the diatribe quietly until Meade came to the part about whipping Stuart.

"Did Sheridan say that?" Grant asked. "He usually knows what he is talking about. Let him go ahead and do it."[10]

Sheridan and cavalry rode south to attack toward Richmond and left the Union army behind. As Sheridan predicted, Stuart had to disengage from his offensive and race back to place his forces between Sheridan and Richmond. At Yellow Tavern, on May 16, 1864, Sheridan's cavalry mortally wounded Stuart and freed four hundred union prisoners. Sheridan briefly ran through Richmond's outer defenses, sending a panic into the Confederate capital, and then circled Lee's army, tearing up railroad tracks and supply trains before returning to Union lines.

Sheridan had grown from the quiet shy boy into a respected, confident, and successful leader of men. But Sheridan's character drifted beyond tenacity to a ruthlessness that made him unusually suited to the tasks Grant believed were needed to bring the Civil War to an end. He sent Sheridan to the rolling hills of Virginia's Shenandoah Valley in the summer of 1864. Meanwhile, Lee sent General Jubal Early and a raiding force of several thousand men there to threaten Washington and reduce the pressure on Richmond. Abraham Lincoln was locked in a close reelection battle, and Lee hoped such a raid might lead to a Democratic victory and a negotiated peace. Grant wanted Sheridan to stop Early, but he also wanted more: "If the war is to last another year we want the Shenandoah Valley to remain a barren waste."[11]

Sheridan won battles in August and September to turn Early from the capitol. But on October 19 Early struck at Cedar Creek, tearing through Sheridan's lines in his absence. Returning from meetings in Washington, Sheridan heard the sounds of cannon and ran into bands of soldiers retreating in panic. On his black steed, Rienzi, Sheridan galloped toward the battle through the lines of retreating troops yelling, "Come on back, boys. We're going to lick these fellows out of their boots. We'll make coffee out of Cedar Creek tonight!"[12] His army turned and regrouped, and Sheridan rode through the line a second time, waving his hat and provoking a mighty cheer from the battle-worn veterans. Together they crushed Early, delivering to Lincoln the victory he needed to win the election. The poem "Sheridan's Ride," released as a piece of electioneering rhetoric, turned the victorious general into a beloved hero whose Cedar Creek victory was relived countless times in grade school recitations for two generations.

Sheridan was not done in the Shenandoah. John Mosby led a guerilla force in the area that pecked away at Sheridan's forces, aided by a small cadre of recalcitrant rebel farmers. Sheridan ordered his troops to take all food and slaves and supplies they could carry and arrest all white men under fifty to keep them from helping Mosby. What was left, he said should be burned. He boasted that "a crow would be compelled to carry his own rations," when crossing the valley. He returned to the harsh lessons he learned from his Irish schoolmaster and punished the innocent along with the guilty. It was a policy he was to repeat through Reconstruction in Texas and Louisiana and later with the American Indian tribes of the West.

After the war, Sheridan went to Texas to oversee the return to civil government. His unusually harsh Reconstruction policies led to his being fired by President Andrew Johnson. In 1868 he returned west to command the Department of the Missouri and thereby to subdue the American Indians and place them on reservations. With a mixture of brutal winter campaigns and peace treaties the government expected soon to be obsolete, Sheridan brought the tribes of the Southwest under toe.

The tone was set when Sheridan sent Colonel George Custer to attack the village of the peaceful chief Black Kettle on the Washita River in Kansas in November of 1868. Only days before, the old chief had led a delegation of Cheyenne and Arapahos to Fort Cobb asking for protection. They were turned away. Sheridan welcomed Custer and his Seventh Cavalry back to camp after the massacre with a band blaring. Custer's scouts waved the scalps of dead warriors they called "brutal savages." In his report, Sheridan lied and said he had offered Black Kettle sanctuary. Soon after that Comanche chief Tosawi brought his band into Fort Cobb to surrender, presenting himself to Sheridan. "Tosawi good Indian,"[13] he said. Sheridan's reply, "The only good Indians I ever saw were dead," was soon afterward transformed into the phrase that is Sheridan's best-known legacy, "The only good Indian is a dead Indian."

In 1869, Grant became president, and Sheridan was appointed lieutenant general and moved his headquarters to Chicago. He was now in charge of the entire Rocky Mountains, an immense area that remained largely unexplored. The Sioux and other tribes still controlled vast hunting grounds. Sheridan decided he needed to tour the region and its forts to understand its geography and to get to know its defense needs and potential. It was that decision that put him on the stage from Corinne to Helena and in the proximity of Atkinson and his stories of wonderland.

The first stories of Yellowstone to reach the East came in the aftermath of the Lewis and Clark Expedition in 1805–1806. John Colter, a Kentuckian, was allowed to leave the expedition on its return trip, beginning several years of fur trading and trapping. His travels took him through Yellowstone in the winter of 1807–1808. He reported his observations of hot springs and geysers and added details to William Clark's map of the famous expedition when it was published in 1814. His description of a hot springs area near Cody gave the label of "Colter's Hell" to the entire Yellowstone area. Other mountain men, including Jim Bridger and Osborne Russell, visited and trapped in Yellowstone, relaying back news of its unusual features. Russell's journals, later published, describe his visit to the Shoshone Geyser basin south of Old Faithful in 1839:

> The first thing that attracts the attention is a hole about 15 inches in diameter in which the water is boiling slowly about 4 inches below the surface at length it begins to boil and bubble violently and the water commences raising and shooting upwards until the column arises to the height of sixty feet from whence it falls to the ground in drops on a circle of about 30 feet in diameter being perfectly cold when it strikes the ground. It continues shooting up in this manner five or six minutes and then sinks back to its former state of slowly boiling for an hour and then shoots forth as before.[14]

These were the kinds of stories Atkinson shared with Sheridan at the Montana Road stage stop. Sheridan arrived in Helena on May 16, 1870, like "a Roman conqueror," the *Helena Daily Herald* reported.[15] He addressed a crowd of more than one thousand in front of the International Hotel, where he stayed, reminisced of his days at West Point, and expressed support for the Northern Pacific Railroad, which was seeking to build a line across Montana. According to the newspaper, he danced until dawn the night of his arrival in Helena. But he couldn't shake his curiosity about Yellowstone.

Sheridan soon learned that a group of respected Montana citizens were in the early stages of planning an expedition into Yellowstone. Its leader, Henry Dana Washburn, was surveyor general of the Montana Territory. The thirty-eight-year-old attorney from Indiana had arrived in Montana only a year before with his wife, Serena. He was no stranger to Sheridan. A Vermont native, Washburn served under Sheridan as a general commanding the Eighteenth Indiana Volunteers during the Shenandoah campaign. His troops, which took heavy casualties, fought with distinction at Cedar Creek, and Sheridan was not apt to forget it. Twice elected to Congress as a Republican after the war, Washburn chose to move to the arid climate of Montana as a Grant appointee to relieve the tuberculosis he contracted during the war.

Sheridan found a wealth of information about the wonderland Atkinson had introduced him to only a day before. A detailed map had been published in 1869, drawn by two Washburn employees who had explored the area. One of them, David E. Folsom, had visited the Grand Canyon of the Yellowstone, Yellowstone Lake, and the Lower Geyser basin of the Firehole River in 1869. A heavily edited account of his trip was published in *Western Monthly* in July 1870. It left out many of the details Folsom shared with Washburn, including his proposal to set aside Yellowstone as a national park.[16] There is no record of Folsom meeting with Sheridan, but he was in Helena at that time and working for Washburn. It's possible he shared his idea with the general as well.

The spiritual value of nature had long been recognized in the cultures of the American Indian tribes who had lived and visited Yellowstone for more than 10,000 years. The American Indians, like the explorers and tourists who followed, saw Yellowstone as a special place with deeper meaning than simply a "pleasuring ground," as Congress would later term it. Just as the mountain man's mystical description captured Sheridan's imagination, Yellowstone found a place at the heart of the American mind.

When Sheridan made his stage journey in 1870, the nation was engaged in a frenzied campaign to develop western lands. But with the frontier beginning to be tamed, a new movement to preserve what was quickly being lost was emerging. Cities, towns, and states had previously created parks and commons, including New York's Central Park in 1857 and Yosemite State Park in 1864. But the iconic power of these treasures did not reach so deeply into the character, culture, and evolving values of the wilderness movement. It was the almost mystical landscape of shooting water spouts, smoking mountains, and mud pots that so aptly illustrated the transcendental vision of nature espoused by Ralph Waldo Emerson and Henry David Thoreau. The two New Englanders advocated that individuals should develop their own relationship to the universe and spirituality that tied them closer to nature. The land, the trees, and wildlife had value in sustaining not only life but the spirit as well. "From the forest and wilderness come the tonics and barks which brace mankind," Thoreau wrote in his 1851 essay "Walking."[17]

Emerson saw parks and preserves as human adaptations of nature that could be used to prop up our frailties. "Only as far as the masters of the world have called in nature to their aid, can they reach the height of magnificence," Emerson wrote in *Nature* in 1844. "This is the meaning of their hanging gardens, villas, garden-houses, islands, parks and preserves, to back their faulty personality with these strong accessories."[18]

Folsom's suggestion wasn't the first time the idea of a national park was presented. The lineage of the national park idea goes back to 1832, when artist George Catlin, accompanying an army unit, steamboated into the West to paint the vanishing American Indian. He saw that the wild character of the world he was painting was soon to be lost forever. To preserve a remnant of the native wildlife and tribal culture, he proposed a large tract of the West be preserved as a "Nation's Park, containing man and beast, in all the wildness and freshness of their nature's beauty."[19]

Joseph Henry, a professor, reported to the board of the Smithsonian in 1871 that Catlin proposed "to reserve the country around these 'Yellowstone' geysers as a public park."[20] Many other traders, prospectors, and even missionaries visited the region in the next three decades. But Sheridan's arrival in Helena came just as the mysterious region was about to be discovered by the entire nation.

Sheridan briefly forgot his mission to tour western forts. He already had decided he would cut the trip short so he could observe the Franco-Prussian War developing in Europe. He now spent two days in Helena talking with the explorers and looking for a way to aid their expedition. "There was such general uncertainty as to the character of this wonderland that I authorized an escort of soldiers to go that season from Fort Ellis with a small party to make such superficial explorations as to justify my sending an engineer officer with a well-equipped expedition there the next summer to scientifically examine and report upon this strange country," Sheridan later wrote.[21]

When Sheridan left Helena, he went to Fort Benton on the Missouri River and there caught a steamboat back east. He stopped in St. Paul, where he met with General Winfield Scott Hancock, who served under him as the head of the Department of Dakota. Soon thereafter, Hancock issued orders for an army escort for Washburn's expedition, presumably at Sheridan's behest. The officer who got the job, Lieutenant Gustavus Cheyney Doane, also knew Washburn. His military career to that time had been strikingly uneventful despite service throughout the Civil War. But he desired to be an explorer.

Stationed at Fort Ellis near Bozeman, Montana, sixty miles northwest of Yellowstone, Doane knew of the Washburn expedition preparations, and he'd heard that the old general and others had been lobbying for a military escort with Sheridan and Hancock. But a shortage of officers and American Indian troubles threatened to prevent his participation. The thirty-year-old Illinois native urged Washburn to make a last-minute plea to Hancock to force his superior to send him. Washburn sent the telegram, and Hancock issued Doane's order on August 14,

1870: "Proceed with one sergeant and four privates of Company F, Second Cavalry, to escort the surveyor general of Montana to the falls and lakes of the Yellowstone, and return."[22]

Sheridan had set in motion a series of events that would lead to Yellowstone's preservation. Doane, Washburn, and a colorful Montana politician named Nathaniel Langford would ride into the park that Sheridan skirted on his stage ride north from Utah. The ride was never to gain the fame of his twelve-mile ride from Winchester in 1864. But it was the first step in Sheridan's long march for Yellowstone and conservation.

CHAPTER 2

Jay Cooke, Nathaniel Langford, and the Northern Pacific

> Nothing can prevent this—nothing. . . . There is no end to the
> possibilities of wealth here. . . . Jay, we have got the biggest
> thing on earth. Our enterprise is an inexhaustible gold mine.
>
> —Sam Wilkerson, in a letter to Jay Cooke, 1869

AT THE SAME TIME in the spring of 1870 that Sheridan was meeting with Washburn in Helena, Nathaniel Pitt Langford, the other major player of the expedition that would lead to Yellowstone's establishment, was back east doing what he did best—promoting himself.

Langford would become Yellowstone's first superintendent and for nearly a century be considered one of its most important saviors. But his road to preserving Yellowstone was built on rails. It was bought and paid for by one of the nineteenth century's most colorful financiers, Jay Cooke. Langford and Cooke had a very different idea of how to preserve Yellowstone than would Sheridan. Their conflicting values would lead to the events that made fire pivotal to later preservation and conservation policy.

Langford, a New York native, had carved out a place for himself in Montana society in the mining boom of the 1860s. He was appointed territorial governor by President Andrew Johnson in 1869. But the impeachment fight between Johnson and Congress halted Langford's confirmation, and he suddenly found himself in need of a new job and a cause. He had returned east through St. Paul, working his political and banking connections in hopes of landing comfortable employment and hyping the importance of the upcoming Washburn expedition, which he correctly recognized as the chance of a lifetime. Eventually, he would insinuate his own name alongside Washburn's as the coleader of the exploration. He would write the popular accounts of the trip— the first draft of history—and rewrite it many times to ensure that his version of events survived. When he wasn't obscuring the truth with his own writing, Langford would offer phony evidence to other writers that supported the notion that his role in Yellowstone's creation was central. He cleverly sealed his place in history by using his initials to call himself "National Park Langford."

Langford was one of the thousands of ambitious young men lured west to seek their fortunes in the goldfields scattered across the Rockies. The twenty-year-old had been in ill health when he left St. Paul in 1862 on a 1,600-mile wagon trip to the mining fields of southwest Montana and the boomtowns of Bannack and Virginia City. There he joined vigilantes, private citizens who took the law into their own hands. They were beginning their own reign of terror in an effort to fill the power vacuum of the frontier mining districts. The vigilantes hung twenty-one men, including the sheriff, Henry Plummer, whom they convicted in a trial of murder and highway robbery after his hanging. Historians now question whether Plummer and others who were lynched had committed any crimes at all. As Langford would do for Yellowstone, he wrote the history of those vigilantes, giving both himself and his colleagues starring roles.[1] Langford's fortunes, though never large, came not from gold or from his stories, but from the advantageous marriages of his sisters. One married James Wicks Taylor, a former law partner of Salmon P. Chase, the secretary of the treasury, who got Langford a job collecting taxes in the new Montana territory in 1864.

That same year another event took place in Washington, D.C., that would soon become pivotal to Langford's fortunes and the creation of Yellowstone. Congress and President Abraham Lincoln chartered the Northern Pacific Railroad in 1864, one of several transcontinental railroads created from dreams and capital in the 1860s. The investors told Congress they would build a rail line from Duluth, Minnesota, on Lake

Superior to the Pacific coast, an incredible claim in the midst of a civil war. Much of the region was still under the control of the Sioux and other American Indian tribes, while vast stretches of the Dakotas and eastern Montana had no settlement at all. To subsidize the railroad and encourage settlement, Congress held out a huge incentive to Northern Pacific for laying track: forty million acres of land—an area larger than New England—stretching from Minnesota to Washington. All the railroad had to do was begin construction in two years and raise $2 million in capital.

The task had turned out to be as incredible to investors as it was in reality. In the time allotted, the Northern Pacific was unable to raise the required $2 million and didn't lay a mile of track. By 1869 it seemed only a wizard could possibly realize the dream.

That wizard appeared in the form of Jay Cooke, America's first investment banker.[2] Cooke's creative financing and promotion of war bonds had raised more than $500 million for the Union cause, and by 1870, his power and influence were exceeded only by that of President Ulysses Grant himself. Now he was turning his sights west to increase his fortune.

Jay Cooke was born in Sandusky, Ohio, in 1821, the son of a lawyer who was elected to the Ohio legislature and later to the U.S. House of Representatives. In 1839, Jay Cooke left to seek his fortune in Philadelphia, working for his brother-in-law in a shipping firm. The lanky blond eighteen-year-old, five feet eleven inches tall, carried himself with confidence and an air of success that others noted. He took a job as clerk in the E.W. Clark & Co. Bank, the largest domestic exchange and banking house in the country. He was a talented banker, and within a few months he was promoted to head clerk and over the next few years to full partner.

At Clark & Co., Cooke learned how to market stocks and bonds with newspaper advertising, then a relatively novel idea. The bank did a brisk business in railroad securities and made a killing in Texas bonds by promoting the idea that Texas would be annexed when the United States defeated Mexico in 1848. These lessons about bonds and railroads were not lost on young Cooke. When E.W. Clark went bankrupt in the panic of 1857, Cooke was ready to break out on his own. Like the dot-com millionaires of the 1990s, Cooke's greatest asset was his creativity. Without a bank to back him, he helped several railroads and canals out of bankruptcy in the 1850s by underwriting bonds to raise capital. He was creating the investment banking industry on the sheer force of his wits, savvy, and personality. A man who met Cooke years later was moved by Cooke's spirit and warmth and quick intimacy. "There are some characters that have that power of friendly impressibility and don't know it, and ought not to be blamed for having it," he wrote.3

In January 1861, Cooke founded the banking house Jay Cooke and Company with a mere $150,000 in capital, far less than the dominant banks of Philadelphia or other major cities. But he knew how to market large stock and bond issues. At the time, Pennsylvania was trying to sell $3 million in bonds to raise funds to defend the state in the event of an attack from the South. Cooke proposed the novel idea of marketing the bonds to the public based on both patriotism and their economic value. The state divided the bond issue between Cooke and the Drexel Bank, which was ten times the size of Cooke's company. Cooke's marketing was a big success, and although he made only pennies on the bond issues themselves, he was able to attract many of the investors to deposit money in his bank, significantly expanding its assets and his reputation.

The man most in need of his skills was Salmon P. Chase, secretary of the treasury under President Lincoln. In the 1850s, the federal budget was only $50–$60 million and included very little debt. When the war began, the Union's costs soared and the debt rose from $90 million in 1861 to more than $900 million by 1865. Chase had raised $50 million in a bond issue after the disastrous battle of Bull Run, but only with difficulty. Cooke's brother Henry, an aide to Chase, introduced the two men. Jay Cooke offered his services for free. In 1862, he and Henry opened a Washington office at the request of Chase.

Using the telegraph, they organized a network of 2,500 salesmen to sell the government bonds. Cooke returned to the patriotism theme for marketing but offered the bonds with six percent interest rates backed by gold. His main products were called "five twenties," bonds that could not be redeemed sooner than in five years or later than in twenty. He offered the bonds in denominations as low as $50 to allow the average American to invest. By 1865 Cooke and Company had raised more than $500 million for the treasury. It made less than $300,000 on the transactions, proving Cooke to be a true patriot for the cause. But his service came with other rewards.

Cooke became the largest player in the bond market. This made him one of the most politically powerful men in the country with influence in all facets of business and government. Yet many men remained richer, and he strived to make his fortune as large as his clout. For that he needed to increase his own capital. He returned to the business of his father and of his own success in the 1850s—railroads.

Railroads were to the economy in the post–Civil War period what computers and the Internet were to the economy of the 1990s. Nearly 30,000 miles of track were laid from 1865 to 1873, doubling the nation's railways. Speculators jumped into railroads the way investors placed bets on tech stocks at the end of the twentieth century. Land grants from the federal government made the railroads more valuable for the property gained than as businesses, especially in the West, where settlers were only beginning to fill in the great land between the Mississippi and the Pacific coast.

The forty million acres the Northern Pacific would receive represented more than two percent of the forty-eight states' land mass and more land than nine of the smallest states put together. But to gain title to the land, the railroad's investors had to build the line across swamps, over deep river canyons, through tall mountain passes across a vast wilderness. It gained title to the land only as it laid track. By 1869 the Northern Pacific had still not left the station and its investors were desperate.

They turned to Jay Cooke for salvation. His banking house purchased controlling interest in the Northern Pacific for $5 million and began selling bonds to finance construction. Drawing on his political connections and the clout of investors, including President Grant, Cooke went back to Washington and lobbied Congress to change the law that created the Northern Pacific's land grant. It now allowed the railroad to sell bonds to raise money and gave it a pass on its past failures to raise the original $2 million or begin construction.

Purchase of the Northern Pacific was a great gamble for Cooke, who added his personal fortune to the investment. He had to keep railroad construction moving fast enough to get title to the land so it could be sold to raise more capital and develop business along the route. Even worse, the Fort Laramie Treaty signed by the federal government in 1868 allowed the Sioux Indians to keep their hunting lands smack-dab in the middle of the railroad's planned route.

Cooke reorganized his sales force and spread one thousand agents across the nation to sell the bonds he needed to fund construction. But unlike the war bond campaign, Cooke couldn't rely on patriotism to attract investors. By this time he knew how to get the public's attention through newspapers, lectures, pamphlets, and handbills. But he needed something fantastic to sell, a way to capture the public's attention, a way to position the Northern Pacific above the competition of far less risky investments. That's when Nathaniel P. Langford appeared in his life. Langford needed a job and Cooke needed a story.

Langford had come east looking for employment and support for his upcoming expedition with Washburn into Yellowstone. In early 1870, Langford was working several angles with James Taylor and his other brother-in-law, William R. Marshall, the governor of Minnesota. Both men were major investors in the Northern Pacific.

Langford showed up at the offices of the Northern Pacific in St. Paul in March 1870 applying for a job, but was turned down. He was not deterred. If anything, he was audacious. In June, he finagled a meeting with Jay Cooke in Philadelphia. It was to become a defining moment in the history of Yellowstone. Yet it was all but hidden during Langford's lifetime and long after because Langford wanted to be remembered foremost as an altruistic preservationist.

The two schemers hit it off right away. Cooke remarkably invited Langford to spend two days with him at his personal estate. Langford entertained Cooke with the stories of geysers, grand canyons, waterfalls, and mud pots that he had heard from David Folsom, who had explored Yellowstone the year before, with whom he had traveled west in 1862. Langford was a great storyteller and did not have to exaggerate much to grab Cooke's interest and keep it.

There is no record of what the two men talked about. But it's clear by the events that followed that they had formed a pact. Langford immediately returned to Montana and joined in organizing the Washburn expedition into Yellowstone, now in the employ of Jay Cooke. He also came out of the meeting with a job as a lecturer to promote the region where the Northern Pacific was to run. Langford's future was hitched to the railroad and his future was in Yellowstone.

Cooke's future too was inexorably tied to the Northern Pacific Railroad's march west. And its success in turn was tied to how many millions he could raise by selling bonds. A writer Cooke hired described the region in which the railroad would operate as "a vast wilderness waiting like a rich heiress to be appropriated and enjoyed."[4] Langford's stories of Yellowstone made the place appear like the jewel on the lady's bosom, and Cooke now wanted to lay claim to its treasures.

CHAPTER 3

The Creation Myth

And right there the national park idea was born.
—Horace Albright, as part of a speech given on the fiftieth
anniversary of the creation of Yellowstone, 1922

NOW COOKE AND SHERIDAN each had his own man riding into Yellowstone in August of 1870 with the Washburn expedition. Nathaniel Langford was Cooke's eager agent, gathering his fodder for the lectures he would use to awaken interest in the railroad bonds Cooke was selling. The adventurer Lieutenant Gustavus Doane was finally on a quest, with orders that were born in Sheridan's Helena visit three months before.

Sheridan and Cooke were by no means rivals. Building the Northern Pacific Railroad's line westward was national policy, and as commander of all U.S. Army forces in the West it was Sheridan's job to help it along. As Cooke's survey crews worked their way across the nation, Sheridan's soldiers escorted and protected them. But the two men were soon to develop very different views about who should protect Yellowstone and from whom.

Cooke first envisioned Yellowstone as a grand symbol for his new railroad, a scenic marvel to attract investment in the bonds needed to finance his expansion. Today advertising executives would call it branding. Cooke also hoped he would lure rich investors to follow their investment West as tourists. He initially hoped that at least some of Yellowstone might even fall within the railroad's land grant. In Sheridan's original Helena speech in 1870, the general spoke enthusiastically of how the Northern Pacific would foster Montana's already successful development. But by the end of the 1870s he would gradually change his tune, eventually opposing the Northern Pacific's monopoly control of the area. He would offer a competing vision, one of strong government control, and press for U.S. Army protection of its wildlife and wonders. In 1870 these two agents of Manifest Destiny, the philosophy underlying the development of the West, were starting the wheels rolling on a national crusade to leave part of it wild. Neither could have predicted when they first learned of the land of geysers, hot springs, and waterfalls that spring that their curiosity would help to lead to a national shift in values. Both of their visions have been all but lost to the ages. Both have been relegated to second- or third-rank supporting roles, if given any role at all in Yellowstone's founding.

The Washburn expedition left Helena on August 16, 1870, joining up with Lieutenant Doane and the military escort at Fort Ellis near Bozeman, Montana. The band of explorers, now ballooned to nineteen, rode east to the Yellowstone River and then south into what would become the park, naming rivers, waterfalls, and mountains they encountered. They rode past the Grand Canyon of the Yellowstone, awed by its scenic falls. They circled Lake Yellowstone, losing Truman Everts, a revenue assessor, who was not found until he straggled out of the wilderness thirty-seven days later, after the expedition had returned. The party climbed over the Continental Divide near Shoshone Lake and camped in the Upper Geyser basin, where they discovered and named Old Faithful, because of the regularity of its eruptions. Early in the trip they encountered a fire near Blacktail Plateau that they believed was started by American Indians. Doane wrote on August 26: "The great plateau had been recently burned off to drive away the game, and the woods were still on fire in every direction."[1] On their last night, September 19, the party camped beneath a striking rock face of the Madison River canyon at the junction of the Firehole and Gibbon Rivers.

For most of the twentieth century the public was led to believe that the idea of a national park was invented at this juncture. The 7,500-foot peak overlooking the campsite was even named National Park Mountain in honor of the mythic campfire discussion, and the National Park Service still has a plaque at the site claiming as much. In the 1950s and

1960s the National Park Service presented annual reenactments of the event. The Hallmark Hall of Fame even broadcast a radio play depicting the explorers' campfire conversation in 1963. Roderick Nash, in his classic environmental history, *Wilderness and the American Mind*, first published in 1967, as the new environmental age was dawning, repeated the story as fact.[2] As recently as 1997, Vice President Al Gore repeated the story in celebrating Yellowstone's 125th anniversary.[3] This story has carried great significance for generations of conservationists and environmentalists. It became a creation myth of the environmental movement. Even people who never knew the story were shaped by the myth; the campfire discussion became an allegory for environmental progress and its altruistic roots. A similar campfire discussion is credited with the preservation of the Frank Church River of No Return Wilderness.[4] The immensely popular *Encounters with the Archdruid*,[5] about the modern environmental leader David Brower, by John McPhee, uses the campfire discussion as a narrative device to discuss environmentalism.

The story itself was created by Langford, who long vied for, and until recent times, carried the title of Yellowstone's founder. His version of the founding was included in the park's first history, *The Yellowstone National Park*,[6] written in 1895 by Hiram Martin Chittenden, a U.S. Army engineer who oversaw the building of hundreds of miles of roads in the park. The story carried with it a new appreciation of nature with all the aspirations and philosophical underpinnings laid by Thoreau and Emerson. The campfire creation of the national park idea elevated the legislative acts to follow into a morality tale, an act of fortitude exercised by a confident, maturing nation of high-minded individuals. But as National Park Service historian Aubrey Haines demonstrated in the 1960s, the story simply isn't true.[7]

The story, as Langford told it in his 1905 published journal, starts with the explorers in a heated discussion about whether they should stake personal claims to the best parts of the remarkable region they had just explored. In his entry of September 20, Langford said Cornelius Hedges, a young lawyer, challenged the idea:

> Mr. Hedges then said that he did not approve of any of these plans—that there ought to be no private ownership of any portion

of that region, but that the whole of it ought to be set apart as a great National Park, and that each one of us ought to make an effort to have this accomplished. His suggestion met with instantaneous and favorable response from all—except one—of the members of our party, and each hour since the matter was first broached, our enthusiasm has increased. It has been the main theme of our conversation to-day as we journeyed. I lay awake half of last night thinking about it—and if my wakefulness deprived my bed-fellow [Hedges] of any sleep—he has only himself and his disturbing National Park proposition to answer for it.[8]

What the story and the subsequent tales Langford spun about the park's creation failed to report was his association with the Northern Pacific Railroad. For obvious reasons he didn't want history to show that he was promoting Yellowstone for the benefit of Jay Cooke. The Northern Pacific wasn't interested in small tracts of land carved up around the geysers and waterfalls and divvied up among a bevy of concessionaires. Cooke had a larger goal in mind. First he hoped that Yellowstone might fall within the railroad's land grant. When he realized this was not so, he wanted to monopolize tourism throughout Yellowstone; for that to be successful he knew that the region had to remain intact. It would be at least a decade before the railroad could develop the park. Hedges's idea, as altruistic as it may have been, found fertile soil in the secret motives shared between Langford and Cooke in front of a fireplace at the banker's estate.

None of the original diaries of the Washburn party ever mentioned the campfire discussion, even though far more mundane subjects were recorded. Langford's published journal included many changes from his original diary, which is missing from Langford's extensive papers at the Minnesota Historical Society. The record now clearly shows that the idea for a Yellowstone National Park had been widely discussed before that night. It was not a new idea to Hedges, Langford, or Washburn. And Washburn may well have shared the thought with Sheridan in the spring.

There is no dispute that Langford's account of the expedition, first published in *Scribner's Monthly* in May 1871, created an instant sensation for Yellowstone, however. It offered the nation, in the drawings that accompanied the article, its first look at geysers, descriptions of colorful hot springs, and exciting stories of adventurers exploring the West. At the end, Langford made sure he got a plug in for his benefactor: "By means of the Northern Pacific Railroad, which will doubtless be completed in the next three years, the traveler will be able to make the trip to Montana from the Atlantic Seaboard in three days and thousands of tourists will be attracted to Montana and Wyoming in order to behold with their own eyes the wonders here described."9

Langford also embarked on a Cooke-sponsored twenty-city lecture series, speaking to big audiences in Minneapolis, New York, and Washington, among other cities—all important markets for Cooke's railroad bonds. Langford was later to claim he lobbied for establishment of a national park during these lectures, a claim that news reports do not support. He succeeded in persuading parks chronicler Chittenden to include his claim in the park history by sending him a newspaper clipping that reported his advocacy during the tour. Haines and other historians believed the clipping was faked or from a later date. Langford also failed to make the national park pitch in the *Scribner's* articles, even though he plugged the Northern Pacific. Langford's lecture in Washington, D.C., did, however, prompt Ferdinand V. Hayden, director of the U.S. Geological Survey of the territories, to get Congress to fund his own official expedition to Yellowstone in 1871.

The first official report to result from the Washburn expedition was Lieutenant Doane's. His 25,000-word journal was a straightforward, unemotional report of his observations on the journey, filled with scientific data and maps.10 Hayden called it "remarkable."

"For graphic description and thrilling interest, it has not been surpassed by any official report made to our government since the times of Lewis and Clark," Hayden commented.11 Doane completed the report on December 15, 1870, and sent it on to Sheridan, who passed it on to Congress, and it was published on February 24, 1871.

The report convinced Sheridan to go ahead with his already stated plans to send a military expedition into the area in 1871. The curious hunter and former amateur ornithologist wanted to know more about what was becoming the last best place untouched by settlers, American Indian wars, and mining. He ordered Captain John W. Barlow, chief engineer of the U.S. Army's Missouri Division, to lead a small contingent that would accompany Hayden but as an independent group. The army's team, including Doane, would explore the park far more extensively than the civilians.

Jay Cooke had other influences on the park's beginning. He convinced Hayden to allow artist Thomas Moran to tag along at Cooke's expense. Eventually, his paintings and sketches, most out of scale or artistically enhanced romantic images of the features, introduced the American public to the unique beauty of Yellowstone and coincidentally helped Cooke sell bonds. Hayden even allowed Cooke to cover the expenses of transporting his expedition west.

Sheridan had ordered Barlow also to bring along a photographer to add photos to his report and to help him in popular articles the general urged him to write. But a great fire was to intervene on the return journey. All of Barlow's photographs were burned in the Chicago Fire of October 8, 1871. The fire and its aftermath were to consume most of Sheridan's attention in the closing months of 1871, as city officials requested his aid in stopping looters and ending the chaos that followed the historic blaze. Sheridan reacted as he always had, quickly and with authority. He brought in six companies of troops to restore order. Mayor Rosell Mason, on Sheridan's recommendation, declared martial law, placing the general in charge of the city. Despite his shaky constitutional ground, Sheridan recruited one thousand men to patrol the unburned portions of the city. When a local businessman was killed by one of the volunteers, Illinois Governor John Palmer, who opposed Sheridan's action, demanded that President Grant bring the military under control. Sheridan backed away from martial law, but under orders of his old friend Grant, he kept four companies in the city until the end of the year. On the same day the Chicago fire began, a forest fire destroyed the town of Peshtigo, Wisconsin, killing 1,200 people. Sheridan sent troops north to aid in the rescue and care of the survivors there too.

Even as Barlow and Hayden were arranging their Yellowstone expeditions, Sheridan was authorizing a military escort for another, very different Yellowstone trip. He sent Captain Edward Ball and ninety-six cavalrymen to accompany W. Milnor Roberts, the Northern Pacific's engineer, who led surveyors mapping out the final stretch of rail in the Yellowstone valley north of the park, in the middle of the Sioux hunting lands.[12] In addition to laying out the path for the future rails, Roberts was laying the foundation for determining the actual parcels that would be involved in the land grant. The survey team worked from Bozeman east, failing to reach its goal, the mouth of the Bighorn River. It would be five years later that Sheridan's favorite subordinate, George Armstrong Custer, would meet his fate along the Little Bighorn River, a result of Sheridan's aggressive challenge to the Sioux's rights under treaty.

Ultimately, it was the Northern Pacific Railroad that engineered the political deals that led to setting aside Yellowstone for public use. In the fall of 1871, A. B. Nettleton, an agent for Jay Cooke, wrote Hayden upon his return from Yellowstone with a suggestion from a Cooke associate, U.S. Representative William Darrah Kelley of Philadelphia. Kelley recommended that Hayden include a call for protection of Yellowstone's geyser basins in his official report, Nettleton said. Kelley said that Lieutenant Doane's report had been his primary influence,[13] thus indicating the direct line between Sheridan's chance meeting with the mountain man in 1870 and the passage of the legislation that created Yellowstone Park.

Now Cooke had to make his choice. He wrote his engineer Roberts in Montana on November 6, reporting Hayden's recommendation for a park: "Would this conflict with our land grant, or interfere with us in any way?" Roberts telegraphed his reply on November 21: "Geysers outside our grant advise Congressional reservation."[14]

Cooke had set his forces in motion even before Roberts replied. Langford had been back in Helena for only a few days when, on November 9, he received a letter from Governor Marshall of Minnesota, his brother-in-law, who told him to return east for important Northern Pacific business. Langford hopped the stage to Corrine, Utah, and arrived in Washington, D.C., on November 14. He began a lobbying effort that included getting his *Scribner's* article into the hands of every congressman. He worked closely with U.S. Representative William H. Clagett of Montana in writing the park bill, which was introduced on December 18, 1871. The bill called for the creation of "a public park or pleasuring ground" where "all timber, mineral deposits, natural curiosities or wonders" be kept "in their natural condition." It gained final passage with little opposition in the House on February 27, 1872, and Grant signed it on March 1.

The combined forces of Cooke and Sheridan, then, both playing behind the scenes, helped the United States establish the world's first national park. Its romantic ideal became a preservation model for the nation and the world. The seeds planted by George Catlin, Ralph Waldo Emerson, Henry David Thoreau, and others germinated in more complex values and motives than simply a love of nature, or a desire to protect the wilderness, or even to ensure that its curiosities would be preserved.

But now that a national park had been created, what did that really mean? How would it be managed? How could the nation preserve Yellowstone and still allow its use? These forces could come together behind a piece of legislation. But in the next decade the national park idea and the experiment called Yellowstone were going to be tested during a time when the West had yet to be won.

CHAPTER 4

Yellowstone's
Preservation Imperiled

These employees are largely made up of inefficient young fellows, ignorant of the ways of the west, and utterly incompetent
to perform the duties for which they are ostensibly employed.
. . . A couple of cowboys could put the whole brigade to flight
with blank cartridges.

—L. B. Carey, writing about the men who
patrolled Yellowstone in 1884

NATHANIEL P. LANGFORD was rewarded for his lobbying
efforts on behalf of Yellowstone by his appointment as the park's
first superintendent. He had no budget and no support staff, and he visited the park only twice. He would accomplish little during his five-year
stint, but instead spent most of his time at his other job, U.S. bank
examiner for the territories and Pacific coast states.

Langford's inaction, historians Aubrey Haines and Paul Schullery
said, furthered the interests of his Northern Pacific benefactors.[1]
Notably, he issued no leases to concessionaires in the park who might
stand in the way of its future control by the railroad. He developed no
rules for controlling hunting on park land, and in fact parties from the
Bottler Ranch, a large commercial hunting business nearby, made regular forays into the park's northern range. His laissez-faire management
of the new federal reservation displayed little of the zeal for preservation he was to portray in his later writings. In his first and only report
as Yellowstone's superintendent in 1873, he even explored opening the
park to logging.

"Leases have been sought for the construction of saw-mills in parts of the property where timber could be spared," he wrote. "The manufacture of lumber will prove a lucrative employment whenever the erection of public houses shall be commenced. In fact, with roads such as I have recommended, the business might be extended to reach the settlements of Montana, in most of which lumber commands a high price. A large portion of the park is covered with a heavy growth of pine timber, fit only for manufacture into lumber."[2]

The idea of using park resources to pay for park protection is often viewed with disgust by environmentalists, who see the profit motive and preservation as diametrically opposed. Inevitably, they argue, the need to meet the bottom line forces managers to trim or even ignore preservation goals. This view is not universally shared. The Chinese finance much of their park protection with money made from park resources. The Audubon Society uses oil-well receipts to pay for maintenance of some of its preserves. An entire generation of free market environmentalists has recommended turning parks and national forests into trusts, which would finance their protection via user fees, leases, and timber sales. Had Langford's intentions been true to preservation, he could have offered Congress and the nation a different model for protecting parks that well might have survived. But the Northern Pacific Railroad always viewed Yellowstone as an attraction, part of its western market area to be exploited, "appropriated and enjoyed." Langford's real job was to protect Yellowstone from development by possible competitors to the Northern Pacific while the rails crept west. With American Indians, bill collectors, and other huge obstacles in its path, preserving Yellowstone was low on the priority list of the Northern Pacific.

Langford's ideas on timber did, however, give him a different perspective than that of the traditional pioneers and capitalists rushing into the West to exploit resources and move on. His logging proposal illustrated the new thinking that came from wanting to protect as opposed to simply exploit a chunk of land. His resources were in one place and he wanted to protect its assets. Financially, one of them was timber. The nation's timber industry, then based in the North Woods of Wisconsin,

Minnesota, and Michigan, was engaged in an unfettered frenzy to cut down and sell as much of the forests as it could lay its axes on.

But Langford now was in charge of a single piece of ground. The forests he controlled needed protection as an asset, even if they were eventually to be logged. That led him to propose Yellowstone's first fire policy: "It is especially recommended that a law be passed, punishing, by fine and imprisonment, all persons who leave any fire they may have made, for convenience or otherwise, unextinguished," he wrote. "Nearly all extensive conflagrations of timber in the mountains may be directly traced to negligence in extinguishing camp-fires. In the timber regions, these fires are generally kindled against stumps and dry trunks of trees, by which, unless carefully extinguished, they often, after many days, communicate with the forest, and spread over immense tracts, destroying large quantities of valuable timber. Nothing less than a stringent law punishing negligence and carelessness, can save the extensive pine timber fields of the park from destruction."[3]

As Langford was lackadaisically running Yellowstone, Jay Cooke was reaping the rewards of his investments there in time and money. The buzz around the Washburn and Hayden expeditions and the congressional effort to preserve Yellowstone helped make Cooke's initial bond-selling campaign a success. His agents had sold $100 million in bonds by early 1873. Unfortunately, the railroad was spending the capital faster than he could raise it. Storms washed out roadbeds and bridges collapsed, slowing the pace of construction. The Northern Pacific had borrowed to its limits at the banks and resorted to paying its workers in script. Jay Cooke was too busy to pay much attention to the park he helped set aside.

The railroad-pumped economy was driving trading volume on the New York Stock Exchange to new heights. Just like the dot-com economy of the late 1990s, a speculation-driven bubble was forming that was destined to burst. Cooke was the man caught on the bubble. He struggled to stay afloat, selling more government bonds and buying back Northern Pacific bonds with his own money to keep it from going bankrupt and to show to investors his own confidence in the bonds.

The day of reckoning came on September 18, 1873, when, on his last day of power, Cooke happened to be entertaining President Grant at his estate. In the morning his New York partner announced that his office was closing. In the afternoon, Cooke was forced to follow suit. Jay Cooke, the nation's most powerful banker, was in ruins.4

The markets immediately collapsed as frightened investors lost their nerve and tried desperately to sell everything they could. The New York Stock Exchange closed for the first time in its history on September 20. Cooke's failure triggered the panic of 1873, which closed five thousand plants and businesses nationwide and sent millions of American workers into the streets without work.

Still, remarkably, investors kept the railroad intact. Frederick Billings, an influential lawyer in California who grew up in Vermont, led a syndicate of investors who created a reorganization plan that foreclosed the existing mortgage on the railroad and substituted stock for the outstanding bonds. The assets, including the vast land grant, were purchased by a committee of bondholders. Over the objections of dissident bondholders, the bankruptcy judge accepted the settlement. The Northern Pacific had laid rail only to Bismarck, South Dakota, 450 miles from Duluth, when the panic of 1873 drove it into bankruptcy. Work stopped, and it wasn't until 1879 that new bond sales could provide sufficient capital for the reorganized company to resume construction. The deadline Congress had set on the charter had passed and the firm never got it extended. Yet miraculously—many say illegally—the firm survived. Under Billings's leadership, rail was laid at the lightning rate of a mile and a half a day between 1881 and 1883.

With the railroad busy just trying to stay afloat, Yellowstone had few advocates in Washington for the appropriations necessary for management. There were no rules to stop tourists from carting off pieces of the elaborate ivory rock formations. Many of the park's early visitors brought sledgehammers and picks to chip off the most beautiful features. Hardy visitors were finding their way into Yellowstone in wagons and on horseback from surrounding territories and on the railroads, which were still hundreds of miles away from the park. Little separated it from the frontier. In 1877, Chief Joseph and the Nez Percé evaded federal troops by crossing into the park from Idaho on their long famous retreat. They even briefly took several tourists prisoner, but later released them unharmed.

Sheridan's transformation on conservation and Yellowstone did not happen overnight. And Sheridan remained a friend of the Northern Pacific throughout most of the decade. The railroad's interest and the army's were the same—to tame the region and make way for development and eventually settlement. Both wanted the Sioux out of the way, and the Sioux hunting grounds were directly in the path of the railroad's planned route. Sheridan was counting on settlers brought by the railroad to kill the game, especially the bison, that kept the hunting grounds promised in the Fort Laramie Treaty of 1868 of paramount importance to the Sioux. Ever since he had been military governor of Texas shortly after the Civil War, Sheridan had advocated the slaughter of the bison herds across the West as a way to starve the region's American Indian tribes into submission. He often expressed praise for the buffalo hunters, who killed an estimated 31 million bison between 1868 and 1881. "These men have done in the last two years, and will do in the next year, more to settle the vexed American Indian question than the entire regular army has done in the last 30 years," Sheridan said in 1871. "They are destroying the Indians' commissary. Send them powder and lead, and let them kill until they have exterminated the buffalo."[5] Sitting Bull, the Sioux chief who defeated Custer, in a sense acknowledged as much: "A cold wind blew across the prairie when the last buffalo fell . . . a death-wind for my people."[6] In 1874 Congress passed a bill to protect remaining bison herds, but Sheridan recommended that President Grant veto it. Grant left the bill to languish at the end of the session without signing it and it died.

By the end of the 1870s Sheridan appeared to rethink the wisdom of his earlier policy of bison extermination. When Sheridan received reports in October 1879 that buffalo hunters had killed two thousand more bison near Miles City, Montana, he sent a telegram to Washington: "I consider it important that this wholesale slaughter of the buffalo should be stopped."[7] Yet as late as 1881, he expressed little guilt for his extermination policy. "If I could learn that every buffalo in the northern herd were killed, I would be glad."[8]

These contradictory statements reveal a more complex picture of the man known to history for laying waste to the Shenandoah, hating American Indians, and slaughtering the buffalo. Like many people, Sheridan sought to reconcile his views of the past with the changes in attitude that came with new experience. Clearly the General's life took a turn when he first met the mountaineer on the road to Helena in 1870. As he learned more about Yellowstone, wildlife, and the shifting events of western settlement, his sense of a conservation ethic grew.

Sheridan was too busy with American Indian affairs to visit the park himself in the 1870s. But he sent several expeditions to map the country and conduct scientific study. In 1875, Captain William Ludlow led the most important of these with an entourage that included Secretary of War William Belknap, Sheridan's hunting partner retired General William Strong, and a young Yale scientist named George Bird Grinnell.

Grinnell was soon to become one of the most well respected naturalists and conservationists of the century. Born September 20, 1849, in Brooklyn, New York, Grinnell grew up wealthy. In 1857, the Grinnells moved to Audubon Park, New York, where he attended a school taught by the widow of artist John James Audubon, Lucy Bakewell Audubon. There Grinnell first developed the interest in nature that was to lead him to a life of conservation.[9]

At Yale, Grinnell became a student of O. C. Marsh, the university's first professor of paleontology. Marsh, whose specialty was Rocky Mountain vertebrates, had developed a professional friendship with Sheridan. Sheridan's interest in science had remained strong ever since his early days as an amateur ornithologist in Texas, and he allowed the paleontologist to go along on military explorations of his district. In the summer of 1870, Grinnell was invited to join a six-month O. C. Marsh expedition to Nebraska, Wyoming, Kansas, and Utah to collect vertebrate Pliocene and Cretaceous fossils. Later, Sheridan invited Marsh to go along with General George Custer's 1874 Black Hills expedition. Marsh was unable to make the trip and sent Grinnell in his place. Grinnell gained the trust and respect of both Custer and Sheridan, and both invited him back for future western trips. It was Sheridan himself who invited Grinnell to accompany Ludlow on his military exploration trip to Yellowstone, asking the graduate student and writer to report on the status of the wildlife in the park.

Ludlow, Grinnell, and Strong returned with horror stories of thousands of elk slaughtered for their hides by commercial hunters. "It is estimated that during the winter of 1874–75 not less than 3,000 elk were killed for their hides alone in the valley of the Yellowstone between the mouth of Trail Creek and the Hot Springs,"[10] Grinnell wrote in the report of the expedition edited by Ludlow.

Grinnell's reports elevated him to national leadership in the relatively new movement for wildlife protection. He came to be seen as a savior of Yellowstone and later of Glacier National Park in Montana, much as Muir became known for preserving Yosemite. His clear voice for conserving wildlife from the sportsman's perspective grew into one of the most powerful models for future conservation leaders. The 1875 Yellowstone expedition and Grinnell's subsequent reports in effect made Sheridan and Grinnell partners in the fight to protect Yellowstone. When Grinnell founded the Boone and Crockett Club in 1887 along with T. R. Roosevelt, Sheridan was a founding member. They made Yellowstone wildlife protection the group's first major cause.

After receiving his doctorate in paleontology in 1880, Grinnell bought *Forest and Stream*, a magazine devoted to hunters and nature lovers. He used the example of Yellowstone to bring national attention to the dwindling game herds and bird populations lost in the wake of development and market hunting. In the magazine Grinnell would regularly credit Sheridan for the conservation stands he took during the next decade to save the park. But knowledge of most of these efforts was lost to history until the late twentieth century when they were rediscovered by historians. Even then, new knowledge about Sheridan's conservation interests did not fit neatly with his image as an American Indian–hating, buffalo-exterminating, scorched-earther in the polarity of good and evil expressed in the simplified rhetoric of environmental campaigns; thus this aspect of his life was largely ignored.

Sheridan's interest in Yellowstone's wildlife was paradoxical in light of his views on bison hunting. Yet since his days as a young lieutenant hunting and bird watching in Texas, he had watched the great herds of deer, elk, and other species disappear along with the bison. Like so many people of his time and ours, he was conflicted between his and society's development goals and the needs of conservation. As he gradually succeeded in defeating the Plains Indians, in part by eliminating the bison, his interest in conservation grew. Conservation as Sheridan advocated it called for a strong federal government exercising a stern hand if necessary to protect Yellowstone and its resources. It was in fact the natural evolution of a man who fought for the federal union over the powers of single states. Protecting a small part of the West for wildlife allowed him to compartmentalize his interest in wildlife without threatening his larger and more important mission to end the American Indian threat to settlement.

But Sheridan and Grinnell did not see the American Indian wars and their conservation goals in conflict. Both of them envisioned a Yellowstone primarily as a game preserve and a scenic wonder that needed to be protected from poachers, vandals, and interlopers. They included the tribes, who had regularly hunted and traveled through the park for centuries, as threats to the park's integrity. American Indians not only joined in the slaughter of big game but also were responsible for many of the fires observed.[11]

The symbiotic relationship between Grinnell and Sheridan must also be considered. Grinnell was the main promoter of Sheridan's conservation views, which he trumpeted to a nation that viewed Sheridan as a hero. Sheridan's advocacy for Yellowstone, in turn, gave Grinnell a popular figure to lead his campaign on behalf of conservation. Another factor that shouldn't be dismissed is Sheridan's transition from bachelorhood to marriage. In 1875 he married Irene Rucker, the daughter of an army officer; at twenty-two, she was half his age. Longtime friends such as William Tecumseh Sherman said the marriage took the edges off the old warhorse.

It was not until 1881 that Sheridan himself visited Yellowstone for the first time, cutting a trail north along the Snake River from Jackson Hole to Yellowstone Lake. Finally the General was to see with his own eyes the geysers, hot springs, and waterfalls the Montana mountaineer had revealed to him eleven years before. Already a peak southeast of the lake carried the name of Mt. Sheridan, in honor of his support for earlier expeditions. One of his strongest observations written in a report of the trip was "the forests on fire for miles, at five or six different places."[12]

When he returned to the park in 1882 with a much larger entourage, Sheridan saw firsthand the impact of market hunters on the park's game herds. He later wrote a report expressing outrage at the destruction of the thermal areas by tourists and rock collectors, the destruction of game, and at the number of campfires left burning.[13]

Sheridan had by this time also discovered what he considered an even more sinister threat to the park's character.[14] By the fall of 1882, the Northern Pacific had reached Livingston, Montana, only forty miles north of the park. Jay Cooke and Langford were gone. But the railroad's plan to monopolize Yellowstone was alive and well.

The Department of the Interior was leasing a huge chunk of the park, including its most valuable features, to the Yellowstone Park Improvement Company. The company was a front for the Northern Pacific Railroad, which was building a line from Livingston to the park boundary. The railroad had plans to run lines throughout the park, carrying tourists to the best spots, where, with the support of Congress, it hoped to have monopoly control over park management. Sheridan had already lost all faith in the Department of the Interior because of his dealings with American Indian agents, whom he viewed as either corrupt or too given to humanitarianism. He had already called for the Bureau of Indian Affairs to be turned over to the army. Now the Yellowstone affair convinced him the department could not be entrusted with the "people's park."[15]

Secretary of the Interior Henry M. Teller was from Colorado, and like many westerners was seeking ways to improve the local economies through federal lands. He had already weakened regulations on logging on federal lands. In 1882, he granted the Yellowstone Park Improvement Company control over 4,400 acres in the park, including Old Faithful, Mammoth Hot Springs, Lake Yellowstone, and the Grand Canyon of the Yellowstone, for an annual rent of $2 an acre. In addition, the government gave the company control over transportation, the right to farm, cut timber, and even mine coal within the park. Cooke's commercial vision appeared to be finally coming true.

Sheridan immediately became the leading voice in opposition to this move. In his annual report to the Department of War in 1882, Sheridan expressed regret "to learn that the National Park had been rented out to private parties."[16] He laid out his own vision for the park, including expanding its boundaries to include additional wildlife habitat to the east and the south. "The improvements in the park should be national, the control of it in the hands of an officer of the government," he said in his report. And he left no doubt to which officer of the government he believed Yellowstone could be trusted. "I will engage to keep out the skin hunters and all other hunters by use of troops from Fort Washakie on the South, Custer on the east, and Ellis on the north, and, if necessary, I can keep sufficient troops in the park to accomplish this object, and give a place of refuge and safety for our noble game," Sheridan wrote.[17]

With Sheridan's explicit opposition, the lines were now drawn. Yellowstone was either going to be developed for the benefit of the Northern Pacific Railroad's tourism business or it was going to be protected by the federal government for the public. This was the great ideological battle that had been brewing ever since the park was established. This was the choice that Grinnell and other supporters of the Sheridan view were citing in dozen of editorials, newspaper and magazine articles, and lectures. In a sense it was similar to the debate that took place in the 1990s when Disney wanted to develop a historical theme park on the battlefields of northern Virginia, where Sheridan had built his reputation, and the twenty-first-century debate over whether snowmobiles should be allowed in the park. The conflict between private interest and federal protection became the defining moment in Yellowstone's future. It also was a pivotal turn for conservation in America. Other scenic areas, such as the Poconos in Pennsylvania and the Adirondacks in New York, included extensive private holdings that today fragment the wildlife habitat and reduce their value as sanctuaries from the bustle of modern life. Canadian national parks have long been dominated by the railroad.

Sheridan had a different vision of what should be done at Yellowstone. He was a Hamiltonian, a believer in a strong central government, and a disciplinarian. Only a stern hand could bring the Rebels and the American Indians under control. The same could be said for poachers and monopolists. The little general began what writer Emerson Hough called in Grinnell's *Forest and Stream* Sheridan's "Greater Yellowstone Movement."[18] His plan was to extend the park's eastern boundary by forty miles and its southern boundary by ten miles. This three-thousand-square-mile addition to the park was a bold challenge to the railroad's design on the land. It was also an amazingly visionary thought, among the first holistic views of nature preservation proposed based on the needs and ranges of wildlife. It would be eighty years before twin-brother bear biologists Frank and John Craighead would envision a Yellowstone ecosystem that spread beyond the park's boundaries. But to the strategic general, who had hunted and toured the region, park expansion was the natural answer for protecting its wildlife.

In addition to Grinnell, Sheridan received support from what at first seems an unlikely source, William "Buffalo Bill" Cody, who had scouted for Sheridan during the American Indian Wars in the 1860s. Cody wrote that the slaughter of game on which he gained his name, "does not find favor in the West as it did a decade or so ago."[19] Cody's voice brought the western mainstream into the fold as well as the mythic West. He essentially said that the old West is going fast and protecting wildlife and Yellowstone was a way to preserve a piece of the days before settlement.

To clinch his case, Sheridan called on a more powerful partner, Missouri Senator George Graham Vest. As chairman of the Senate Committee on Territories, Vest was in the best position to challenge the administration's Yellowstone policies. Sheridan sent his report on Yellowstone to Vest in late 1882 with his recommendations, including those of expanding the park and putting the army in charge. "The suggestions made in my report are the only ones left for us to do to save this noble game," he wrote Vest.[20]

Meanwhile the Northern Pacific was attempting to increase its stranglehold on the park. It was working behind the scenes to get its plan for rails in the park approved. If it couldn't get rails directly into the park, its supporters called for reducing the size of the reserve so it could at least run a line to mines in Cooke City (named for Jay Cooke), isolated on the northwest corner of the park.

Vest, influenced by Sheridan, introduced a comprehensive bill on January 3, 1883, to expand Yellowstone's boundaries and stop the Northern Pacific's effort to gain monopoly control. It was a remarkable proposal for the time. It gave the park's regulations, long ignored, the force of law. It protected most of the park's wildlife from hunting, increased appropriations to enforce these rules, and prohibited the granting of monopolies. It also granted Sheridan's key recommendation: It authorized the use of troops to manage the park.

Don't forget that while all of this was happening, the United States was still deeply involved in the American Indian Wars. Tens of thousands of emigrants were flowing into the West following the Civil War, chasing dreams of free land, gold, and economic success. The idea of allowing a railroad, the most modern method of transportation to run into the people's park to take them to its most famous attractions was not then, nor perhaps would it be now, considered inherently a threat to the park's integrity. But the wanton exploitation of wildlife, in the wake of the bison's near demise across the West, struck a nerve that sent strong signals to an increasingly urban East. Grinnell's public campaign against poaching was beginning to sway national opinion. Teller, the secretary of the interior who handed Northern Pacific's minions the Yellowstone monopoly, gave in on that front. He decided to prohibit all killing of game within Yellowstone.

That was enough to prevent Vest's bill from passing. But the Missourian didn't give up. Vest attached a rider to the Sundry Civil Appropriations Bill that forbade the secretary of the interior from granting monopolies in the park. Sheridan's recommendation to authorize the use of troops in the park was added as an amendment. The bill became law on March 3, 1883. Northern Pacific's front company still got its leases to areas surrounding the attractions in the park, but only for a ten-year period and only on a measly ten acres of land.

In retrospect, the forces of government preservation appear to have fought the forces of commercialization to a draw. Some concessions had been made, but Sheridan's dream of a Greater Yellowstone was still unrealized. Vest had been a great and powerful ally, but Sheridan now went higher to promote his park expansion plan. In the summer of 1883, he convinced Chester A. Arthur, the president of the United States, to come along on an expedition to Yellowstone.

Arthur, Sheridan, and their entourage, including Vest, traveled by rail from Chicago to Green River, Wyoming, on August 2. Then they went by wagon the 220 miles to Fort Washakie in the Wind River Mountains southeast of the park. From there, the party rode horseback 230 miles through Jackson Hole to Old Faithful. Arthur made it to Mammoth Hot Springs by August 31. For Arthur, whose health was failing, the trip was a welcome respite. He and Vest caught 105 pounds of trout in one day, but Sheridan strictly forbade anyone to hunt. Along the trail, the Democratic president and lifelong Republican Sheridan became fast friends. The stories of their trip sent back east by Sheridan's brother Michael added to the public's fascination with Yellowstone. Arthur's health went downhill after the trip, and he was never able to aid Sheridan's campaign beyond bringing more national attention to the area.

Despite the fierce battle over the park's future, Sheridan had not broken his ties with the railroad. On their return journey from Yellowstone, Sheridan and Arthur took a wagon to the Northern Pacific line in Cinnabar and then rode to St. Paul, where they helped celebrate the completion of the Northern Pacific transcontinental line.

Arthur's well-publicized trip added to the support for protecting Yellowstone. After the trip Vest was able to stave off attempts by westerners to return the park to the public domain and reopen it for private development and homesteading. And he had stopped the Northern Pacific from running a spur line into the park. But he was never able to get the appropriations needed for the Department of the Interior to manage Yellowstone. Nor was Sheridan able to convince Congress to expand Yellowstone's boundaries.

In the 1880s, under weak and even corrupt leadership, Yellowstone foundered. Congress authorized a park police force in 1883, but it was made up mostly of political appointees who were unqualified and unwilling to stop people not only from poaching wildlife but also from carrying away pieces of the crystalline rock formed by the geysers and hot springs. The last straw was the scheming of the fourth park superintendent, Robert Carpenter. Carpenter, another lackey for the Northern Pacific, had tried to secure land within Yellowstone for the railroad so it could reach the Cooke City mines. When his conspiracy was discovered in Washington, he was removed and replaced by David Wear, who brought in a group of experienced backwoodsmen to patrol the park. Wear began to have some limited success in bringing the poaching under control. But time had run out for Yellowstone. The U.S. Congress was fed up with this experiment in preservation, and many congressmen, especially in the West, suggested it be reopened for settlement. Typical was the view of John A. Reagan, a congressman from Texas. It was not the place of government to get involved in "show business" or to provide "imperial parks for the few wealthy persons," he said.[21]

On August 4, 1886, Congress cut off all Department of the Interior funds to the park. The very idea of protecting large expanses of land as national parks or other reserves was now in peril. To prevent chaos there, two days later, on August 6, Lucius Quintus Cincinnatus Lamar, secretary of the interior under President Grover Cleveland, wrote the secretary of war requesting troops for Yellowstone under the authority of the 1883 Sundry Appropriations Act.

Once that was granted, Sheridan was now in charge of Yellowstone National Park. Once again his nation was calling on him to act in an emergency. He was asked once again to ride to the rescue, just as he did at Cedar Creek, in Texas, and in Chicago. The situation in the park worsened with each passing day. "Since action of Congress, lawlessness in the park has rapidly increased on part of lessees and others," Wear said on August 13 in a telegram to Interior officials.[22]

This was a job, Sheridan decided, for the cavalry.

CHAPTER 5

The Cavalry Rides to Preservation's Rescue

The presence of the visible power of the Federal government, as represented by this little garrison, has proved a more efficient protection to the park than could have been hoped. It is reasonable to suppose that the same moral effect would follow if the forests were placed under the control of the organized and disciplined military forces of the nation.

—Charles S. Sargent, *Garden and Forest Magazine*, September 10, 1890

CAPTAIN MOSES HARRIS rode at the head of a dusty blue column of the First Cavalry up the final grade of the Gardiner Stage Road on August 20, 1886, through rolling hills of sagebrush to the crest of a hill overlooking a wide valley surrounded by steep rocky cliffs and pine-covered mountains. The steaming porcelain travertine hill called Mammoth Hot Springs, one of the world's most stunning natural wonders, appeared directly in his path. At the bottom of the road between Harris's column of cavalry and the thermal feature was the 141-room, three-story Mammoth Hot Springs Hotel.

It wasn't the magnificent crystal rock formation that immediately drew Harris's gaze, however, but another, more ominous, natural phenomenon. On the mountainside to the east, just across the valley from the hotel, a huge forest fire was burning out of control. In the late afternoon heat, lodgepole pines were torching, and the woods popped, cracked, and exploded like a scene out of the Civil War veteran's battlefield past. Harris led two lieutenants, twenty enlisted men, fifty-six horses, seventeen mules, three army wagons, and one ambulance down the final hundred yards to where he would establish Fort Sheridan at the foot of the hill. His nose filled with the scent of sulfur and wood smoke as he considered how to bring order to the chaos that had placed him in control of the 2.2-million-acre national park.

Harris was the kind of man General Phil Sheridan instinctively turned to when he had a difficult and critical job to do. The feisty general preferred men like himself, who turned their faces into the battle and rode forward until they won or were killed. Harris's first order as the new superintendent of Yellowstone National Park addressed what he sized up as the immediate threat to his command. He ordered his troopers to put out the fire.

Armed with shovels, buckets, and axes the soldiers crossed the Gardiner River and attacked the fire, already several hundred acres in extent and growing fast. The inexperienced troopers had little effect on the fire but a profound impact on the future of the nation. The cavalry's firefight that day was the federal government's first entry into wildland fire fighting.

On August 13, Sheridan himself had issued the orders for Harris and his men to ride to Mammoth Hot Springs. There, Harris was "to perform the duties in the Yellowstone National Park that recently devolved upon the Superintendent of the Park and his assistants."[1] Harris's men, horses, and supplies were loaded on to the Northern Pacific Railroad and sent to the end of the line, Cinnebar Station, ten miles north of Mammoth.

Sheridan's vague orders masked the huge job that lay before Harris and his soldiers. He had no laws to back up his enforcement of behavior in the park. Congress had just cut off all funding. Many in Congress wanted the national park dismantled and the park opened up again to settlement. Even Yellowstone's supporters were skeptical that the military could preserve the integrity of the park. The Northern Pacific Railroad was still hoping that it could win control over the area it helped preserve for its own development. Poachers, skin hunters, and rock collectors were looting the park with impunity now that Congress had removed Superintendent David Wear's authority. To make matters worse, two other large fires were burning out of control along with the blaze that Troop M first saw as it headed into the valley.

Harris had no special qualifications for the job of acting superintendent. He had never seen the park until the day he rode in. Captain Gus Doane, William Ludlow, or other officers who had explored the park seemed more obvious choices. But Sheridan knew what he was doing when he picked Harris. The task would take creativity and leadership as much as courage.

Moses Harris was born September 6, 1839, in Andover, New Hampshire. He joined the army as a young man, and when the Civil War began, he was sent with his unit to protect Washington, D.C. Harris fought in several campaigns as a cavalry trooper before he was offered a commission as a second lieutenant in August 1864 during Sheridan's Shenandoah campaign.

The young lieutenant made his mark while he was second in command of a squadron of 150 cavalrymen on August 28, 1864, at Smithville, Virginia. The generals ordered the squadron to attack head-on a Confederate force ten times its size. With sabers drawn, the smaller Union force plunged into the rebel brigade, which had slowed to fire its pistols. One shot felled the commanding Union captain, and Harris then led the charge. The tiny force broke the Confederates into a panicked retreat,[2] and for his gallantry and inspired leadership there Harris would later be awarded the Congressional Medal of Honor.[3]

Several weeks later, Harris saw action at Cedar Creek, the battle of Sheridan's greatest glory. Thousands of soldiers broke and ran under the pressure of Confederate General Jubal Early's morning attack. Harris and his troops stood their ground even though, in the words of historian of the cavalry R. P. Page Wainwright, "subjected to an enfilading fire."[4]

"The personal example . . . of the brigade, regimental, and squadron commanders [Harris among them] kept the men up to their places until the return of the Sixth Corps."[5] Sheridan made the ride from Winchester, reinforcements arrived, and the rest is history.

Harris proved repeatedly that he could deliver when the odds were against him. But like many veterans, his rise through the ranks was stymied by the glut of officers available after the war. In 1872 he was finally promoted to captain and was put in charge of the First Cavalry's Troop M, which he would eventually lead into the park from Fort Custer on the Bighorn River east of the park.

The day after Harris arrived, he surveyed the park accompanied by Wear. He assigned soldiers to each of the six patrol cabins scattered through the park, which Wear's assistants were vacating, and many of his other troops to fight the fires. Wear told Harris the fires were set deliberately by "a class of frontiersmen, hunters, trappers, and squaw men"[6] who flaunted the park's rules and challenged the authority of the United States. Harris would later blame American Indians as well for setting some of the fires he encountered that first season. Like Sheridan, Harris saw his duties patrolling the park as a natural extension of his duties in the American Indian wars.[7] In Harris's mind, fighting fires would become inexorably linked to restoring order to Yellowstone. What was needed to prevent fires was what his mentor Sheridan called "firm control." Whatever the motive, many of the fires, Harris later reported, actually started with unattended campfires.

Now that he had people attempting to put out the fires he first encountered, Harris got down to the business of setting up a management system for the park. He developed a set of rules that he expected park visitors to follow and troopers to enforce. They included a ban on cutting green trees, removing minerals, hunting, trapping, and uncontrolled grazing in the park. He told campers to "only build fires when actually necessary."[8] For Harris, fire was as much the enemy as the "unscrupulous hunters" living just outside Yellowstone's boundaries.[9] He carried out the task that Sheridan had given him with as much determination as he did his stand at the battle of Cedar Creek. But he could not subdue these enemies through force of arms. His technique for dealing with people who broke the rules was simple—he'd throw them out of the park. Fire control proved to be far more complicated. Yet it was a natural outgrowth of the army's efforts to stop vandalism and bring order to the park.

The view of forest fire in America was rapidly changing in the waning decades of the nineteenth century. American Indians had long used fires to drive game, open up forests, or improve habitat by encouraging tender young browse and grasses. Settlers had burned forests and grass-lands to open the lands for agriculture and in some areas to clear out smaller trees to improve the growth of larger ones. But as forests began to be viewed as capital assets—as Langford had suggested in his 1873 Yellowstone report—fire was increasingly seen as a threat to those assets, and to humans caught in its path. Fire's danger, once out of con-trol, had been demonstrated at Peshtigo and in other fires in the North Woods of the Midwest. Sheridan saw firsthand the destruction from fire in Chicago. In 1881, more than 130 people were killed in forest fires in Michigan. The transformation of the United States from wilderness to frontier to farmlands and communities reshaped Americans' wildland fire policy.[10] At a time when the nation was developing a love of wild ani-mals and wild places, it was losing its tolerance for wildfire. The logic that bred the idea that fires needed to be stopped helped pioneer the opposition to the cut-and-run ethic that still dominated the new indus-trial America. Forests were no longer some unlimited intangible but the natural landscape of places that had been settled, established, or sur-veyed. Fire was a threat to these landscapes people valued. Now that the wilderness was tamed, fire must be brought under human control. It was in this frame of mind that Harris went to work in Yellowstone.

The Yellowstone Harris found was a landscape long shaped by cli-mate, geology, and fire. After all, Yellowstone's unique geysers and hot springs are the result of millions of years of volcanic activity. These geo-logical features lie at the top of a huge hot spot rising from the crust of the earth. As the continent has moved gradually over this hot spot for billions of years, its location has shifted from Oregon, through Idaho, to its current site. The most cataclysmic event in the region's history was not the fires of 1988. It was the ancient volcanic eruption that created the caldera, essentially a huge crater, where Yellowstone today lies. The massive explosion sent molten rock more than 160 feet into the air and spewed hot ash and lava thousands of miles from the park with a force 2,500 times that of Mount St. Helens in 1980.

After the volcanic eruption 630,000 years ago, the next major natu-ral event in Yellowstone was the receding of glaciers there 12,000 years ago. After that, forests developed over the landscape, covering much the same area as today. As the climate changed, the forests and grasslands were transformed, often by fires. We know this thanks to the extensive Yellowstone fires of 1988, which prompted dozens of research projects that have dramatically increased scientists' knowledge of the area's fire history.

The most significant is an analysis of charcoal deposits in the park's lakes conducted by Cathy Whitlock, Sarah H. Millspaugh, and Patrick Bartlein of the University of Oregon.[11] They found that the frequency of forest fires in the park has been correlated with the level of drought during July for the last 17,000 years. Measurable fires occurred most frequently during that period 9,900 years ago, when the climate was warmer and drier. Since then, as the climate became cooler and wetter, the frequency of fires dropped to fewer than two or three fires per one thousand years in the area around the lakes. This is an area dominated by the lodgepole pine forests that cover seventy-seven percent of the park.

Lodgepole pine, the species that covers most of the high elevation forests of the Rocky Mountains, is evolutionarily tied to fire. Most lodgepole tree cones are "serotinous"; this means that the cones open and spread their seeds only with exposure to extreme heat during fires. Other stands of lodgepole trees with "nonserotinous" cones open with less heat. Even in the worst fires, where the cones are mostly incinerated, the cones protect some of the precious seeds so they can restock the stand. When fires were more frequent in Yellowstone, species such as Douglas-fir, which develop a thick bark that can withstand frequent smaller fires, probably were more numerous than lodgepole pine. But in the period of less frequent fires that has typified the last seven thousand years, the lodgepole pine became the dominant species.

Fire turns living plants and dead organic material into usable nutrients that can be cycled through the often relatively nutrient-poor ecosystems of the region. Soil fertility is enhanced by fire, and fire acts as an essential recycler of carbon and other mineral elements in the ecosystem as plants and trees burn. But the research showed that this recycling process was stretched out over centuries in Yellowstone's past.

Throughout the northern Rockies, including Yellowstone, the climate is too dry for decomposition during most of the summer and too cold during the winter. The result is that plant growth far exceeds decomposition, and biomass builds up on the soil. Periodic fire recycles this biomass and makes up for the lack of decomposition. But in the moist areas of the higher elevations, fires burned to any extent only during periods of extreme drought. The last series of extreme droughts in Yellowstone came during the early 1700s. Fire scars, tree rings, and other evidence show that huge fires, comparable to those in 1988, burned then. Relatively large fires also burned in the 1860s, just as explorers were beginning to reach Yellowstone.

On drier areas, such as the lower elevations in the north, fires were more frequent historically. In the northern grasslands, fires have always been more frequent, burning at twenty- to twenty-five-year intervals. These are the areas Harris first saw, where the fuels were most flammable and where humans have the most impact on the size and frequency of fires.

Yet Harris was to learn the lesson of forest fires that Robert Barbee, Yellowstone's superintendent in 1988, and modern firefighters would relearn a century later: Once a large fire gets going and conditions are right, even the U.S. Army can't stop it.

The fire Harris saw as he entered the park in August was still burning when he filed his first annual report in October 1886. Other fires reported were extinguished by snow, not by the troopers he had sent to fight them. "Destructive forest fires have been raging in the park during the greater portion of the present season," he reported. "The facility with which forest fires can be started and the impossibility of extinguishing them, when once under way, by any available methods, render it extremely difficult in this high and wind-swept region to guard against them."[12]

Harris's major challenges in managing the park were the lack of a major road system, primitive communications, and the perennial problem of park managers—money. He also suffered from what the military today would call mission creep. The army's stop-gap deployment to Yellowstone lasted thirty-two years, long past Harris's own command.

Harris was forced to improvise a system that would not only protect park resources but also accommodate visitors, two tasks far beyond the experience of the U.S. Army. The Northern Pacific, trying every political connection it could, continued to seek a line into the heart of Yellowstone. The other concessionaires Harris allowed in to build and run hotels were often corrupt or found his military approach stifling, and that limited development.

Harris shared his mentor Sheridan's belief in the necessary role of the army and the federal government in preserving Yellowstone. "I have been very forcefully impressed with the danger to which [the park] is subjected by the greed of private enterprise," Harris wrote in his annual report. "All local influence centers in schemes whereby the park can be used for pecuniary advantage. In the unsurpassed grandeur of its natural condition, it is the pride and glory of the nation, but, if under the guise of improvement, selfish interests are permitted to make merchandise of its wonders and beauties, it will inevitably become a by-word and a reproach."[13]

By the time Harris left the park in 1889, he and his troopers could point to some important successes. Without a legal framework or adequate funds he put the first dent in the rampant poaching and specimen collecting that had taken place since the park had been established. His troopers also appear to have become pretty fair firefighters. In 1888 more than one hundred fires were reported, but burned acreage was limited to five acres. Early in 1889, the Harvard botanist Charles S. Sargent proposed in *Garden and Forest*, the popular magazine he edited, that all forestlands under control of the federal government be withdrawn from possible sale or entry and be placed under the protection of the U.S. Army. Harris's tiny force was already changing the thinking of the growing movement to protect federal lands. "The presence of the visible power of the federal government, as represented by this little garrison, has proved a more efficient protection to the park than could have been hoped," Sargent wrote.[14]

When Harris was reassigned, Frazer Augustus Boutelle was named as his successor. Captain Boutelle, the man who fired the first shot in the Modoc War, the major American Indian conflict in California, was awarded the acting superintendent command despite heavy lobbying for the job by now Captain Doane, the army's first man in Yellowstone. Boutelle took on the firefighting task in 1889 with vigor and vision. His untamed zeal led to his short tenure in the park. However brief, his efforts established many of the firefighting policies and systems on which others would model future fire-control efforts throughout the nation.[15]

Boutelle based his strategy on fire prevention. He insisted that visitors camp only in designated campgrounds so their fires could be monitored. These were the first campgrounds specially designated in the nation, setting a precedent that modern campers take for granted. Few understand that it was fire control that brought people from the crowded cities into the wilderness only to set them feet apart in tents. Boutelle would throw visitors out of the park if they didn't camp in the right places or if they left their campfires unattended.

Boutelle linked a series of lookouts with telegraph lines, telephones, and roads so fires could be discovered, reported, and responded to quickly. It was basic military strategy similar to the army's approach to fighting American Indians. Limit the weapons of war—with American Indians, rifles; with fire, ignitions. When a fight starts, get to the scene fastest with the most troops to overwhelm the enemy before it gets reinforcements.

Ironically, the strategy that defeated the American Indians was the alternative strategy for firefighting—to starve the enemy into submission. By limiting the fuel available, fire cannot climb from the ground into the trees and can be kept under control. Sheridan defeated the Sioux by driving the bison nearly to extinction. But Boutelle never considered such an option in fighting fires. It would be a decade before foresters first recognized that fire was a natural dimension of the forest and that cogent arguments could be made for the alternative strategy of starving the fire rather than stopping it. By then, though, the army model of direct suppression was deeply embedded in land management orthodoxy.

Boutelle's problem was not vision. Nor was it motivation. His problem was tact. His call for more equipment got him into trouble with the

Department of the Interior. Soon after he took over, he realized his men didn't have some of the basic tools necessary to carry out his firefighting program. He requested by telegraph funds to buy twenty axes and twenty rubber buckets. It was a simple and relatively inexpensive request. He heard nothing. Boutelle wrote three follow-up letters, all ignored by Secretary of the Interior John Noble. Boutelle lost his patience and likely his perspective, perhaps because, as he wrote, he had been "personally fighting forest fires for some days and nights."[16]

"I shall not be ignored," Boutelle now wrote. "In the Department in which I have served for twenty-eight years I have been accustomed to have some respectful actions taken on my papers."[17] This slight of the Department of the Interior finally got Noble's attention. However, it didn't get the response Boutelle was seeking. Noble instead responded in kind, calling Boutelle "troublesome" and "quick to attribute delinquencies to others."[18] Boutelle kept the exchange going with a wounded reply in his annual report about the seriousness of the situation. "Rubber buckets were indispensable," he wrote. He further noted that a Mr. Leavis of Pennsylvania "had donated $40 from his own pocket" to purchase the buckets. "'If this great United States Government or the Secretary of Interior has not money to buy you a few rubber buckets for the protection of this wonderful and beautiful country,'" Boutelle quoted Leavis, "'I have!'"[19]

In all, Boutelle's small force suppressed sixty-one of the seventy fires he reported in 1889. Yet the fires that were not controlled burned large portions of the park. In 1890, the fire season was unusually fierce, and Boutelle continued his crusade to get Noble and Interior to recognize the severity of the problem. "Forest fires raged uncontrolled on every side of the park and destroyed millions of acres," he said in a fit of hyperbole that no doubt confirmed Noble's view of his credibility. The truth was that fighting forest fires was difficult, backbreaking work. In a fire in Gibbon Canyon, Boutelle said, the steep climb "was so difficult that two men had epileptic fits from the effort."[20]

When Boutelle once again brought up the rubber bucket incident, his report was returned for reconsideration. Boutelle had done him a "great injustice,"[21] Noble said. Before the year was out, Boutelle was sent to fight the Sioux.

Boutelle's system still didn't make a dent in the large fires that burned for weeks despite all of his efforts. But his men were able to put out many small fires that had cropped up near roads and lookouts and could be attacked quickly. Yellowstone's firefighters adapted other basic strategies used to fight wars for use in their fire control program that firefighters elsewhere would copy. Fire patrols were set up that reported fires back to headquarters, which dispatched men to the fire to dig fire lines, which they were then typically ordered to hold. If the fire was too great, they were ordered to fall back and reestablish a new line. Coupled with the goal of overcoming frontier and American Indian attitudes toward fire, the army was developing not only techniques for firefighting but also philosophy.

Second Lieutenant F. J. Arnold highlighted these new techniques in a report on an August 8, 1898, fire that was heading toward the park near what is now West Yellowstone. At 9 p.m. Arnold got news of the fire at the Riverside Station on the Madison River and passed it on by telegraph to the acting superintendent, his commanding officer. An hour later he got his orders to take twenty men with tools and rations and proceed to the fire at once.[22]

After marching all night the soldiers arrived at the fire at 6 a.m. It had spread to a square mile and was burning briskly. The troopers immediately went to work, and wielding eight shovels and an axe, they brought the fire under control by noon. The afternoon breeze brought the fire back to life, however, and it overwhelmed the force. Even with twenty additional firefighters from Mammoth Hot Springs arriving on the scene at 1 p.m., the platoon was required to retreat back to the Madison River, a mile and a half away. The next morning the rested soldiers lined up like a picket along the front of the fire chopping away trees and throwing dirt on fires cooled by the night air. They extinguished the fire by 9 a.m. and then mounted soldiers patrolled the lines for two days until it was clear they had won the battle.[23] By then, the federal model of wildland protection, preserved by Sheridan's orders to send in the cavalry, was firmly in place.

Sheridan never returned to Yellowstone, but he continued to press his goal of expanding the park's boundaries to protect more wildlife habitat. In 1887, Theodore Roosevelt, then a young New Yorker who had moved west to ranch and hunt, called George Bird Grinnell, Sheridan, and other prominent sportsmen to a dinner in Manhattan to discuss the creation of a hunting organization. The next month the Boone and Crockett Club was formed with Roosevelt as its president. The group would take up the cause for Yellowstone, calling for additional funding, authority, and expansion of the park. In 1888 it made Sheridan a founding life member. But the wear of so many campaigns finally caught up with the fifty-seven-year-old general. He died later that year of a heart attack in New York.

Through Grinnell, and now Roosevelt, the Yellowstone campaign continued on two fronts, as these two giants of conservation took the mantle from the Civil War hero. The army was finally given authority to prosecute poachers in Yellowstone with the passage of the Lacy Act in 1894. The bill, considered the first wildlife protection law passed in the United States, placed states in charge of wildlife protection but gave the federal government authority to prosecute interstate violations and violations in Yellowstone. The Boone and Crocket Club also pressed Congress to establish a set of forest reserves, modeled on Yellowstone policy. The designation was intended to protect federal forestlands from the same private monopoly control Sheridan had fought in Yellowstone. Bills creating such reserves were killed in 1888, 1889, and 1890. Finally, in 1891, Congress gave the president authority to set aside federal forests in the reserves. President Benjamin Harrison wasted little time in designating the first of these, the Yellowstone Reserve adjacent to Yellowstone in Wyoming. It included much of the area Sheridan had proposed adding to the park in 1882. Later, other adjacent lands were added in Montana and Idaho. Sheridan's vision of a Greater Yellowstone overseen by the army was now fulfilled.

The budding conservation movement now had in Yellowstone its first successful model for preserving large areas. Its leaders were advocating alternatives to the frontier-driven policies of cut-and-run development ranging from wilderness preservation to utilitarian wise-use policies. The army's protection in Yellowstone appealed to both camps.

The best-known voice of wilderness preservation in the late 1800s was the prolific nature writer John Muir, born in Scotland and raised in

Wisconsin. His books and articles echoed the ideas of his own heroes, Henry David Thoreau and Ralph Waldo Emerson, and painted romantic images of places untainted by humans. Muir founded the Sierra Club in 1892 and led the campaign in 1890 to make Yosemite a national park. He loved Yellowstone and wrote several articles about it in which he praised the army's management. "Under this care the forests are flourishing, protected from both axe and fire; and so, of course are the shaggy beds of underbrush and the herbaceous vegetation," Muir wrote in his 1901 book *Our National Parks*.[24]

Yellowstone's success spread the army to other parks as they were established. Yosemite, Sequoia, and Kings Canyon in 1890 and Glacier in 1910 were established as national parks under army oversight. The army transferred the techniques of fire control developed in Yellowstone to these places even though the forests were very different.

Charles Sargent was the chief advocate of such army control of parks and forests. In the 1880s, he pressed his plan for withdrawal of all national forests from entry and called for the appointment of a national commission to develop a plan for permanent administration of the lands. Sargent's plan went beyond fire control, as we've seen. He envisioned the army training professional foresters at West Point, much as it already trained engineers. His plan called for an army experimental forest to develop forestry techniques for managing the federal forests. Officers with forestry training would be placed in charge of the forest reserves with enlisted guards who would fight fires and prevent illegal logging. To Sargent and his supporters the army was the natural outfit for protecting forests. The U.S. Army Corps of Engineers was already protecting hundreds of thousands of people from flooding through maintenance of dams and levees along the nation's major rivers and harbors. So, protecting parks and forests seemed like a natural extension of the army's role in the West.

In 1896 the National Academy of Sciences convened a commission on forestry at the request of President Grover Cleveland. The Department of the Interior asked the panel to develop legislation to protect the forests and to determine the impacts of forests on climate, soil, and water conditions. It also asked, "Is it desirable and practicable to preserve from fire and to maintain permanently as forested lands those portions of the public domain now bearing wood growth, for the supply of timber?"[25]

Sargent was named chairman of the commission. He had been chairman of the New York State Forest Commission and originator of the Adirondack Forest Preserve, and had written books and articles on forests for several decades. Henry Abbott, an army general, engineer, and authority on stream hydraulics and physics, gave the military advocates a strong voice on the panel. The commission also included Muir as an ex-officio member, and a geologist, a zoologist, an agriculture professor, and a young forester, fresh from his schooling in France. This was Gifford Pinchot's first entry onto the national scene, but it would not be his last. He was the first native-born American with a forestry degree, and he was a man with a mission. He had seen the carefully crafted forests of France and Germany, models of efficiency and order. He appreciated the work the army had done in bringing order to Yellowstone, and when the commission began its work, he at first agreed with Sargent on military control of the forests. But eventually he viewed the command structure as too autocratic. Pinchot wanted forests to be used, not simply saved from destruction by fire or uncontrolled logging.

Sargent and Muir's more experienced voices won the day, and Pinchot would have to wait for a more opportune time. "Fire and pasturage . . . chiefly threatened the reserved forest lands of the public domain," the commission said in its 1897 report.[26] The panel recognized, as Harris had reported in 1886, that "no human agency can stop a Western forest fire when it has once obtained real headway." But the commission recognized that Yellowstone's troopers had shown that prevention and prompt action made fire control cost-effective as a means of reducing the losses from forest fires. It recommended that the army take over management of the forest reserves and put its firefighting savvy to work there. "Many of the duties are essentially military in character, and should be regulated for the present on military principles," the commission concluded.[27]

The commission also recommended the creation of 21 million additional acres of forest reserves, which Cleveland quickly approved. The army had demonstrated that the federal government could and should expand its permanent estate of public lands both for future use and preservation. Muir argued in an 1897 *Atlantic Monthly* article that fire was an even larger threat to the forests than logging. "It is not generally known that, not withstanding the immense quantities of timber cut every year for foreign and home markets and mines, from five to ten times as much is destroyed as is used, chiefly by running forest fires that only the federal government can stop," he wrote.[28]

The cavalry had originally come to Yellowstone's rescue with a limited mission and no obvious agenda. Only a decade later it had proven that the federal government could realistically control its immense federal domain. The troopers who diligently fought the fire in the eastern hills overlooking Mammoth Hot Springs had not only begun, by chance, the federal government's firefighting program. Harris's troops had also ensured that a large chunk of the American landscape would remain in the public's ownership. Since the government could manage these lands, Americans would hold in common a legacy that would strengthen its sense of freedom and security.

The cavalry had charged into national park management and won Sheridan's last battle even though he did not survive to see it. The pugnacious warrior-turned-preservationist had helped create the nation's public lands legacy, saved it from monopoly control, and then initiated the system on which future management would be based.

CHAPTER 6

The Gospel of Fire

God has cared for these trees, saved them from drought, disease, avalanches, and a thousand straining, leveling tempests and floods; but he cannot save them from fools—only Uncle Sam can do that.

—John Muir, *Our National Parks*, 1901

JOHN MUIR AND GIFFORD PINCHOT broke away from the rest of the National Academy of Sciences Forestry Commission in October 1896 as it toured the Grand Canyon. The fifty-eight-year-old naturalist and the thirty-year-old forester took off like kids cutting classes for a day-long jaunt along the south rim. Carrying only canteens, two hard-boiled eggs, and a sandwich apiece, Muir and Pinchot walked into the wild world where they were both most at home. Together they crawled into the chasm, exploring its sharp crevices and gazing with awe at the muddy churning of the Colorado River as it pounded over huge rocks below.

As always, the grandfatherly Muir spun stories and delivered a running commentary about the geology, flora, and fauna of the carved plateau. "When we came upon a tarantula he wouldn't let me kill it," Pinchot recalled.[1] Together they leaped into headstands to catch a unique perspective of the soft, multitextured tones of sandstone and burgundy that turned pink with the alpenglow.

When the sun went down, they started a campfire and built beds of cedar boughs in a thick stand of forest on the edge of canyon. Muir carried the conversation into the new day. As the sun rose, they broke camp. "We sneaked back like guilty schoolboys, well knowing that we must reckon with the other members of the Commission, who probably imagined we had fallen over a cliff," Pinchot wrote.[2]

The summer tour of the National Academy of Sciences Forestry Commission did more than set the course of public land management; it nourished the remarkable relationship between Muir and Pinchot, which was to have such a powerful effect on the conservation and environmental movements generations later. Muir, already a popular nature writer, had established himself as a leading voice for protecting public lands. In his writings, Muir mixed intricate details about botany, geology, and wildlife with a religious passion for what he saw as God's creative genius behind nature. His romanticism connected the growing conservation movement with the philosophical underpinnings of Thoreau and Emerson. Indeed, Muir spoke at Thoreau's funeral and later befriended Emerson when the literary giant visited Yosemite in 1871. Yet Muir was to move beyond the human-centered transcendentalism of the earlier romantics. Nature in his eyes was a far greater power than man and had value in and of itself.

Pinchot, the product of the emerging New York merchantile elite, had rejected the commercial interests of his father and grandfather, who had amassed a great fortune cutting down eastern forests, for a life of public service. He chose the infant profession of forestry, becoming the first native-born American trained in the established schools in Europe. As practiced by Europeans, forestry approached trees as a crop, which, when harvested, replanted, and protected from fire and disease, could provide a sustainable supply of lumber and other products while also yielding other public benefits such as scenery, wildlife habitat, and watershed protection.

Pinchot and Muir first met in 1893 in the Pinchot family brownstone in New York City. Encouraged by Pinchot's parents, the two men met several more times in the early 1890s. Through correspondence, Muir encouraged the young forester in his choice of studies and travels. But their relationship blossomed when they walked through the mountains of Montana, around Idaho's lake country, through the coastal forests of the Pacific Northwest, south through the Sierras, and finally in the Southwest with the Forestry Commission. Their common love was the outdoors. Whenever they could, they hiked when the rest of the party chose to ride in stage or train. Pinchot proved his worth with Muir when he was willing to sleep outside in the rain without a tent.3

For Pinchot, the Grand Canyon escapade was one of the high points of his life, "Such an evening as I have never had before or since," he wrote more than forty years later.4 Muir also expressed pleasure in the memory in his letters to Pinchot for the next decade, transforming the mutual moment into a bond that held them together until their eventual break that became the powerful parable of preservationism.

Muir's childlike enthusiasm for nature was instilled in him in his youth along the coast of Scotland, where he was born in 1838. There he played among seaside castles and rich meadows until he was eleven. Then his parents immigrated to Wisconsin, where the young boy was forced to work from dawn until dusk to help the family carve a farm out of the wilderness. He still found time to explore the surrounding forests and savannahs, teaching himself about science, math, and the classics and developing a keen intellectual awareness. He attended the University of Wisconsin for two and a half years, where he added formal studies of botany and geology to his lust for learning. After a thousand-mile walk to the Gulf of Mexico, Muir shipped off to California and then walked from San Francisco to the Yosemite Valley, arriving in 1869. It was a life-changing event for the thirty-year-old traveler, who was soon to lay down roots in one of the nation's most dramatic landscapes. He farmed and sawyered for a living and began writing about his observations of the natural tapestry that surrounded him.

Muir's first article, "Yosemite Glaciers," challenged the prevailing professional view that Yosemite's valley floor had been formed by a single cataclysmic event. Instead, Muir wrote, the valley was formed by a slow process of glaciations over millions of years. He turned out to be right and gained a national audience for his popular works on nature. As the nation was turning its eyes west, Muir was presenting people with an alternative nirvana to the gardens of plenty promised by the partisans of the plow. "These blessed mountains are so compactly filled with God's beauty, no petty personal hope or experience has room to be," Muir wrote in *My First Summer in the Sierra*.5

By 1876 he was advocating legislation to preserve forests from commercial exploitation and seeking to convince the nation that the time for unfettered development was over. In 1892 he joined with Robert Underwood Johnson, his editor at *The Century Magazine,* to form the Sierra Club. Having operated a sawmill, Muir was not averse to cutting trees. Despite his reputation as the father of the preservationist movement, Muir took a surprisingly open mind into the Forestry Commission debates. "It is impossible in the nature of things to stop at preservation," he wrote in *The Century Magazine.* "The forests must be and will be not only preserved but used. . . . The forests, like perennial fountains, may be made to yield a sure harvest of timber, while at the same time all their far-reaching uses may be maintained unimpaired."[6]

Muir, Pinchot, and the entire Forest Commission were opposed to the cut-and-run philosophy that was to that time endorsed and supported by programs designed to give away federal timber. Both men had a common view that fire was an enemy of the forests they sought to protect. They both advocated management programs based on the control of fire—programs modeled after the army's in Yellowstone. They both advocated raising the "firm control" of the federal government to carry out their goals of protecting the land. Each offered alternative paths that could be traced back to General Phil Sheridan.

On the 1896 western tour the two men were building the relationship of mentor and student that was to become the heart of the defining parable of the conservation and environmental movements. The clash between the older Muir's preservation values and Pinchot's utilitarian dream of scientific forestry management created the bipolar rules of engagement for most of the conservation debates that would follow. The story, amplified for both political and emotional effect by later followers of the two men's philosophies and institutions, masked the complexities of environmental history and of the pivotal role of fire policy therein.

The story goes something like this: Muir, the mentor, instructs the young Pinchot on the intrinsic values of nature. Together they convince their common friend and president, Theodore Roosevelt, to protect millions of acres of national treasures in national parks, forests, and refuges. But in the end the student chooses wise use over preservation and sells out to the evil interests of power and commercialism. Pinchot's misdeed, said Muir and his later followers, was backing the flooding of the Hetch Hetchy valley—a landscape nearly as scenic as the nearby Yosemite—to supply water for San Francisco. Their fight became the yin and the yang of conservation. Future conservationists defined their own place in the conservation political milieu by whether they took Muir's side or Pinchot's. Future debates were defined against the backdrop of preservation versus wise use.

The story, although true in many respects, is only a piece of the complex conservation picture that had developed at the end of the nineteenth century and the beginning of the twentieth. Its one great fallacy is that the two men turned T. R. Roosevelt into a conservationist. His active involvement with the Boone and Crockett Club, which he cofounded with Grinnell, was far more influential than either man's efforts in the late 1880s and early 1890s. It was the Boone and Crockett Club that had taken up Sheridan's fight to save Yellowstone from the railroad monopoly. It also had championed the law that gave the army authority to prosecute poachers in Yellowstone. Finally, the Boone and Crockett Club, with Roosevelt as its president, had led the effort to establish national forest reserves, beginning with the Yellowstone Reserve that followed along the lines of Sheridan's Greater Yellowstone vision. Using the forest reserve law he helped create, Roosevelt, once president, added 150 million acres to the forest reserve system.

The reality is that, despite their differences, Muir, Pinchot, and Roosevelt shared a common view that only the combined forces of the federal government could counterbalance the power of capitalism in protecting the nation's treasures of nature. The states didn't have the collective will. Private efforts were doomed to fall short. To all three, conservation and federal action were inescapably tied together.

But from the beginning Muir and Pinchot's different core values signaled different visions for how the government would control the land. By the time the commission had released its recommendations in 1897, the two men were moving away from the bonds they had built on the edge of the south rim.

Even before the Forestry Commission gathered, Pinchot had a different plan for managing the public lands than leaving it to the army. In 1894, Robert Underwood Johnson sponsored a symposium to discuss Charles Sargent's plan for army protection of all forest reserves. Pinchot, only beginning to get notice for his writings in Sargent's *Garden and Forest Magazine*, offered a counterproposal. He called for "a forest service, a commission of scientifically trained men," to manage the forest reserves instead of the army.

Despite these views, Sargent invited him on to the Forestry Commission in 1896 but soon regretted it. Sargent, like Muir, preferred the forests preserved, not managed for timber production. In fact, at the time Sargent was more adamant about preservation than Muir was in his writings. The lines between preservation and management were drawn squarely on both how the reserves would be managed and by whom. Even as Muir's friendship with Pinchot grew on the trip, they grew further apart politically.

When Pinchot considered writing a minority report challenging Sargent's preservation plan, the elder botanist became angry at the young forester's insolence. Pinchot backed down and Sargent's recommendations ruled the day with Muir's strong support. In addition to its call for expansion of army control, the report recommended 21 million acres of the West for additional forest reserves. President Grover Cleveland followed through and with his signature expanded the nation's protected forests.

But Pinchot was not deterred. Even if the army had organized a forestry school at West Point, as Sargent suggested, Pinchot believed its chain of command to be too autocratic. He wanted foresters to have enough autonomy to react to local conditions. He found other shortcomings in Sargent's plan as well: He pointed out that it lacked a central bureaucracy to coordinate support for and to defend politically the foresters' on-the-ground work.

Muir and Pinchot also shared a rudimentary understanding of the ecological processes on which the forests they both loved were built. Both men were familiar with the writings of George Perkins Marsh, a lawyer, congressman, and diplomat generally credited with inspiring the science of ecology. In his 1864 book, *Man and Nature*, Marsh compared the destruction of Vermont's forests and farmland to the deforestation he had seen in Europe as an ambassador to Italy. He argued that changes humans cause to nature can have long-term destructive consequences. But he also offered hope, arguing that people can make choices that preserve the integrity of the natural world and benefit it and them. "We are never justified in assuming a force to be insignificant because its measure is unknown, or even because no physical effect can now be traced to it as its origin," Marsh wrote in *Man and Nature*.7

Their familiarity with Marsh and their own keen observations of forests led Pinchot and Muir to recognize that fire had shaped many of the forests of the West. Muir, writing about the old-growth Douglas-fir forests around Puget Sound, noted that moss and decay in the moist areas made the forest appear as if it had been there for centuries. Then, as he moved up the slope, he found trees ranging from fifteen to fifty years in age.

"These last show plainly enough that they have been devastated by fire, as the black melancholy monuments rising here and there above the young growth bear witness," Muir wrote in *Steep Trails*. "Then, with this fiery, suggestive testimony, on examining those sections whose trees are a hundred years old or two hundreds, we find the same fire-records, as though heavily veiled with moss and lichens, showing that a century or two ago the forests that stood there have been swept away in some tremendous fire at the time when rare conditions of drought made their burning possible. Then, the bare ground sprinkled with the winged seeds from the edges of the burned district, a new forest sprang up."8

Pinchot expanded on Muir's lessons in a remarkable article published in *National Geographic* in 1899, when he was head of the U.S. Department of Agriculture's small Division of Forestry. "A few observers who have lived with the forest, such as John Muir of California, have grouped fire with temperature and moisture as one of the great factors which govern the distribution and character of forest growth," Pinchot wrote.9 "Fires determine the presence or absence of forest in a given region far more generally than is often supposed." Walking through the same forest, Pinchot noted that young seedlings were found in abundance in unshaded areas where the undergrowth had burned away, leaving only the soil. "I did not see a single young seedling of Douglas-fir under the forest cover, not a single opening made by the fire did not contain them," he wrote. "In a word, the distribution of [Douglas] fir in Washington, where it is by all odds the most valuable commercial tree, is governed, first of all, so far as we know at the present time, by fire. Had fires been kept out of these forests in the last thousand years the fir which gives them their distinctive character would not be in existence, but would be replaced in all probability by the hemlock, which fills even the densest of the Puget Sound forests with its innumerable seedlings."[10]

Though recognizing so clearly the role of fire in the regeneration of forests, Pinchot was prevented by his forestry education from seeing the significance of allowing fire to play a role in future management. Fire prevention was not just an ingrained habit of the army but a bedrock value of European forestry, developed in a wetter region where fires were less common. His professional answer to fire's role in the forest was that forest managers could take its place. Foresters would reseed the land after harvest. They would grow the trees faster and more efficiently than nature. Eventually they would go a step further and replace fire with clear-cuts, mimicking the large openings and land disturbances on the landscape. So in his last line Pinchot offered a caveat to ensure that his reader was not unduly swayed by the entire article, "Relations of Forests and Forest Fires": "I hasten to add that these facts do not imply any desirability in the fires that are now devastating the West."[11]

Both Pinchot and Muir distinguished between the fires of long ago and the fires of their own time. For Muir, fire was just another force unleashed on the land by the unbridled armies of commercialism and greed. Spread by railroads and careless shepherds, loggers, and miners, fire was an invader into his paradise. He could see no hand of God in the blackened aftermath of a racing crown fire. Just as he saw God in the towering sequoias, Muir saw the devil in forest fires. Fire even invaded the sky. "For all of the summer months, over most of the mountain regions, the smoke of mill and forest fires is so thick and black that no sunbeam can pierce it," Muir wrote in *Our National Parks*. "There is no real sky and no scenery, nor is a mountain left in the landscape."[12]

The focus of past environmental historians on the political and philosophical battles of Muir and Pinchot obscured the role of fire control in the development of federal land policy. Both men supported a system of strong federal control over public lands and a proactive program of fire prevention and suppression. No matter who had eventually won the philosophical arguments that led Roosevelt to organize the modern public land bureaucracy, fire control was to be a central element.

Pinchot's unifying idea was scientific management, another one of the national trends that had emerged following the Civil War. He believed, like other progressive reformers of the time, that science could be used to transcend political pressures to cure social ills. If the power of the federal government were used to empower foresters, they could use their science to expand efficiently and apportion the resources of the forests. Science would tie them together. Science would shield them from commercialism.

Pinchot's ambition, his political savvy, and his administrative insight made him, as historian Char Miller declared, one of the creators of modern America.[13] He is best known for creating the U.S. Forest Service in 1905. But perhaps his greatest contribution was his work in transferring the power exercised in American society over public land management from the military to the civilian executive branch. Pinchot used the model created by Sheridan to protect Yellowstone, developed by Moses Harris and perfected by his successors, to give the federal government control of its immense public landscape. His achievement would not only transform government natural resources policy but also lay the groundwork for the New Deal a generation later.

Pinchot's success could not have happened without ascension to the presidency of that ultimate man of action—T. R. Roosevelt. An unconventional vice president in a Republican Party dominated by laissez-faire capitalists, Roosevelt took office on September 14, 1901, when President William McKinley was gunned down. Fourteen years earlier Roosevelt had joined with Grinnell in establishing the

Boone and Crockett Club, carrying on Sheridan's campaign to save Yellowstone from the monopolists and poachers. Now for the first and perhaps only time a conservation leader lived in the White House. A former rancher, active hunter, committed conservationist, and retired Rough Rider, Roosevelt could converse with either Muir or his close friend Pinchot on equal terms about nature.

In May 1903, Roosevelt completed the triangulate by visiting Muir in Yosemite. He joined the aging wilderness philosopher in sleeping in the open for three nights, including one on the edge of a cliff above the Yosemite Valley covered in a four-inch blanket of snow. The two men did not have the same kind of personal connection they each had with Pinchot, but Roosevelt was clearly influenced by his brief time with Muir. He wrote, "There is nothing in the world more beautiful than the Yosemite, the groves of giant Sequoias and redwoods, the Canyon of the Colorado, the Canyon of the Yellowstone, the three Tetons; and the people should see to it that they are preserved for their children and their children's children forever, with their majestic beauty all unmarred."[14]

Each of those places today is a national park, and protection to Roosevelt undoubtedly initially meant protection by the army. He knew of the army's record in Yellowstone and the other national parks. He shared Pinchot and Muir's revulsion of forest fires, which were viewed not as natural events but instead as the result of human incursions into the wilderness. "The most reprehensible waste is that of destruction, as in forest fires," Roosevelt said in a speech in 1908.[15]

When he chose between Muir's preservationist, caretaking view of federal control and Pinchot's, Roosevelt followed the path blazed by his friend toward scientific management. "Social and economic problems should be solved," Roosevelt said, "not through power politics, but by experts who would undertake scientific investigations and devise workable solutions."[16]

When Roosevelt took office, Pinchot was already head of the Division of Forestry in the Department of the Interior. This position had no authority, but gave the forester a platform from which to espouse his forestry crusade. In 1901 the division was changed to a bureau, and Pinchot began working to convince Roosevelt, his tennis and wrestling partner, to give it more authority. Roosevelt delivered, moving management of the forest reserves from Interior to the Department of Agriculture and into the willing hands of Pinchot.

Even though he saw the army as autocratic, Pinchot realized that it would take the same sense of loyalty and pride that made men follow Sheridan to their deaths to prevent his own foresters from succumbing to the lure of greed and commercialism. His rangers would need a sense of professionalism and camaraderie like that of the military to set them apart from the economic and cultural pressures of the communities they would serve. Pinchot brought in the brightest young foresters in the nation to transform the country's landscape management.

Many of these early followers of Pinchot were graduates of Harvard or Yale. Pinchot wanted men with formal educations in science and forestry, but he also wanted those, who, like himself and John Muir, appreciated the outdoors. He was developing a new breed of public servant, a cross between soldier, policeman, and technocrat, who must be able to independently make decisions that follow the direction set in Washington. He would train and filter out the best of these foresters at summer camps his bureau sponsored in Washington State. There, the men studied the growth rates of Douglas-fir, learned surveying and mapping, and began to build what would become lifelong friendships, sleeping under the stars, singing around the campfire, and climbing the mountains together.

The several hundred men who became the heart of the Forest Service were the vanguard in his crusade for public forestry and, secondarily, for federal control of forest policy. Together, they would turn the Bureau of Forestry into a close-knit team of technicians, ready to take over the forest reserves when Pinchot was able to make his move.

They spent their winters in Washington, preparing for their summer rides through the West, surveying the public timber, and mapping out the places Pinchot hoped to turn into his Bureau of Forestry empire. Their opportunity came in 1905 when President Roosevelt transferred the forest reserves to the control of the Department of Agriculture and the bureau. But their real coup came ironically enough in 1907 when powerful western congressmen attached a rider to the agriculture appropriation bill that would remove the president's authority to designate any more forest reserves. Roosevelt ordered Pinchot to write up proclamations to protect as much federal forest as possible before the deadline to sign the bill. Thanks to the summer rides of his young men, Pinchot was prepared. Working around the clock, he and his corps of foresters pieced together the necessary paperwork to add twenty-one new reserves and to expand existing ones, a total of 16 million new acres of reserves.

After these magnificent early conservation victories this close-knit band of brothers viewed themselves as an exclusive club: Pinchot's young men. "I have always been proud of being one of Gifford Pinchot's young men," said Elers Koch, one of the original Forest Service employees who grew up near Yellowstone. "It was as fine, enthusiastic, and inspired a group of public employees as was ever assembled."[17]

Pinchot's scientific forestry worked where the soil was rich, where the climate was right—in short, where trees could grow rapidly and increase in value enough to cover the costs of management. However, millions of acres of national forests were unproductive lands, difficult to access, or grew trees such as lodgepole pine that carried little commercial value. Even when managing the extensive private forests of George W. Vanderbilt's Biltmore estate, Pinchot was unable to cover the costs of forestry with the sales of timber. Although Pinchot would argue forestry in terms of economics, he was more interested in growing trees for their larger public purposes than to generate income. This economic blind spot contributed to the fundamental error he and his successors in the Forest Service made with respect to fire. Had he been forced by economics to pay for the management his zealous approach called for, he well might have remembered the lessons of his own *National Geographic* article on forest fire, that fire is a natural force of forests from which they evolved.

Nowhere was the questionable economic value of future national forests more apparent than in the Yellowstone Reserve in Montana. John B. Leiberg, a U.S. Geological Survey geographer, conducted a survey of the forests of Montana in 1904. In his survey of the Absaroka

Division of the reserve just north of the Yellowstone National Park boundary, Leiberg wrote, "The large preponderance of lodgepole pine, is wholly the result of these fires, the great complexity and variation in the age of the stands indicating successive ones during the centuries." Sharing Pinchot's view, he painted the fires as devastating events. He concluded that fires were "various, but always evil, without a single redeeming feature."[18]

Yet in Leiberg's brief discussion of the viability of turning the forests into lumber, he foreshadowed the economic challenge to forestry, especially in the high-elevation forests around Yellowstone dominated by the low-valued lodgepole pine: "Most of the timber is exceedingly difficult of access and can only be taken out of the reserve with much labor and expense."[19]

Years later Yellowstone's defenders fought subsidized timber harvests on the national forests surrounding the park, arguing that they were destroying wildlife habitat important to grizzly bears and elk in and out of the park. Pinchot's flawed economic model, suggesting that the efficiencies of forestry could more than pay for the costs of applying it generally across forest types, became deeply embedded into the U.S. Forest Service's budget and resulted in so-called deficit timber sales. In these instances, the agency justified selling timber for less than the costs of putting it up for sale and replanting it because foresters believed the management alone was a value the public and the government were getting in return. That management included building roads deep into the forests and often fruitless attempts to turn unproductive, high-elevation sites to tree plantations. These efforts caused river sedimentation that hurt fisheries and disturbed areas that would recover only over hundreds of years. These activities would never have been considered by private foresters because they could never get a return on their investment. They grew out of the almost religious devotion to the efficiencies promised by the science of forestry. Foresters could grow trees to maturity in nearly half the time as nature using forest science. Mixed with an open checkbook, the Forest Service was able to spread its gospel across the nation. Pinchot and his colleagues led the nation into a trap that was to be repeated often in the twentieth century.

Acting as politicians, they wrapped themselves in a coat of objectivity, picking and choosing the science they, the experts, deemed appropriate for the problem they aimed to solve. This flaw in the scientific management model allowed Pinchot to ignore his own scientific understanding of the role of fire in forests to carry out his crusade for producing the greatest good for the greatest number over time.

All that was needed to carry through Pinchot's vision for national forestry was a crisis, a threat to which he could point that would justify forestry's preeminence, and a way to fund his dream. The threat, Pinchot warned, was that the nation was about to run out of timber. "The United States has already crossed the verge of a timber famine so severe that its blighting effects will be felt in every household in the land," Pinchot said.[20]

The timber famine became for Pinchot and his zealous followers a mantra, a rationale not only to justify the agency's control over the national forests but later for regulation of private forestry as well. This was a crisis that called for conservation, efficiency, and leadership. Foresters were prepared to save the nation from such a catastrophe. Overharvest remained a major problem on private forests, Pinchot said. But the biggest threat to public and private landowners alike was fire.

In 1908, at the height of his influence Pinchot convinced Congress to give the Forest Service the funding tool it needed to reach his ambition. Since no one could predict how bad a fire season would be, no agency could set a realistic budget for fire control. In the Forest Fire Emergency provision, Pinchot got Congress to authorize the secretary of agriculture to pay the costs of firefighting in supplemental appropriations after the fire season was over. Congress would advance the agency an estimated budget and then pay the bills when the smoke cleared. Here was a bureaucrat's fantasy.

As long as the public considered fighting fire critical to the nation and the spending was not extravagant, the Forest Service would have a blank check. No other part of government had such a mechanism except the military. The blank check transformed the firm hand of the federal government to the handout. Creative Forest Service managers in the future, unhindered by budget restraints or economic concerns, could built the agency's power and gain the public respect as long as they could show they could control fire.

Harris and the army had shown how it could be done, but Harris had also expressed doubts that humans could ever really control a forest fire once it got going. Pinchot knew the natural role fire played in the forest, but he believed his foresters could take its place. Pinchot developed the bureaucracy to control fire and also the language to control the debate. Scientists like his foresters could not only stop cut-and-run loggers, renegade sheep herders, and destructive miners; they had progressed so far in the early twentieth century that they could now control nature.

"I recall very well indeed how, in the early days of forest fires, they were considered simply and solely as acts of God, against which any opposition was hopeless and any attempt to control them not merely hopeless but childish," Pinchot wrote in *The Fight for Conservation* in 1910. "It was assumed that they came in the natural order of things, as inevitably as the seasons or the rising and setting of the sun. Today we understand that forest fires are wholly within the control of men. So we are coming in like manner to understand that the prevention of waste in all other directions is a simple matter of good business. The first duty of the human race is to control the earth it lives upon."[21]

CHAPTER 7

Fire and Rain

Major Powell launched into a long dissertation to show that
the claim of favorable influence of forest cover on water flow
or climate was untenable, that the best thing to do for the
Rocky Mountains forests was to burn them down.

—Bernard Fernow, 1902

O N   A   C O L D   E A R L Y   S U M M E R   evening high in the Colorado
Rockies, explorer John Wesley Powell set up camp in the shelter
of a pine forest. Thick clouds trapped the cold air against the slopes and
chilled the one-armed Civil War veteran to the painful nerve endings in
his stump. He gathered kindling from the forest floor and placed it at
the base of a towering ponderosa pine, so it was sheltered from the driving wind. Once lit, the welcome fire warmed the former teacher, who
reveled in the light of its bright yellow flame.

Soon the fire ignited the thick orange bark of the pine. The flames
rose, licking the cones and rushing through the needles, crackling and
popping as they grew. In a few minutes the tree flared into a giant torch,
"which illumined a temple in the wilderness domed by a starless night,"
Powell wrote.[1] The wind carried sparks and embers to the surrounding
trees, and before morning the forest was ablaze, the storm carrying the
fire through the crowns. Trunks exploded. Trees crashed to the ground
and the roar of the fire echoed off the rocks and cliffs as the forest was
consumed. Powell's conflagration burned "scores of miles" of forest—a
thousand square miles, by his account—and lasted for days, destroying
"more timber than has been used by the people of Colorado for the last
10 years," he claimed.[2]

Powell's late 1860s forest fire, and his matter-of-fact way of telling the story, set him apart from the preservationists and foresters who were his peers in conservation at the end of the nineteenth century. Powell wasn't embarrassed by his incendiary behavior, though it was likely just carelessness. He reveled in the telling, as we'll see dominating a meeting with Secretary of the Interior John Noble in 1890 with an elongated version that left little time for the foresters who had sought the influential ear of the cabinet member. Unlike them, Powell didn't consider forest fire evil. He had seen many forest fires in his frequent visits in the West and considered them as natural as the arid landscape or snow-capped peaks. Powell did not follow the route blazed by Sheridan and Harris through Yellowstone, a path that was built on the control of fire on federal lands. Their route led to a vast federal forest and rangeland estate that today is viewed by most Americans as a birthright, part of our collective heritage. They left us with more than 600 million acres, mostly in the West, of national forests, national parks, wildlife refuges, and Bureau of Land Management lands. The occasional western rebel who suggests selling off vast portions of these public lands is quickly shouted down in the cacophony of our national debate.

But Sheridan's path also led the nation into a policy of fire suppression that has dramatically changed the forest ecosystems of the West. Scientists continue to argue whether these changes have overwhelmed the capacity for restoring the health of forest ecosystems and the productivity of the trees themselves, yet few people today believe the fire policies of the last century were good for the land.

The path that Powell blazed led a different direction. His vision for the American West was based on regulating water, not fire. He did not disagree with Sargent, Muir, and later, Pinchot that fire needed to be controlled. But he had a different idea of who should be doing the controlling and how central fire suppression was to the region. For Powell, fighting fire was not a crusade, certainly not a national one. But then and now a person in government who admits to burning down a forest, and even approving of it, has to be ready for a fight. But no one would ever accuse John Wesley Powell of cowardice.

No man on the conservation stage of the late 1800s, save for Sheridan, faced death more often. A schoolteacher in Illinois, Powell joined the Union army and rose quickly through the ranks to command an artillery battery of six cannons and 132 men. On April 5, 1862, he found himself camped along the Tennessee River near a little Methodist church called Shiloh. The same day, Sheridan was in Chicago buying horses as a quartermaster. Muir had fled to Canada to avoid service.

Confederate troops surprised the Union forces under Grant's command and began chasing them back toward the river. Powell and his men sat in their encampment listening to the sounds of battle, awaiting orders that never came. At 10 a.m. Powell couldn't take it any longer. He ordered his men to hitch up their horses and head toward the cracking rifles, cannon roars, and rebel yells. Powell's tiny force waded up the road through the retreating forces of General William Tecumseh Sherman and scores of badly wounded soldiers. Suddenly they were in the clear. Powell realized his men had now gone too far, and ordered them back to a sunken farm road that was the Union's last defense. The troops quickly placed their guns in position and joined the fragile line that stood between survival and defeat. Grant ordered the tiny force to hold the line at all costs until he could deploy a new, stronger defensive position closer to the river.

The two sides traded fire for hours as the Rebels slowly enveloped the roadside defense. At 4 p.m. Powell placed several cannons near the corner of a peach orchard in full bloom and directed their aim at a line of Rebels hiding along a fence. He climbed off his horse, but as he raised his hand to signal the gunners, a bullet struck his forearm, shattering the bone. When Powell tried to remount, he realized he was hit. All around him soldiers were running away as Confederates charged his position at double time. A sergeant helped Powell, who was bleeding profusely, onto his horse. He desperately clung to his saddle as he made the three-mile ride back to the river landing, his battery following close behind. By dark the Confederate's attack had been halted and 24,000 men were either dead or wounded in one of the bloodiest battles in history. Three days later Powell's arm was amputated two inches below the elbow. Grant's army and his reputation survived Shiloh and with it the Union cause.

The thirty-one-year-old Powell returned from the war in 1865 to teach science at Illinois Wesleyan University. He didn't teach for long. With the support of his old commander Grant and several scientific institutions, Powell was able to get backing to lead an expedition into the Rocky Mountains to collect specimens and survey the geology of the region.

Two years later, also with Grant's help, Powell organized a daring plan to explore the yet uncharted Grand Canyon of the Colorado River. The perilous nine-hundred-mile trek captured the public's attention, first in progress reports he mailed back during the trip, and later in *Scribner's Monthly* and eventually in his 1895 book *Canyons of the Colorado*. In this classic adventure tale, Powell includes an account of his own actual one-armed cliff-hanging rescue, daring runs of huge rapids, and crashes of their little wood boats. It ends with the fatal choice of three of the explorers to avoid the last, most fearful of whitewaters and to exit the canyon overland, where they were never seen again. Powell made the right choice, riding the rapids into history.

Powell turned his notoriety into a federal appropriation to continue his surveys of the Colorado River country. The result was a landmark treatise, *Report on the Lands of the Arid Region of the United States*, published in 1878. In the report Powell demonstrated that lack of abundant water in the West was the limiting factor to permanent settlement. Only through an intricate irrigation system, which included reservoirs to capture the spring flow and regulate its release through the growing season, could croplands be sustained. Powell challenged the prevailing view, supported by scientists such as Yellowstone explorer Ferdinand Hayden, that tree planting and other human activity would increase rainfall in the West and improve its climate.[3]

He also challenged the primary legal mechanism for settling the West, the Homestead Act, which limited the amount of land a settler could obtain through improvement to 160 acres. Powell proposed increasing the amount to 2,560 acres, the amount of land he said could sustain thirty-five to fifty cows in a grazing operation. Where irrigation was not possible, Powell said, this was the only viable method of agriculture feasible across most of the region. All of these recommendations fell within a grander scheme, to organize the formation of cooperatives—commonwealths, he called them—for water use and grazing, developed along the natural boundaries of watersheds.

Powell's report was written before the voices of forest preservation were to dominate the public discussion of conservation. Powell was offering an alternative plan for settling the West, not protecting it. Forests were a part of his plan but only as their growth affected the hydrology of the watershed. Forests also offered timber for the farmers, ranchers, and miners who lived nearby, a supply, Powell believed, that would be more than adequate long into the future. Through cooperative land and water ownership, these local residents would control the watershed, including the forests in its upper reaches. They would be in charge of controlling fire in their region and would share the costs. His was a nineteenth-century version of sustainable development.

A decade before Powell's views on forests would place him squarely in opposition to Sargent, Muir, and Pinchot, the thrust of his new ideas was rejected by Congress when presented with it. The biggest challenge for watershed democracy was that watershed boundaries crossed existing political boundaries. Senators and congressmen were not excited by the prospect of changing state and territorial boundaries from which they had been elected. The Homestead Act, political historian Robert H. Nelson wrote, was considered one of the great accomplishments of the Republican Party, "a triumph for the little man, free market individualism and personal initiative."4 Powell was asking to change the third rail of the politics of his time. In the absence of his reforms, thousands of farms were doomed to failure, but the industrial developers and capitalists in Chicago, New York, and other urban centers saw little advantage to them in Powell's vision. Instead, they exploited the land laws that were enacted, such as the Timber Culture Act, the Desert Land Act, and the Timber and Stone Act, to convert public lands to private lands, to steal timber, and to gain access to the resources they could use to feed the growth of the rising industrial giant. Nelson contended that private parties and companies that wanted to exploit western resources and had the support of the federal government and the public had little choice but to subvert these laws, resulting in graft, theft, and eventually a public outcry. In essence, Nelson said, rejection of Powell's vision led to the preservation laws that set aside forests and parks. Scientific management—the control of resources by foresters and other professionals shielded from commercialism—thrived as an alternative to the fraud and abuses of the westward settlement that resulted from the irrational policies Powell unsuccessfully challenged, Nelson said.

Clearly, had Powell's ideas taken root, millions of acres of national forests and rangelands would be in private ownership today. Whether those owners would be better stewards of the land, water, and forests is a wonderful debate question that can never be resolved. Clearly, public access to these lands would be limited. But Powell's vision did not preclude setting aside national parks, such as Yellowstone. Had his views won out, it is likely that Charles Sargent's vision for the army would have muscled out Pinchot's national forestry model. Foresters would still have found their place in American society and as managers of the decentralized western forests. But there would have been inherently more diversity in their management programs. Economics would have played a larger role, and low-value, hard to reach timber—such as in the forests around Yellowstone—would have remained wild.

Powell's irrigation development ideas survived and were used to transform western deserts into what historian Mark Fiege called an "irrigated Eden,"[5] an entirely new ecological creation of human-made waterways, wetlands, and lakes connected to rivers that have laid the foundation for a western economy that still survives.

Powell's views on forests and governance provide the counterpoint on which the prevailing policy can be judged. A central case for preserving forests was to protect the ability of the watershed to catch and store water so that rivers, so vital to settlement in the arid West, would continue to flow. Foresters argued that if trees were properly managed as a crop, a sustainable harvest could be made while remaining trees stored the water for slow release throughout the year. Powell agreed that forests at lower elevations helped prevent snow from melting quickly and aided stream flows. But at higher elevations, he and his supporters argued, more water stored as snow evaporated than melted and flowed into the rivers. He did not believe higher elevation forests were better off burned down. In fact, he recognized that trees were the best cover for preventing erosion, which, left unchecked, would fill with silt the reservoirs he wanted built. But he did not accept the notion that blanket forest preservation was necessary to protect the watershed.

Throughout Powell's twenty years of traveling the West, forest fires were regular events, creating a "haze of gloom" through which "rays of the sun can barely penetrate, and its dull red orb is powerless to illumine the landscape," he wrote in his 1878 report. "The geological work of our Survey is cut off during the very dry months by the smoke; the men can't get lines of sight from height to height because of the fires produced in the mountains and the smoke settling down over the land," he told a House committee in 1890.[6]

Powell saw a dramatic change in the size and ferocity of the fires as settlers replaced American Indians as the cause. "Before the white man came the natives systematically burned over the forest lands with each reoccurring year as one of their great hunting economies. By this process little destruction of timber was accomplished," Powell wrote in 1878. "But protected by civilized men, forests are rapidly disappearing. The needles, cones and brush together with leaves of grass and shrubs below, accumulate when not burned annually. New deposits are made from year to year until the ground is covered with a thick mantle of flammable material. Then a spark is dropped, a fire is accidentally or purposely kindled, and the flames have abundant food."[7]

This remarkable insight, nearly a decade before Moses Harris led the nation into a policy of fire suppression, offered a view of startling contrast on how and why settlement was spreading fire across the landscape. Powell had observed the changing fire regime, and he offered a program to address the issue. In the park-like groves of ponderosa pine he called for managed grazing by cattle and sheep to crop down the flammable grasses and plow other fine fuels into the soil under hundreds of hooves. "But if the pasturage is crowded, the young growth is destroyed and the forests are not purposely replenished by a new generation of trees," Powell wrote. "The wooded grounds that are too dense for pasturage should be annually burned over at a time when the flammable materials are not too dry, so that there may be no danger of conflagration."[8]

The old major was offering a different strategy for his battle with fire. Where Harris and Captain Gus Boutelle, Harris's successor as acting superintendent in Yellowstone, and their supporters in the forestry and preservation communities sought to control the ignition and the outbreak of fires, Powell was aiming at the supplies of fuel. In essence he wanted to fight fire the same way that Sheridan had successfully defeated the Plains Indians and conquered the Shenandoah. He wanted to starve it.

Powell's establishment of the U.S. Geological Survey and his expansion of the agency around the science of geology laid the foundation on which the philosophy of scientific management was built. The agency offered a civilian alternative to the military-based surveys of his time. It also challenged the Army Corps of Engineers as the major source for scientific expertise in government. But Powell never envisioned it as a land management agency. He didn't want the Geological Survey to control people. For him the federal role was paternalistic and cooperative. His beliefs about government and his attitude toward fire were therefore very similar. Neither fire nor men were to be controlled by the federal government. Instead federal scientists would work with the citizens of a watershed and the natural processes themselves to "conquer" the rivers and build a sustainable democracy in the West. His limits on control ironically stopped at the riverside. The waters were a natural force that could be harnessed. There he trusted in his own scientific expertise to overcome the forces of the ages.

Powell's apathetic approach to fire suffered by its association with American Indians and forest-clearing settlers, especially sheepherders, groups viewed as threats to forest protections by both preservationists and foresters. Sargent was a friend of Powell's. But when Powell began expressing his views against federal fire control, Sargent harshly admonished him in the August 1890 issue of *Garden and Forest*: "Major Powell's recent remarks about our forests must bring great comfort to all the army of men who live illegally in one way or another on the forests of the public domain. As long as the officer, whose duty it is to furnish scientific information to the Government, declares that the forests of the western mountains are an injury to the country, timber thieves will continue to cut and shepherds will continue to burn these forests with new energy and with diminished dread of punishment."9

Later that year Powell walked into a meeting on forestry organized by forest advocates with Secretary of the Interior John Noble. The December 30, 1890, meeting was set up to discuss closing headwater areas of the public domain to public entry. Leading the delegation was Bernard Fernow, a German-born forester, who headed the Department of Agriculture's tiny Division of Forestry. Before Pinchot rose to prominence, Fernow was the nation's top forester. Educated in the forestry of his homeland, Fernow carried most of Pinchot's forestry beliefs without the younger man's political and bureaucratic skills. But he remained a major influence in American and Canadian forestry.

Powell came into the meeting, perhaps defensively, because the forest advocates were treading on his bureaucratic turf and challenging his vision for watershed democracy. Before Fernow and the others were able to explain their intentions, Powell stole the stage. He jumped right into his challenge of the foresters' main scientific claim for taking over the headwaters, that forests conserved water flows. He combined it with his refutation that planting trees would change the climate of the West. Then he told his story of the Colorado forest fire he set two decades earlier. Fernow was furious. "He had used up our time when our chance came to speak," Fernow said. "We consumed not more than two minutes, stating that we had not come to argue any theories, but to impress the Secretary with the fact that it was under the law his business to protect public property against the vandalism of which the Major had just accused himself."10

Powell had won the day but was soon to lose the battle. The next year, led by Theodore Roosevelt's and George Grinnell's Boone and Crockett Club, Congress gave the president the authority to set aside forest reserves from development. Powell's forest science was, by and large, correct as far as it went. Regular burning in the mostly ponderosa pine forests he knew in the Southwest is exactly the policy most modern foresters support. Forests do hold water back, but not to the degree that foresters of the 1800s saw. Grazing, however, removed the fine fuels that naturally burned frequently underneath the ponderosas and contributed to the growth of the underbrush that would, by the end of the twentieth century, increase the size of fires. Like Muir and Pinchot, Powell recognized that fire was one of the great forces that shaped the West he loved.

But if his science was sound, his attitude was out of step. Pinchot, writing years later of the 1890 meeting, which he did not attend, made clear that Powell was no model for modern conservation. Pinchot used Powell's unpopular view toward fire as a way to dismiss the old major's decentralized approach to land management. "His account of how the fire caught other trees and then went roaring off through the Western mountains gave no slightest indication of regret. It was interesting, and that was all," Pinchot said.[11]

From that 1890 meeting on, fighting fire, government control, and conservation were linked. The debate between advocates of fire protection and those supporting what was called light burning continued long after Powell's death in 1902. It broke along similar political lines as those in the Noble meeting. Fire protection advocates were also government control supporters led by the U.S. Forest Service and the legions of foresters who were to grow out of the forestry schools of Yale and Cornell started by Pinchot and Fernow. Advocates for Powell's idea of light burning were private timberland owners who were more interested in protecting their standing timber than in increasing the productivity of their forests two and three generations in the future. Sustained yield forestry wouldn't catch on with private timberland owners until a generation later. Pinchot's crusade to prevent a timber famine didn't capture the imagination of the timber people who would benefit from a future scarcity. Fire protection advocates had to convince forest owners that paying for fire suppression would cost less than they would lose when fires came to their land.

It was a hard sell, especially in California's pine country. Thomas Barlow Walker was one of the lumber barons and land speculators who had cut over the white pine country of the Midwest's North Woods and moved west seeking new opportunities. The Minneapolis businessman settled his Red River Lumber Company in Westwood in northern California near Mount Shasta and in the 1890s began buying up all the forest lands he could get. By 1909 he had 750,000 acres and had become the largest landowner in the state.

Walker, who had seen giant forest fires burn up communities such as Hinckley, Minnesota, in 1894, considered them an act of God, just one of the many risks of his high stakes business. In his sugar and ponderosa pine–dominated California forests he developed a sophisticated system of burning, based on long established practices in the South, to clear out the undergrowth and reduce the combustible fuels that could carry fire during the dry season into the crowns. He was putting into practice what Powell had preached. His views were shared by many in the Shasta region, where historically fires had burned frequently, leaving open, park-like forests. Light burning was a practice that made sense in the longleaf pine forests of the South and the ponderosa pine forests of the Southwest and California. It had no application to the high-elevation lodgepole pine forests of Yellowstone, where fire was historically infrequent due to the increased moisture and shorter dry season. There fire presented a threat only in dry summers and a serious threat only in the driest years.

As the first decade of the twentieth century was coming to a close, the U.S. Forest Service, firmly established, was seeking to put in place its own system of fire protection, based on the army model still solidly in place in the national parks. Powell's model had a firm foothold in California. The chaotic events of 1910 would reshuffle the deck. But the control model—of government and fire—established by Sheridan and Harris was firmly in place.

CHAPTER 8

The Big Blowup

All along the line, from north of the Canadian boundary south to the Salmon the gale blew. Little fires picked up into big ones. Fire lines, which had been held for days, melted away under the fierce blast. The sky turned a ghastly yellow, and at four o'clock it was black dark ahead of the advancing flames.

—Elers Koch, 1942

THE STORY OF THE 1910 FIRES begins and ends with Ed Pulaski. His personal story of heroism on August 20 became the saga on which the future of the U.S. Forest Service was built. When the fires of 1910 were long cooled, Pulaski invented a cross between a hoe and an axe that remains the firefighter's basic tool. As Stephen Pyne, author of the modern classic book about the 1910 fires, *Year of the Fires*, wrote: "Every time a firefighter hefts a pulaski, he or she is retelling the saga of 1910."[1] Pulaski's story was one of more than a dozen similar accounts of courage and hardship in the face of what was the greatest forest fire conflagration of the twentieth century.

The epic of the great fires of 1910 obscured and overwhelmed the earlier stories of fire control's beginnings in Yellowstone. It pushed aside older stories of fire disaster at Peshtigo, Wisconsin, in 1871 and Hinckley, Minnesota, in 1894, where the loss of life and destruction of property was far greater. Those fires didn't have an Ed Pulaski or a political context on which to capitalize. After 1910, a casual observer could easily believe that the Forest Service invented the idea of fire prevention. Moses Harris and Gus Boutelle were nearly lost to environmental history even though their development of the strategy and tactics for firefighting far outweighs the utility of the pulaski. At a time when Pinchot's Forest Service fire protection strategy was competing with John Wesley Powell's light burning strategy for the hearts and minds of forest practitioners, Pulaski's heroism rose above the great defeat to give the young agency the authority it needed to win the debate. The stories of the 1910 fire helped Pinchot's successors, his "young men," to anchor fire protection as the foundation for federal leadership of forestry and conservation. But even Pinchot couldn't have imagined a better device than the pulaski for expanding the doctrine he had instilled in his young men for a once and future Forest Service.

Pinchot wanted to use science to transcend political pressure to protect the land. He sought to empower foresters so they could use their science efficiently to expand and apportion the resources of the forests. If his crusade was to succeed, if his ideas for managing forests and people were to spread beyond his own bureaucratic empire, he needed what author and wildland fire historian Stephen Pyne called an epic story. He needed a creation myth as powerful as the campfire story of Yellowstone. That opportunity came with the great fires of 1910.

Pinchot's mentor and partner in conservation, Theodore Roosevelt, had stepped aside in 1909, after the elevation of his vice president, William Howard Taft, to the presidency. Under Roosevelt, Pinchot had been given carte blanche to further the cause of conservation. But Taft did not share Pinchot's or Roosevelt's expansive view of government. Pinchot quickly got into squabbles with other Taft appointees, including Secretary of the Interior Richard Ballinger. Taft, when forced to choose between the two men, fired Pinchot in the first days of January 1910. Taft chose Pinchot's long-time friend and confident, Henry S. Graves, dean of the School of Forestry at Yale, as his new Forest Service chief. Graves, in turn, surrounded himself with many of the same corps of young men that he helped Pinchot shape.

IN AN ORGANIZATION built on youth, Pulaski was an anomaly. He was forty years old when he joined the Forest Service in 1908 as ranger of the Wallace, Idaho, district in the Coeur d'Alene National Forest. Except for his dreams and perhaps his care for the land and outdoors, he had little in common with the young men Pinchot had chosen to manage the nation's forests. There was no Yale in his background.

Born in Seneca County, Ohio, Pulaski quit school at fifteen and headed west. He worked his way through the mining camps of the day—Butte, Montana, the Salmon River boomtowns, Silver City, Idaho—and came eventually to the Coeur d'Alene Mountains. In between prospecting and mining he worked as a ranch foreman, and along the way he developed a host of craftsman's skills, including black-smithing, carpentry, plumbing, and machine repair. He took pride in the skill of his hands, said C. K. McHarg, a Forest Service regional inspector and friend. Pulaski married twice, the second time to Emma Dickerson, with whom he adopted a daughter, Elsie, who was seven in 1910. His demeanor was modest, but at six foot three with steel-blue eyes, he had a strong presence. He was the kind of person who, working in mines, on railroads, and for himself, carved civilization out of the western wilderness of the nineteenth century. Even if he wasn't like the Yale boys, he quickly proved to them his worth. His boss, Forest Supervisor William G. Weigle, said it best: "Mr. Pulaski is a man of most excellent judgment; conservative, thoroughly acquainted with the region, having prospected through the burned area for over 25 years. . . . He is considered by the old-timers as one of the best and safest men to be placed in charge of a crew of men in the hills."[2]

The Forest Service was confident it was ready for anything nature could throw at it as the 1910 season started. William Greeley, the Missoula-based regional forester for the Northern Rockies, had negotiated a series of cooperative agreements with lumbermen in the region to coordinate fire protection across all ownerships. Greeley, a westerner, had gone east to attend Yale after graduating from the University of California in 1901. He was a student of Henry Graves and also one of Pinchot's rising stars. Greeley became supervisor of the Sierra South Reserve in California in 1906, 2.5 million acres of forest that Pinchot later renamed the Sequoia. In 1908 he was promoted to regional forester at the ripe old age of twenty-seven.

Under Greeley's plan each landowner would pay his share of estimated firefighting and prevention costs based on the amount of timberland he owned in a protective district. Since the Forest Service was the major landowner in the area, it would lead the fire control efforts. Because it had an emergency account to handle the costs that would occur, the service could ensure that lack of funding wouldn't keep men and equipment from the fire lines.

Greeley oversaw more than 40 million acres of national forest in Montana and in the northern half of Idaho, a land mass the size of Washington State. He served as the general of the massive 1910 campaign that the Forest Service fought against the series of 1,700 fires that grew to a crescendo from August 20 to 22, which from then on would be known as the Big Blowup. At his side would be Gus Silcox, who would bear the burden of procuring and distributing supplies to this first major firefighting campaign of the twentieth century.

They had the money, the means, and the power to put their fire control program to the test. Their basic strategy and tactics had been initially developed and employed by the army decades earlier in Yellowstone and other national parks and more recently carried on by the newly formed Forest Service. But they had never seen a day like August 20, 1910. The task for Greeley's team remained daunting. There were no lookouts, and the service depended on intermittent patrols to detect fires throughout most of the country. The Idaho-Montana border country was still a vast wilderness from the St. Joe River on the north to the Salmon River on the south. There was little way to quickly move crews into the backcountry even when fires were discovered.

The year had started off surprisingly wet. Heavy snows in the mountains had caused massive avalanches throughout the region. In the Coeur d'Alene Mountains snow levels were above normal, according to a forest ranger survey. Beginning in the spring, the weather turned hot and dry. The regular spring rains were scanty, and Elers Koch, another of Pinchot's young men, wrote in the official Forest Service history of the 1910 fires, "The hills hardly got green that spring."[3] As supervisor of the Lolo National Forest in Montana, Koch was especially prepared, having faced an active fire season in 1908. He and Weigle both had built trails and trained crews to fight large fires.

Their success in controlling fires in 1908 stood in contrast to the severe fires that burned across the Midwest and the East. Despite the best efforts of states and local governments long faced with the threat of forest fire, the 1908 blazes burned through villages and towns and spread a smoky cloud over most of the eastern seaboard. The Forest Service declared that year's fire season, in which it played a minor role, "one of the worst in the last quarter century."[4]

The 1910 season would not hit the East as hard. But in the West, drought quickly became a serious threat. Snow had already melted away on the high slopes of the Bitterroots, a full month earlier than usual. Severe lightning storms in June started a rash of fires throughout the Rockies. On July 10, Koch wrote, the Northern Pacific Railroad reported that it was laying off three thousand to four thousand men due to drought-related crop failures along its line. The Forest Service fire-fighting machine went to work, organizing crews and sending them out with shovels, axes, and saws to dig fire lines and isolate the growing blazes. By July 15 Greeley had put three thousand men to work, exhausting the local labor market. When they could, Greeley's men enlisted loggers and miners, who were both relatively experienced and reliable. Rangers also canvassed saloons and poolrooms to find workers willing to engage in the back-breaking, dangerous tasks of containing fire. "We cleaned out skid row in Spokane and Butte," Greeley said. "A lot of the temporaries were bums and hoboes. . . . They loafed on the job; some of them quit on the job." Yet his distaste for the unwashed did not keep him from placing thousands of them across the landscape, which was quickly filling with fire.[5]

The fires were not limited to the Northern Rockies. More than 3,600 men were fighting fires in Washington State. Crown fires raced over the Canadian border into Minnesota. More erupted in neighboring Wisconsin. In Montana the army was scrambling to protect Glacier National Park. Guests in Yellowstone were once again getting a front-row seat for an army forest firefight in the park. The fires flourished despite the army's efforts because they were started by lightning away from the roads. More troops were called to fight the two fires that burned several thousand acres for three weeks before they were brought under control. Other soldiers were put on patrol to prevent fires from escaping from the roadsides and camps. These efforts were seen by then superintendent Major H. C. Benson as the reason Yellowstone was to escape the major fires that were to mark the 1910 season. Without them the "park would have been practically destroyed."[6]

As the fire season was heating up in the Northern Rockies, fires also were burning in California, both wild and intentional. The dry conditions didn't keep the vocal advocate of light burning, Thomas Barlow Walker, from burning the underbrush from his private forestlands near Mount Shasta. By July, however, the Widow Valley burn had gotten out of control and grown into a full-fledged crown fire that threatened Modoc National Forest lands. Supervisor Chris Rachford wired Walker's Red River Lumber Company headquarters in Minneapolis asking for help in bringing the fire under control. Walker's son Clinton, who was managing Red River, wired back on July 28: "Endless hopeless job fight fires—think it not right principle—better burn now than few years later."[7]

The Widow Valley fire burned through 33,140 acres, nearly all on Walker's land, and completely destroyed more than 30 million board feet of merchantable timber before it was stopped on the edge of the national forest by federal firefighters. The Forest Service would for years hold up the Widow Valley burn as an example of the failure of light burning.

Despite more than three thousand small fires and ninety major blazes, Greeley was optimistic enough to tell reporters on July 31, "We are holding our own against all the fires within the jurisdiction."[8] In the Rockies though, the situation had grown so threatening that on August 8 President Taft called out the army to join in the firefight that the Forest Service was waging. But weather conditions seemed to be easing, and on August 9, Koch told reporters that every fire on his forest was out, or practically under control.

Like so many firefighting optimists for generations to come, Koch was forced to eat his words the next day. High winds and low humidity pumped up the fires across the entire region, extending the fire lines and forcing Greeley and Silcox to find ever more bodies to throw into the fight. Silcox emptied stores and even towns of supplies to equip the firefighters, but many camps came up short.

Somehow they kept the men coming, scattering more than nine thousand firefighters across the region by August 19. Again, the weather calmed, and for those on the line it appeared that their toil and testing had paid off. "Many miles of fire line were held, and with the end of the season approaching, it looked as though the loss might not be too great," Koch later wrote.9 On the Coeur d'Alene, Weigle had 1,800 firefighters with fire lines nearly surrounding the remaining blazes. Pulaski had a crew of 150 firefighters spread out along the divide between the Coeur d'Alene River and the St. Joe River up Placer Creek about ten miles from Wallace, Idaho. On the evening of August 19, he left the crew and rode to Wallace to bring back supplies. Pulaski wrote his mother, telling her not to fear, for the danger had passed. Actually, Pulaski was far more realistic than his superiors. He told his wife Emma: "Wallace will surely burn so be prepared to save yourselves."10

The wind came up with the sun on August 20. By 8 a.m. the southwest breeze had turned into a gale. The humidity, already low, virtually disappeared. The conditions for burning were suddenly ideal across a 150-mile swath of forest that most years is hard to ignite. The drought had prepared the ground; nature tossed in dry lightning strikes by the hundreds. Sparks from passing trains as well as miners, homesteaders, campers, and even firefighters themselves had started dozens of fires. Across the Northern Rockies, these smoldering fires came alive all along the hundreds of miles of fire line. Backfires, set in the previous weeks to reduce the threat, exploded in minutes from ground fires to crown fires. Fanned by winds exceeding sixty miles per hour, many of the fires took control of their own destiny, turning into hurricanes of heat. The steep topography, narrow canyons, and river valleys were transformed into chimneys. Fire is the rapid oxidation of fuel. When the forest is dry and flammable enough, and oxygen is plentiful and forced through these natural flues, it triggers a chain reaction that sustains itself. Hungry for oxygen, the fire's core creates its own sucking winds that are both fed by the gale and generate a storm of their own.

As the morning advanced, pillars of smoke rose up from the canyons toward the stratosphere like giant thunderheads. "The air felt electric," Koch wrote, "as though the whole world was ready to go up in spontaneous combustion."11

Every fire grew to an intensity rarely seen in modern times. Hundreds of thousands of acres were burned within hours, creating their own winds of more than eighty miles per hour and producing the power of the atomic bomb dropped on Hiroshima every two minutes.[12]

The thousands of firefighters who were on the offensive the day before were now facing the most fearful sight of their lives. Greeley had unwittingly placed them in the worst possible places on one of the most dangerous burning days in several centuries. "The whole world seemed to us men back in those mountains to be aflame," Pulaski told his wife. "Many thought it really was the end of the world."[13]

Some followed the cool-headed leadership of men such as Lee Hollingshead, a twenty-two-year-old fire guard who led a crew of sixty men south of Wallace. When they became surrounded by fire, most worked their way through the fire line to a previously burned-over area for safety. Nineteen weren't so astute; they panicked and ran down a hill to a small cabin and took cover inside. When the burning roof fell in they rushed out into the full force of the firestorm. Eighteen of them died within feet of the cabin. The nineteenth man, Peter Kinsley, fell while going through the door, but from there managed to crawl to a small creek. The skin of his face and hands was mostly burned off, as were his clothes. Yet despite his condition, he walked out to the St. Joe River two days later and survived.

By all accounts Pulaski was completely composed, even resigned to his fate. He had returned to Wallace to get supplies for his firefighters when the fires started growing that fateful morning. He wasn't going to leave his crew in the hills without leadership even though he would have to leave the relative safety of town. His wife, Emma, and daughter, Elsie, walked up Placer Creek with him and the packers until they came to the end of the road. "I may never see you again," Emma said he told them.[14] Soon they could see the flames, and the packers refused to go farther, dumping their loads. Pulaski rode on, gathering firefighters as he went. Because most of them didn't know the country, they knew they had to stay with him, even though he was heading toward the fire, not Wallace. The smoke of the gathering firestorm had turned the midday dark.

His voice almost gone from yelling orders above the roar of the fire, Pulaski told the forty-five men he had gathered to grab some blankets and do what he said. His plan was to ride and walk to Wallace, ten miles away. He knew the odds were against him but he didn't see any other choices. "Trees were falling all about us under the strain of the fires and heavy winds and it was almost impossible to see through the smoky darkness," Pulaski said.[15] They moved quickly downhill, joined by a young bear chased to the floor of the deep narrow canyon by the flames.

They traveled nearly five miles before the fires became so close that even Pulaski knew Wallace was an impossible dream. But still he led his men downhill. Then he remembered the old tunnel of the War Eagle Mine only a short distance ahead. He gave up his horse to an old man and hurried the men to the mine. The fire was so close one man was killed by a falling tree aflame. "We reached the mine just in time, for we were hardly in when the fire swept over our trail," Pulaski said.[16]

Flames, hot gases, and smoke were sucked into the adit, igniting timbers at the opening and filling the tunnel with deadly fumes. The woodsman ordered his crew to lie face down on the water-covered floor of the tunnel and cover themselves with blankets so they could breathe what little air was left. All but Pulaski were fear-stricken, crying and praying as the furnace raged only a few feet away.

One firefighter couldn't take it any more and broke for the door. Pulaski pulled his revolver. "The first man who tries to leave this tunnel, I will shoot," he said.[17]

The ranger braved the heat and smoke to put out the fire on the mine timbers by scooping up water with his hat. Some of the wet blankets even caught fire and Pulaski carefully re-covered the scared men. One by one they lost consciousness. Finally Pulaski succumbed.

The fire continued to burn northeast toward Wallace, a town of six thousand, five miles from the tunnel. Late in the afternoon residents saw what appeared like a giant thunderhead rising from the direction of the St. Joe River to the south. Many thought it meant that rain was on the way and hoped for relief. But the cloud turned into a black mass of smoke that turned the setting sun into a great red ball of fire.

When the flames crested the ridge at 9 p.m. the wind was still blowing hard. Men, women, and children ran through the streets trying to flee. The roar of the fire was punctuated with the crash of falling trees, the whistle of trains, and the screams of the fearful. Many found refuge in the special trains sent from Missoula and Spokane. Others stayed and watered down their homes and buildings. Firefighters lit a series of backfires that successfully protected most of the town.

When the fire came to Wallace, Emma grabbed Elsie and all she could carry and joined neighbors gathering on the rock-covered tailings dam of a local mine. She watched as the fire "leaped from one mountain to another as though the whole world was afire."

"Some where in those burning mountains," she knew Ed Pulaski was leading his men.[18]

Emma, Elsie, and many Wallace residents spent a restless night on the tailings dam watching a real-life fireworks display, "though beautiful, most terribly cruel."[19]

Wallace survived largely on the efforts of its residents, its city government, and the army. The Forest Service was mostly gone, out in the hills fighting to protect the forest. At the moment when the communities needed them most, Greeley's rangers were fighting to save the lives of their crews and themselves.

At the War Eagle Mine one man came to, crawled over the others, and dragged himself outside. Small fires sparkled across the burned landscape. Then, covered by the dark of night, the man made his way down the creek to Wallace, arriving at 3 a.m. Ed Pulaski and his crew were dead, he reported. He wasn't the only man who thought Pulaski was gone. Other men in his crew awoke at 5 a.m. to find their savior prostrate, his clothing burned into rags and his shoes burned off. His face and hands were burned. "Come outside, boys, the boss is dead," one man said as he breathed fresh air. From within the tunnel a voice called out, "Like hell he is."[20] Ed Pulaski crawled out of the War Eagle Mine and tried to stand up. He was blind, and like most of the men could hardly walk. Nevertheless, Pulaski and his men managed to work their way toward Wallace and safety. All but five of the forty-four firefighters he guided to the tunnel survived.

The fires raced on through August 21, many running thirty to fifty miles over the two days. Finally on August 22, the wind stopped and the humidity rose. As quickly as the fires had exploded they laid down. A light rain the night of August 23 calmed the fires further. Then on August 31, the season-ending rain came and the fires died, though a few continued even into the winter of 1911.

In less than three days more than a million acres of forest burned. Eighty-five lives were lost in the two-day blowup. Seventy-eight were firefighters, many the dregs of the frontier boomtowns Greeley so disdained. Not one of the dead was a ranger, crew leader, or forest guard. None of the thousands of soldiers, trained to follow orders even in the worst of situations, were victims. But if Greeley had little respect for the majority of his volunteer force alive, his portrayal changed once they were dead. The fallen firefighters were now "heroes," and Greeley insisted they get a decent burial.

Still, Greeley and Pinchot's other young men didn't think to ask themselves why these men had died. Few actually were protecting communities. The major value lost was the timber. More than 3 million acres had burned throughout the whole season, including 8 billion board feet of timber. Yet much of this wood was largely inaccessible to logging. Many of the trees that were retrievable were salvaged in a large, focused logging operation.

For Pulaski himself, it would be days before he actually could see. To fully regain his eyesight would require an operation. Surprisingly, despite the impact that his story of courage was to have on the future of the Forest Service, the agency refused to pay for his medical expenses. He suffered from his injuries for the rest of his life in relative silence, professionally going about the business of a ranger. He managed the salvage of the burned white pine and saw to it that crews replanted millions of seedlings to reforest the burned mountainsides. His teams rebuilt the trails, laid new telephone lines, and staffed the guard stations that kept a vigil in an effort to ensure that another Big Blowup wouldn't occur. Pulaski refused to repeat the story of his survival for historians until 1923, when, pressured by friends, he entered an essay contest sponsored by *American Forests* magazine. The contest, titled, "My Most Exciting Experience as a Forest Ranger," paid $500 to the winner. Pulaski dictated the story, "Surrounded by Forest Fires," to Emma, describing his remarkable trip into the War Eagle Mine. He won, allowing him to pay some of the continuing medical costs of the injuries to his eyes, lungs, and throat that never completely healed.

As Stephen Pyne said, Pulaski spoke louder with his hands, embedding history into the tool he perfected and promoted. Pulaski had worked on early versions of the cross between an axe and a hoe with other rangers prior to 1910. It allowed a firefighter to cut through roots or dig out the bare area of fire lines without changing tools. He perfected it in 1913 and presented it to his superior, who soon made it as much a part of the firefighter's gear as the shovel. The pulaski keeps the story of the 1910 fires alive in every fire camp even today. But even as Pulaski's tool tells the story, Pinchot, Greeley, Koch, and Silcox were the primary authors. They turned the 1910 fires into the Yellowstone campfire story. They used it to crush Powell's light burning strategy and to institutionalize the blank check for firefighting. Their values would endure unchecked for most of the century, until another large conflagration, seventy-eight years later in Yellowstone, would begin to unravel the mythology that Pulaski's tool stood for. But even today, fighting fires is viewed as a noble cause, with its modern heroes who bravely walk up the trails toward unknown dangers carrying their pulaskis.

CHAPTER 9

The End of the Trail

This country existed and maintained a general timber cover
before man was born and for millions of years before the
Forest Service came into being. Surely its existence as wild
land capable of sheltering game and holding the watershed
together cannot now be altogether dependent on the efforts of
the Forest Service?

—Elers Koch, 1935

I F T H E F O R E S T S E R V I C E had wanted to show it knew how to
fight big fires, it might have made Elers Koch the hero of 1910.
Instead, Koch became a lonely voice whose message about the limits of
firefighting would be muted until Yellowstone's fires of 1988. The Lolo
National Forest supervisor became the main historian of the fires, and
subsequently his modesty obscured the Forest Service's one true success in August of 1910.

The Montana native had gone back east to forestry school at Yale,
graduating in 1903. He had gone to Pinchot's summer camp in Washington and was captivated by Pinchot's personality and passion. After
graduation, he joined the Bureau of Forestry, becoming a charter member of the exclusive corps of Pinchot's "young men."

His firefighting apparatus had been battle-tested in 1908 when large
fires burned through the Montana forest. So when fires started burning
along the Idaho-Montana border and through the slash of timber company lands in 1910, Koch's forces were quick to react. They already had
miles of thin fire line cleared through the forest and roads built into
places like the Ninemile valley northwest of Missoula. "Fire or six large

fires were handled in succession, but one by one they were beaten," Koch later wrote.[1] His experienced firefighters stayed on the line when the Big Blowup arrived on August 20, and the Ninemile valley lines all held. The fires burned their share of the forest, but under Koch's leadership and his direction of the men he trained, not a firefighter was lost.

Koch went on to become one of the Forest Service's most respected firefighters, rising to fire chief of the region that included Montana and Idaho in 1919 and eventually to regional timber management chief in 1921, where he served until retirement. He established the first formalized fire training in the service and the first boards of review to learn from the experience of previous firefights. He pioneered the agency's lookout network in the Northern Rockies and invented a map-orienting table to pinpoint and communicate the location of fires. He even invented a fire tool that carried his name—the Koch—a handle that could be mounted on either a grubbing hoe or a shovel. When he wrote the official history of the 1910 fires in 1942, as he neared retirement, it's clear he remained a strong supporter of fire control. He had, though, already challenged the unyielding, doctrinaire manner in which the agency had carried out the policy since 1910. In the 1930s he tried but failed to inject reason and a sense of economics into the system, advocating that large areas be left wild, where fires would be allowed to burn. But after 1910 the Forest Service locked itself and the nation on an unyielding path blazed by the army in Yellowstone. The road to conservation was built on the foundation of fire exclusion. Koch was the only fire boss who could wrestle the Big Blowup to a draw. But he could not stop his fellow 1910 veterans from racing through the lines of logic and science with the same ferocity of the fire that chased Ed Pulaski into a hole. The veterans espoused the idea that if just given enough manpower and technology they could bring even the worst fires under their control and essentially eliminate fire from the landscape to the benefit of all.

Despite his own success Koch saw the 1910 fires for what they were: "a complete defeat for the newly organized Forest Service forces."[2] Koch, more than William Greeley and Ferdinand Silcox, his superiors during the blowup, had to deal with the long-term effects of the fire's fury. He served in the same region throughout his entire career. Both Greeley and Silcox departed for Washington, D.C., positions and for other careers only a few years after 1910. As Greeley and Silcox went on to develop a national vision for forestry, Koch always saw it through the glasses of a Montana native. "If I had any success in controlling big fires, it is because I have never believed in generalship from the rear," he wrote in his memoirs.3 Even as the region's timber chief he led fire crews, walking the lines, scouting through thickets and downed timber, jumping from log to log to avoid still hot ashes and coals. His judgment came after hiking and riding horseback through thousands of miles of the forests he knew intimately. On that experience, Koch concluded that fighting fire was a losing proposition throughout much of the Northern Rockies, especially the wild, craggy divide where the 1910 fires had thrived and spawned repeated blazes. Koch's assessment came after leading firefights year after year, nine of which he classified with 1910 as really bad years. He had lived on the land for more than sixty years and could place this cycle of fire in the context of the climatic shift from his youth. The early third of the twentieth century in the Northern Rockies and in much of the nation was a time of drought. It forced thousands of homesteaders off their land in the northern plains, and turned Oklahoma, Kansas, and Texas into the dust bowl, forcing thousands of dirt-poor families onto the road to California. It was a condition of nature largely ignored by Greeley, Silcox, and the others who shaped the nation's wildfire policy, however.

The politics swirling in the wake of the Big Blowup forced Pinchot's young men to press for all or nothing. The 1910 fires were still burning across the Rockies when Pinchot's political foil, Secretary of the Interior Richard Ballinger, took the podium on August 25 in San Francisco and flatly challenged the Forest Service's fire control strategy: "We may find it necessary to revert to the old Indian method of burning over the forests annually at a seasonable period."4 He was joined in his criticism by the Forest Service's most arch enemy, Idaho Republican Senator Weldon B. Heyburn, who had led the effort to halt the expansion of the national forests. Heyburn called the Forest Service's Idaho and Montana firefight "spectacular but ineffective." His solution was to open the forests to more settlement because, he said, by not allowing settlers, prospectors, and miners to remain on the land, the first line of defense was gone, leaving the timber "easy prey to flames."[5]

Pinchot, a civilian since January 1910 and therefore not directly responsible for coping with the disaster, came to the defense of his protégés against Ballinger and Heyburn, his old foes. "To my mind their conduct is beyond all praise."[6] He turned the tables on the Monday-morning quarterbacks. He blamed men like Heyburn, who had hindered the agency's preparedness by challenging its budget and mission. Fire was preventable, Pinchot said, if the agency were given the manpower to detect fires early, respond rapidly, and regulate the disposal of slash by loggers. In other words, just give the bureaucracy more money and more power and they could ensure that there would be no repeat of the Big Blowup. Yet he told the *New York Times* only a few weeks later that the 1910 fires had to be considered in the same category as earthquakes and hurricanes—a natural event that no one should be held responsible for controlling. Such a catastrophe, he argued, was not a reason to cut the Forest Service's budget. "When a city suffers from a great fire it does not retrench in its fire department but strengthens it."[7]

Pinchot and the agency's supporters succeeded in convincing Congress to approve the Weeks Act of 1911, which for the first time allowed the agency to establish national forests in the East, and more important, it provided matching funding to states that cooperated with the Forest Service on fire prevention and control. Even though the emergency fund neared $1 million for the 1910 fires, the agency was given the power to spend even more, even picking up many of the costs states might incur. The blank check gave the Forest Service a powerful incentive to convince states to follow its lead toward fire exclusion instead of light burning or even a mixture of the two. For the decade following the 1910 fires, the Forest Service would devote its efforts to undercutting the last vestige of Powell's forest program, light burning or "Paiute burning," as Greeley derisively called it, resurrecting a term that had been around since the early days of the light burning debate.

The only way a state could cash in on the cooperative fire program was to put in place the kind of fire prevention, detection, and response programs the Forest Service advocated. In addition to this pork it could pass around to the states that chose its approach, the agency had a powerful populist argument against the practice of light burning. The main advocates of the practice were men such as Thomas Barlow Walker, timber barons who owned hundreds of thousands of acres of old-growth forest. The Southern Pacific Railroad, one corporate giant that had no reputation for conservation, also pushed light burning because of the thousands of acres of mature forests in California and the Southwest that were dominated by ponderosa and sugar pine, the forest type that light burning best protected. The practice of light burning killed the young trees that were the focus of forestry, the brood stock on which faster growth and a future crop depended. But it protected the larger, standing old-growth timber that was of primary immediate value to the timberland owners.

Greeley became the leading critic of light burning and the leading advocate for fire suppression. In his autobiography, *Forests and Men*, written in 1951, Greeley began with his fundamental philosophy: "Fire prevention is the No. 1 job of American foresters." Over his entire career, "smoke in the woods" was the yardstick by which progress in American forestry should be measured.[8] "Paiute Forestry or the Fallacy of Light Burning," his essay published in *Timberman* magazine in 1920, laid out his argument. "Light burning, in actual practice, is simply the old ground fire which has been the scourge of the western pineries, under a new name," Greeley wrote. "Its use means a deliberate continuation of the destructive surface fires which were steadily and irresistibly eating up the pine forests of our western states until they were placed under protection."[9]

Light burning killed the young trees necessary for reproduction of the forest, Greeley argued. It also scarred many trees, making them susceptible to insects and disease. He ignored the historic role fires played in the forests of the West and once again warned of the threat of a future timber famine. "If surface burning is not stopped, the end is total destruction just as complete and disastrous as when a forest is consumed in a crown blaze that kills everything at once."[10]

Greeley's views never changed. His on-the-ground experience waned after he left his regional job, amplifying the significance of the 1910 fires on his views. The 1910 experience loomed large in Silcox's views as well. He was another young man who had been attracted like a moth to Pinchot's light.

Ferdinand Augustus "Gus" Silcox, was born on Christmas Day in 1882. The Georgia native attended the College of Charleston, and then, in 1905, he too earned a master's degree in forestry at Yale. A born woodsman, Silcox shared Pinchot's personal charm. He also was an organization man with a social conscience, though not the aristocrat that Pinchot was. His brilliance was quickly recognized, and he became Greeley's assistant in the Missoula regional office. Silcox left the Forest Service and forestry soon after 1910, but returned as chief of the service in the 1930s. Like Greeley, his experience on the ground came in the heat of battle, and both men's shared experience in 1910 blinded them to any scientific information that challenged their view.

Remember, both Muir and Pinchot himself recognized the role of fire in rejuvenating native forests. Frederick Clements, who developed the science of ecology in the United States, published research paid for by the Forest Service in 1910 that showed in detail how the lodgepole pine forests that grow throughout the high elevations of the Northern Rockies, including Yellowstone, were directly tied to fire.[11] But all of the scientific evidence was ignored by the Forest Service's top foresters, who were supposed to be the vanguard force for scientific management.

Greeley, arguably the man most responsible for the 1910 defeat, in the years following those fires was more interested in expanding the cooperation for fire control programs to private forestlands, a process he had started even before the Big Blowup. Forest Service Chief Henry Graves placed Greeley in charge of selling states on the cooperative fire control program, which Greeley carried out, Graves said, like "an evangelist out to get the converts."[12] For Greeley it was a way to fight the 1910 fires again, and he was "spurred on by the vivid memories of blazing canyons and smoking ruins of little settlements and rows of canvas-wrapped bodies."[13] Greeley knew from the start his vision of a blanket of fire prevention and control would not be realized without the timber industry's support. Pinchot had spent decades demonizing men such as Walker and Frederick Weyerhaeuser as "land skinners" who were as much a threat as fire, in his view, to cause the mythical timber famine he warned about. The timbermen's allies in Congress, men such as Heyburn, were not likely to support a plan devised by the Forest Service they despised. Greeley saw the industry in grayer terms. He heard its complaints about taxes and the risks of investment. The wasteful practices and cut-and-run strategies were the natural reaction of capitalists to the availability of a cheap natural resource, Greeley believed. Instead of regulating the industry or furthering Pinchot's more ambitious agenda of turning forestlands public, Greeley sought to offer the timber barons incentives to help him erect a national fire control program.

In 1914, the Forest Service, the Bureau of Corporations, and the Federal Trade Commission, three of Theodore Roosevelt's progressive-era reform agencies, teamed up to investigate the timber industry's conservation practices. Greeley played a leading role in writing the final report. It showed that the industry's speculation and its wasteful business practices had contributed to the devastation of the forests he and Pinchot had fought to save. But Greeley in the report praised the industry's fire protection programs and recognized its role in the development of the West. The report recommended that the government help pay for fire protection on cut-over private lands, adopt tax changes to encourage long-term investment, and offered only tepid support for federal forest regulations. Pinchot, now chairman of the Society of American Foresters, reacted immediately. He called the report "one of the ablest I have ever seen, and altogether one of the most dangerous," placing the "commercial demands of the lumber industry as supreme over the need of forest conservation and the right of the public."[14]

Now Greeley's mentor became his tormentor. This major break in the forest fraternity was all but lost on environmentalists, for whom the break between Muir, the preservationist, and Pinchot, the wise-use advocate, became the sole dividing line by which people recognized their place in the environmental milieu. Pinchot's and Greeley's fight continued when, in 1920, Greeley replaced Graves as Forest Service chief. The battleground moved to Congress as Greeley sought to expand beyond states to private forest owners the cooperative curtain of fire protection the Forest Service had established in the 1911 Weeks Act.

Ever since the 1890s, when Pinchot reached the national stage, his vision was for federal conservation. He took the view, developed by General Phil Sheridan, George Bird Grinnell, and other early conservationists, that only the federal government had the power to withstand the political and financial power of the monopolistic capitalists. "These are men who already destroyed this country and reduced to desert conditions an area larger than the forests of Europe," Pinchot told the Senate Agriculture Committee in 1923. The only control, he said, "these gentlemen have any fear of is national control."[15]

This core value never seriously changed even as he tried to develop a working relationship with the Weyerhaeusers and other industrialists. To him, Greeley was going over to the enemy, putting the Forest Service, "in the position of throwing contempt upon its basic reason for existence."[16]

Pinchot had built the federal land estate not on scientific management but on his keen political savvy and on the remarkable opportunity the Roosevelt presidency had presented. His first real defeat came through the lessons he had taught Greeley. When Congress was debating Greeley's bill to expand cooperative fire fighting and reforestation, he confessed to "packing the stand at the committee hearings with fire witnesses. . . . Not many a man with a real forest fire story to tell escaped the witness chair."[17]

Greeley's bill, the Clark-McNary Act, which expanded the fire protection benefits that the federal government would provide states and private forestland owners through the Forest Service, sailed through Congress in 1924, in part because Pinchot's attention had been diverted to his campaign to become Pennsylvania's governor. In 1928, the same funding was spread to the National Park Service and other agencies under Forest Service administration.

The army had left the national parks during the First World War and had been replaced by the National Park Service in 1916, which was organized in the same martial model as the Forest Service, but with a mission aimed at providing visitor services and preservation. It kept the army's vision of full fire suppression in the national parks. But it did not have the means for implementation until Greeley included them in his fire protection net under the control of the Forest Service.

Greeley had in place now the tools for a truly national network of fire control, an accomplishment even Pinchot had to marvel at. The Forest Service was clearly recognized as the leading firefighters. And the agency had the money to pay other federal agencies, the states, and private landowners to carry on the fight the way it chose. Now, all the agency needed was unlimited manpower. The Great Depression, the election of Franklin Delano Roosevelt, and the establishment of the Civilian Conservation Corps (CCC) handed the Forest Service this final component. Once again a 1910 veteran, specially equipped to exploit this opportunity, stepped forward to carry the flame.

Like many other foresters, Silcox left the agency during World War I for the army. The military recognized his organizing skills and his educational background and placed him in charge of labor problems in Seattle and Portland. He liked the work, and when the war was over he didn't return to the Forest Service, but remained in industrial relations in the private sector. He returned in 1933 as Forest Service chief after a career in the timber industry. But his stint on the private side made him even more skeptical of its motives rather than becoming its pawn. Greeley, who took a job as a timber industry lobbyist, quickly found that Silcox was more like Pinchot than him. Silcox's overall agenda was aimed squarely at turning forests into vessels for social change. The forests' trees could provide homes for the homeless and jobs for the struggling. In 1937 at the height of his term as chief he expressed his views passionately in a challenge he wrote to employees. "We of the Forest Service must reexamine our responsibilities; reanalyze our opportunities; revitalize the forest movement in relation to human beings," he wrote. "We must rededicate ourselves to a broader public service. As trustees we must manage the Nation's forests so they may become tools—and better tools—in the service of mankind."[18]

Franklin Delano Roosevelt himself was greatly influenced by Pinchot. He told Yale forestry students that a Pinchot lecture on deforestation and soil erosion in China "started me on the conservation road."[19]

Ironically, the polio-stricken president's last effort as a healthy man was fighting a forest fire. He was sailing in the Bay of Fundy off New Brunswick on August 10, 1921, when he spotted a forest fire. He went ashore and used pine boughs to thrash out the flames. He dove into the water to clean off the ashes and returned home weary, chilled, and filled with pain. The next morning the paralysis he suffered for the rest of his life set in.[20]

Roosevelt likely called on Silcox because of his background in managing labor. He replaced Robert Stuart, another 1910 veteran, who either jumped or fell from his office window in 1933. For President Roosevelt, the national forest and parks provided a place where he could immediately put the young and unemployed to work on conservation projects, reforestation, fire prevention, and trail repair. He created the CCC during his first hundred days in office to do just that. The idea came in part from Pinchot, who had started a similar program in Pennsylvania as governor. When the Depression sent thousands into unemployment, Pinchot set up emergency relief camps to house, by 1932, almost 15,000 workers to build highways and country roads. The camps were organized much like army camps. Pinchot's program took in more than 20,000 miles of Pennsylvania county roads in 1931, and by 1935, seventy percent had been paved by his force.[21]

Roosevelt's administration used the same model, only it brought in the army to train the workers and set up the housing. The army, out of the public lands business since 1916, was once again recognized for its unique ability to organize such a large work program quickly.

The CCC turned into a minor miracle, largely meeting its goal of hiring 250,000 men in only four months, placing them in camps across the nation and putting them to work. By 1935, 600,000 men earning $30 a month were sending $25 a month home, spreading the relief to homes nationwide. The millions of dollars spent on food for them and on equipment for use in their work were allowing several business sectors to survive and even thrive in the midst of economic ruin. More significantly, the Forest Service, the Park Service, and states were using the manpower to carry out a bureaucrat's dream program. CCC workers built thousands of patrol cabins and lodges, strung thousands of miles of telephone lines, cleared campgrounds, planted millions of trees, built bridges, installed flood control dikes, and maintained trails. Most important, especially in work for the Forest Service, they built fire breaks and roads deep into previously primitive areas to carry out the agency's mission to fight all fires. CCC crews also became the core of the Forest Service's firefighting force, providing it for the first time a nearly unlimited number of laborers to carry out its firefighting vision.

For Silcox, it made his larger vision—that of federal control of timber harvesting—a real possibility. Silcox's focus was a surprising turn for the agency that had cozied up to the timber industry under Greeley. Silcox envisioned federally operated timber mills cutting wood from national forests. The timber industry, suffering like the rest of the nation through the Great Depression, feared a federal grab for the forestlands they controlled. At Silcox's side was young Robert Marshall, who shared Silcox's social perspective.

Marshall, a friend of Pinchot and Silcox, was a leading advocate for another new idea in national forests, leaving the land in a pristine state as wilderness. The son of a prominent New York lawyer, Marshall spent his youth roaming the Adirondacks, turning himself into an accomplished climber. He earned three degrees, including a Ph.D. in forestry, from Johns Hopkins University, as he rose through the ranks of the Forest Service, eventually becoming assistant chief for Recreation and Lands. The idea of national forest wilderness itself came from another of Pinchot's young men, Aldo Leopold.

Aldo Leopold was younger than Koch, Greeley, or Silcox and did not have personal ties to Pinchot as they did. Born in 1887 in Burlington, Iowa, he spent his youth along the Mississippi bluff country hunting for ducks, exploring the woods and prairies, and immersing himself in the mixed landscape of farm fields, backwaters, and wilds. He too went to Yale, graduating with a master's degree in forestry in 1909. That year, the twenty-two-year-old joined the Forest Service as an assistant on the Apache National Forest in Arizona.

As a young forester Leopold began to ponder ways to keep large roadless portions of national forests wild. His focus was the headwaters of the Gila River near Silver City, New Mexico, which he had explored, fished, and loved. In December 1919 he met with the Forest Service's first landscape architect, Arthur Carhart, who had proposed leaving Trappers Lake in Colorado undeveloped. The two men were challenging what was believed to be the heart of Pinchot's wise-use philosophy—that forests were meant to be put to their best and most productive use. Carhart's appeal to aesthetics and the preservation of scenery sounded too much like Muir to Forest Service leaders. But Leopold built his argument on an expansion of Pinchot's idea of use to include recreation. He helped Carhart stop cabin development on Trappers Lake and later in the Boundary Waters region of northern Minnesota. In 1921, in an article in the *Journal of Forestry*, Leopold urged the preservation of wilderness as just another of many recreational opportunities the agency could provide in national forests. Coming soon after the establishment of the National Park Service, the idea of increasing the Forest Service's recreational mission was becoming attractive to its leadership. But when he offered a detailed proposal for protecting the Gila area as wilderness, Leopold was shot down by Greeley as too radical. Finally, in 1924, Leopold's plan to protect more than 500,000 acres of the Gila was approved. Two years later, Greeley went even further and called for an inventory of all de facto wilderness areas within the national forests. In 1929, several areas across the system were protected by regulations until further management plans were written. In 1935 Marshall and Leopold joined with others in founding the Wilderness Society, dedicated to preserving the last of the nation's wildlands.

What Marshall and Leopold didn't recognize immediately was the impact of the agency's charge to control fire across all its land. And Marshall, a major supporter of Silcox's socialist dream for the agency, was not able to reconcile its goals for people and the land. In fact, the thousands of miles of new roads built to fight fires in the early 1930s had opened up large portions of forests that were still wild until then. Both men wrote many articles critical of the roads' threat to wilderness. Even though more than four hundred miles of road were built in Yellowstone even before the twentieth century, it left most of the park roadless without special designation. Koch, the Northern Rockies

Region timber management chief, was never identified with Leopold or Marshall as a wilderness advocate. But his experience in firefighting brought him to a remarkably similar position based primarily on economics.

Koch saw the CCC and the other New Deal programs that enriched the Forest Service bureaucracy as counterproductive. The thrift that was built into the agency from its years of tight budgets was largely lost as managers were encouraged and promoted based on how much money they could attract and spend. Worse, the values of thrift and good management the agency was protecting were suffering under the opening of civilization to the woods. To explain what he meant, Koch wrote a remarkable essay in 1935 for the *Journal of Forestry* called "The Passing of the Lolo Trail."

The former supervisor who had walked in the footsteps of Lewis and Clark so many times was mourning the loss of a national treasure, the trail where the two explorers and their expedition had faced their greatest challenge. The high ridges of the Idaho-Montana border's Bitterroot Mountains had driven the explorers to the edge of starvation as early snows nearly trapped them in the headwaters of the Clearwater River. In 1935 roads built by the CCC and other New Deal programs had opened the area to automobiles, turning the trip into a three-hour drive from Missoula. "Only ten years ago it was just as Lewis and Clark saw it," Koch wrote.[22]

The Forest Service had opened up the wilderness with roads, telephone lines, and airstrips, built "white painted lookout houses" and "poured in thousands of firefighters year after year in a vain attempt to control forest fires," he said.[23] "Has all this effort and expenditure of millions of dollars added anything to human good?" he asked. "Is it possible that it was all a ghastly mistake, like plowing up the good buffalo grass sod of the dry prairies?"[24]

Little of the forests in this area are of a high value for lumber, he explained, with the expertise to back up his statements. Those areas that may have decent timber are in steep country where it will always be hard to build roads for extraction. "It seems obvious that whatever value the area may have, it is not for timber production," he wrote. "Its value lies in whatever pleasure man may get out of its recreational resources in the way of isolation, scenery, fish, and game."[25]

Koch, the only man to stop the 1910 fires, who had led men on the fire lines in every major campaign since, was calling his efforts in the Selway and Clearwater forests in Idaho "one of the saddest chapters in the history of high-minded and efficient public service."[26] "Many fires have been controlled, but when the time is ripe for a conflagration, man's efforts have been puny in the face of nature's forces," he wrote. "Each year we made a greater effort and threw larger forces of men into the battle, but so far as results were concerned there is little difference between 1919 when crews of thirty or 40 men, in a vain but courageous gesture were trailing the leeward end of each five or six gigantic fires and in 1934 when firefighters were counted in the thousands and the fires swept 180,000 acres."[27]

Indeed when burning conditions were right, Koch said, "the whole United States Army, if it were on the ground, could do nothing but keep out of the way." He broke it down to costs and benefits and demonstrated that the Forest Service could never hope to return the costs of firefighting in any form of revenues. Recreation and watershed values are the only others he considered. Before the Forest Service existed, Koch said, there was fair forest cover and the watershed did not seem to suffer. And the recreational values were lower late in his career than when he first started. Lightning started the 1934 Selway fire right under the lookout's nose. Firefighters got on it immediately, but it still took off, he pointed out. "If similar circumstances arose next year or ten years from now it is not at all likely that any different results could be secured in this particular country," Koch wrote. "I can only conclude that by doubling or trebling the fire control cost, the Forest Service might possibly reduce the area burned, but with always the possibility of a great conflagration sweeping beyond all control and nullifying past efforts."[28]

Koch wrote the essay after a board review (his own creation, remember) had recommended even more men and money for firefighting, even on low-value lands such as the Selway. He mailed the essay to Silcox in November 1934, "as a memorandum of a viewpoint which I believe is held at least in part by a good many other foresters."[29]

Silcox ignored him as well as the only other two voices to publicly object to the proposed firefighting plan, Leopold and Marshall.[30] In fact, an overwhelming consensus had grown within the organization that now was loaded with cash and manpower thanks to the New Deal. The longtime dream of full fire suppression on every acre of national forest was within the agency's grasp. Silcox's initiative for federal control over timber harvest had been transformed by 1935 into a new cooperative forestry proposal with the timber industry. He had not lost his ardor for reform, but it was tempered by the reality of politics and personal friendship with J. Phillip Weyerhaeuser, one of the first of the timber barons to embrace sustained yield forestry as preached by the Forest Service.

So Silcox listened to the voices in his agency that offered a chance of ending fires such as the creation blaze of the Big Blowup and the Selway fire of 1934. The new policy called for controlling every single fire by 10 a.m. the day after it was discovered. If the fire could not be extinguished by then, plans were written to put it out by the next day at 10 a.m. This would continue until the fire was controlled. The new policy was approved in a meeting of regional foresters in April 1935, soon after Koch's article went to press.

Now, even drought, hurricane winds, or economic devastation could not stand in the way of the Forest Service. The entire government would follow Silcox's "experiment on a continental scale."[31] The policy standardized fire control and clearly aided the agency's efforts to put out fires faster.

However, Koch was not completely ignored. The Forest Service designated 1.8 million acres of the Selway-Bitterroot country in Idaho and Montana as a primitive area in 1936 under the wilderness regulations Leopold and Marshall had advocated. With the new fire policy in place and an easing of the drought, the Forest Service could use its annual fire statistics to demonstrate its wisdom. Koch, the good soldier, never publicly challenged the policy again, even ignoring the debate in his memoirs.

Marshall, who rose to head the Forest Service's recreation programs in 1937, died in 1939 after convincing Silcox to expand the agency's protection of roadless lands. Silcox died the same year, leaving Koch with the last word on the 1910 fires. That word was *failure*. When he looked back critically in 1935 at the region he had tried to protect over his entire career, he warned about the role the public's view of their efforts would play. "Some day public opinion may rend the Forest Service for having accomplished so little protection for so much money," he wrote to end "The Passing of the Lolo Trail." "Public opinion can be molded, and it is the job of foresters to lead public opinion in the right direction in forestry matters,"[32] Koch said.

CHAPTER 10

Green Fire

Husbandry watches no clock, knows no season of cessation, and for the most part is paid for in love, not dollars. Husbandry of somebody else's land is a contradiction in terms. Husbandry is the heart of conservation.

—Aldo Leopold, 1942

YOUNG RANGER ALDO LEOPOLD was leading a crew on a surveying expedition through the Apache National Forest in 1909 when he saw the wolf wading through the whitewater of the Blue River. He and a crew member had sat down to lunch on a rimrock above and watched as the wolf joined her pack of grown pups in a flat below. The two men grabbed their rifles and shot into the pack without picking a target. They saw the old alpha female down and a pup dragging a wounded leg. Leopold poked the dying wolf with his gun. He described the next events in his essay, "Thinking like a Mountain":

> We reached the old wolf in time to watch a fierce green fire dying in her eyes. I realized then, and have known ever since, that there was something known only to her and to the mountain. I was young then, and full of trigger-itch; I thought that because fewer wolves meant more deer, that no wolves would mean hunters' paradise. But after seeing the green fire die, I sensed that neither the wolf nor the mountain agreed with such a view.[1]

Leopold used the story, written late in his life, to explain his personal transformation from a doctrinaire forester and youthful predator-killer to ecologist.[2] He was one of Pinchot's "young men," who would

129

expand the forester's vision beyond the trees, and his view of the land's health would become central to the evolution of thinking about Yellowstone, fire, and the natural world.

Aldo Leopold's evolution from a predator-killing Chamber of Commerce promoter to an ecological philosopher is one of the most powerful parables of the modern environmental movement. His story of shooting the wolf with the "fierce green fire" in her eyes has brought tears to countless readers and listeners. It has become a standard element of environmental speeches for speakers as varied as Dave Foreman, founder of Earth First!, and former Secretary of the Interior Bruce Babbitt.

Leopold's own story, as conveyed in his brilliant writing and other work, is so powerful because it shows how the Iowa native's thinking, attitudes, and beliefs were transformed by his relentless study of nature and people. The wolf story is the classic, but it is by no means the only example of how his on-the-ground careful observation, his introduction to the ideas of ecology, and his expanding ethical understanding reshaped his thinking on human relationships to the land. His transformation in thinking on fire was just as dramatic. Early in his career Leopold shared the view of others of Pinchot's young men, that people must exclude fire from the forest. He would eventually become a pioneer in the movement to use fire to restore ecosystems. Yet the evolution of his own views on fire and his voice in that debate have been largely obscured by his pivotal role in the development of the Forest Service's wilderness policy and his invention of the science of game management. These two achievements, combined with his even more significant creation of the philosophy of a land ethic, also have, until recently, masked the Sand County sage's many writings on the role of government and private property in conservation.

When the stories of evolution in Leopold's thinking on fire and on government are combined, they present an entirely different path from 1910 to the fires of 1988 and beyond. Leopold's guideposts led away from Sheridan's "firm control" approach to people and fire as his disciple Moses Harris translated it. In the intellectual legacy of Aldo Leopold, science and politics, land and power are tempered with personal responsibility. His views on government and fire have been largely rediscovered since Yellowstone's 1988 events, and their role in his legacy is still evolving. Yet there might not have been any legacy at all. Before Leopold was to spring from the influence of Pinchot and William Greeley, he almost died in the open spaces he loved.

LEOPOLD ROSE to supervisor of the Carson National Forest in northern New Mexico in 1912, the same year he was married to Estella Bergere, a first-grade teacher and the daughter of a concert pianist from nearby Santa Fe. Thus, he joined the ranks of federal land overseers, in charge of 1.5 million acres of pine-covered mountains and rangeland. In his first spring in the job Leopold was checking on sheep operations in the distant Jicarilla Mountains on the Colorado border, on horseback. He got lost and rode for several days through sleet and snow before, cold, wet, and suffering through excruciating pain from swollen knees, he finally struggled to a rail depot and could return home.3 When he arrived at work the next morning, Leopold's face, arms, and legs were swollen so large he could hardly move. His assistant forced him to see a doctor, which saved Leopold's life.

Leopold's kidneys had shut down. Doctors administered sweating pills, which slowly eliminated the impurities that had built up in his tissues and eased the attack. But Leopold was not out of the woods yet. He had Bright's disease, or nephritis, which usually begins as an infection and can lead to permanent kidney failure. The attack sent Leopold to bed and rest for more than a year, forcing him to leave his job with the Forest Service. During this period of imposed idleness Leopold read Thoreau, and reflected on his early experiences, his relationship to wolves, the wild, and life itself. Aldo Starker Leopold, who would create his own legacy later, came into the world on October 22, 1913.

Leopold returned to the Forest Service in its Southwest regional office in Albuquerque, overseeing grazing with a new zeal for protecting and managing the diversity of animal life on the national forests of New Mexico. He found encouragement in the communities that surrounded the national forests. Sportsmen and even ranchers shared his expanded view of the national forests as important animal habitat, and they joined him in the New Mexico Game Protective Association. Yet his ideas got nowhere with the Forest Service, which was heading into its first dark age. Just keeping to its mission of conservation of forests, let alone wildlife, was nearly impossible. World War I prompted the Forest Service to remove its limits on grazing and force its rangers to spend much of their time selling war bonds.

Leopold left the Forest Service, disillusioned with its retreat from the conservation zeal Pinchot had instilled personally only a few years before when Leopold was a student. He became head of the Albuquerque Chamber of Commerce, where he promoted another of his core values: the responsibility to get involved in improving the community. Public service was not a profession to Leopold; it was a way of life. With the addition of a second son, Luna, and a daughter, Nina, Aldo and Estella were deeply rooted in the culturally diverse New Mexican society, and the chamber position allowed him to nurture its best face. But when the chamber's plank turned to road development and business boosterism, he stepped down quietly. And the Forest Service now wanted him back.

Leopold's transformation from forester to ecologist was not a straight path. Ecology itself was still a new and obscure science. He was unaware of the work of early ecologists; he discovered ecology's basic concepts largely himself. His own education came largely through field observations he made after he returned to the Forest Service in 1919, now as the number-two man in the Southwest Region, assistant forester for operations. He may have seen the green fire a decade before, but it was only after 1919 that he was to see the light.

His first major insight was the idea of national forest wilderness, which grew in part out of his readings of Thoreau while ill. Leopold called for setting aside large roadless areas not just for preservation but also for hunting, horse packing, and other activities that demanded scenic solitude. Yet even as he was pressing forward this rather radical idea, he remained in the flow of mainstream views about predators and fire. His views on fire were made public in 1920 during the Forest Service's campaign against light burning. "Piute [*sic*] Forestry Versus Forest Fire Protection," his essay in *Southwestern Magazine*, mimicked the writings of Forest Chief Henry Graves, his professor at Yale, and Greeley, the leading voice for fire exclusion. Light burning, Leopold said, "would not only fail to prevent serious fires but would ultimately destroy the productiveness of the forests on which western industries depend on for their supply of timber."[4]

He laid out the argument based not on his own research or observation but on the writings of Greeley and other foresters. "It can be stated without hesitation that the large percentage of the chaparral or brush areas found in the southwestern states were originally covered with valuable forests, but gradually reverted to brush after repeated light burning had destroyed the reproduction," he added.

After returning to the field and inspecting the dry forests of Arizona and New Mexico Leopold realized that the Forest Service's science was dead wrong and reversed his view. He decided that the basic resource of forests was not trees but soil. Conserving soil, Leopold surmised, was the fundamental job of the land manager. After examining fire scars and tree rings, he determined that the frequency of fire changed dramatically following settlement of the region. With settlement came heavy grazing, severely limiting the amount of grass available for fuel. With the loss of grass came widespread soil erosion that dramatically reduced the productivity of the land. Instead of flourishing in the absence of fire, ponderosa pine forests were turning into dense thickets of stunted trees, impeding the growth on which sustained yield forestry depended.

"Until very recently we have administered the southern Arizona forests on the assumption that while overgrazing was bad for erosion, fire was worse, and that therefore we must keep the brush hazard grazed down to the extent necessary to prevent serious fires," Leopold wrote in "Grass, Brush, Timber and Fire in Southern Arizona," published in the *Journal of Forestry* in 1924.[5] "Let us now consider the bearing of this theory on Forest administration. We have learned that during the pre-settlement period of no grazing and severe fires erosion was not abnormally active. We have learned that during the post-settlement period of no fires and severe grazing, erosion became exceedingly active. Has our administrative policy applied these facts? It has not."[6] Leopold was thus openly challenging the Forest Service fire dogma. But he didn't stop with his observations about erosion. He let the agency's own numbers speak for themselves.

"We have likewise rejected the story written in our own fire statistics, which shows that on the Tonto Forest only about one-third of one percent of the hazard area burns over each year, and that it would therefore take three hundred years for fire to cover the forest once," he wrote. "Even if the most conservative grazing policy, which now prevails should largely enhance the present brush hazard by restoring a little grass, neither the potential danger of fire damage nor the potential cost of fire control could compare with the existing watershed damage."[7]

Leopold saw in the scars of fire on junipers and oak something like the fierce green fire he had seen years before in the eyes of the wolf. The land was telling him something that was forcing him to expand his mind so he could listen. These observations were fundamental to his personal journey from forester to game manager to ecologist. His insight on fire came even before his reconsideration of the wisdom of predator control.

Leopold's work caught the attention of Greeley, who was now Forest Service chief. Predictably, he didn't like what he was hearing from the midlevel bureaucrat. Leopold was focusing too much on the land when he should have been thinking about the practice of forestry, developed in Europe, taught at Yale, and championed by the Forest Service. An assistant forester should be keeping track of budgets and costs, not dirt. Greeley didn't directly challenge Leopold's findings. He didn't have to because they were all but lost in the flood of sycophantic rhetoric about fire control's benefits coming from throughout the Forest Service.

Greeley recognized Leopold's curiosity and his knack for research and urged him to transfer to the Forest Products Laboratory in Madison, Wisconsin, to develop new ways to protect trees and turn lumber waste into products. At the time, 1921, Leopold had no interest in leaving New Mexico. He was still excited about his game management projects in the state and his push to have the Forest Service incorporate wilderness in its management programs. Greeley was surprisingly supportive of these efforts. By 1924, Leopold's work was becoming well-known throughout the agency, though the challenge to its fire policy was considered a minor footnote. Greeley asked him to reconsider the Forest Products Lab job, and this time Leopold accepted.

Aldo Leopold and his family, which had grown to four children with the addition of Aldo Carl Leopold in 1919, packed up their belongings and moved to Madison, a thousand miles away from the native home of his wife and children. They moved into a stucco house in a culturally sterile neighborhood, where Estella dug out her homesickness by planting a lush garden. The move seemed to make sense only in the professional advancement category. But in the history of the environmental movement it was critical.

When Leopold returned to the Midwest, he was leaving the stage of the western forest fire debate. His Forest Service work for the next four years was devoted largely to finding new uses for wasted timber and encouraging builders to use wood more wisely. Greeley's promotion had kept the Forest Service's most creative scientist from devoting his time and focus to the issue that was at the heart of its forest management program—fire.

We can only guess how a spirited and well-funded research program on the role of fire throughout the national forest system might have reshaped Forest Service chief Gus Silcox's decision on the 10 a.m. policy in the 1930s. Had the agency been visionary enough to encourage Leopold's research on fire, it might have made the leap back into the forefront of conservation as it had been in the days of Pinchot.

In fact, the views of Pinchot himself had evolved far beyond his own historic legacy as the wise-use foil to Muir's preservationist zeal. As Pennsylvania's governor, he set aside thousands of acres of state forests to preserve aesthetic values, not timber production. After reading the likes of Leopold and ecologist Frederick Clements and visiting the biologically unique Galápagos Islands, Pinchot rewrote in 1936 his classic 1914 manual, *The Training of a Forester*, to incorporate ecological concepts.[8]

In 1927, the Leopolds were happily acclimating to their new home by taking regular hunting and camping trips into Wisconsin's countryside. They added a second daughter, Estella, to the fold. Leopold became active in the Isaac Walton League, a conservation group of fishermen, and used his post to advocate wilderness designation in northern Minnesota's Boundary Waters canoe country. But for Aldo Leopold, the sporting lifestyle and part-time conservation were not enough. Frustrated with his limited duties, Leopold left the federal government in 1928, seeking once again to devote his efforts toward studying, advancing, and promoting his ideas on game management. The move to the Midwest had broadened the forty-one-year-old scientist's horizons. His thinking was no longer confined to the West, forestry, or even government conservation.

The Forest Service's loss of Leopold was the earth's gain. His expanded focus, first on game management, then on ecology, and eventually on government policy and philosophy, was critical to the subsequent evolution of the environmental movement decades later.

His first benefactor was the Sporting Arms and Ammunition Manufacturers' Institute. Today they would be lumped with the gun lobby and spurned by many inspired by Leopold's land ethic philosophy. In 1928, though, the gun manufacturers and Leopold recognized that they had common interests. Improving game populations would increase hunting, prompting new markets in guns and bullets. Increased hunting, Leopold recognized, increased the constituency and funding for wildlife conservation.

With industry funding, Leopold conducted a survey of game populations and management programs in the Midwest. He soon was able to show that the key to increasing wildlife populations was to increase their access to food and cover—in other words, habitat. But simply setting aside refuges of federal land for wildlife wouldn't be enough, he said. A successful wildlife restoration program would depend not only on refuges but also on habitat improvements on the private lands that surround them. Farmers and other private property owners were an integral part of the team. In the course of his work he was learning and teaching about the complexities of the relationship between wildlife and the land where they lived. Through his research, his guidance, and force of will, Leopold was able to convince the sportsmen-based conservation organizations of the time of the wisdom of a cooperative program between government and farmers for habitat protection and restoration. In addition to game species such as deer and ducks, the new national wildlife program of the American Protective Game Association called for protecting nongame species as well, including songbirds and predators. This effort brought his work increasingly to the attention of other conservationists and the ecological community as well.

IN 1869, GERMAN BIOLOGIST Ernst Haeckel coined the term "ecology" from the Greek word *oikos*, meaning house or place. He used the word to describe the study of the relationship of an organism to its organic and inorganic environment. The field of ecology was pioneered by early-twentieth-century botanists, among them Frederick Clements, the author of the 1910 Forest Service study that showed the role of fire in regenerating lodgepole pine. Clements was the chief advocate for the concept of ecological succession among plant communities. Plant communities, Clements argued, progress through a series of distinct stages to a final climax stage. Soil conditions and climate dictate which species would dominate each stage and eventually dominate when climax was achieved and a natural equilibrium was reached. Fires and other disturbances could disrupt the process, but then it would start over and move toward climax again. Victor Shelford, a professor at the University of Illinois, applied many of Clements's concepts to animal ecology, and their collaborations in the 1930s brought together the fields of plant and animal ecology. But in 1931, Leopold's personal understanding of ecology was already beyond that of the specialists in the field. His vision already encompassed the ecological relationships among plants, animals, soil, climate, and topography. As he was writing his first landmark book, *Game Management*, his mind was racing ahead to the next conservation challenge. The subsequent observations would leave their mark on Yellowstone when they would reshape land management.

Two foreign trips in the 1930s were to steer his gaze back to his forestry roots, which opened his eyes to its limitations. He went to Mexico, just across the border from the eroded forests and rangeland that had first taught him the basics of ecology. There he found the Sierra Madres' soils stable and the watersheds intact. Fires burned regularly through the Chihuahua Sierras every few years, and the only forest effects seemed to be that the pines were a bit farther apart. Deer thrived despite the presence of wolves and mountain lions. "Whereas our own states, plastered as they are with National Forests, National Parks and all the other trappings of conservation, are so badly damaged that only tourists and others ecologically color-blind, can look upon them without a feeling of sadness and regret," he wrote in "A Conservationist in Mexico."[9]

Then he went to Germany, the birthplace of forestry and the model for the control-dominated forestry Pinchot had brought to America. The forest floors were cleared of the litter that fertilized the soil. Healthy hardwood forests were replaced by spruce and pine because the fungi, bacteria, and insects that helped turn organic matter into soil were not thriving. Predators were nonexistent and game animals were fed like livestock.

"The forest landscape is deprived of a certain exuberance which arises from a rich variety of plants fighting with each other for a place in the sun," Leopold wrote of Germany. "I never realized before that the melodies of nature are music only when played against the undertones of evolutionary history. In the German forest one now hears only a dismal fugue!"[10]

These trips and his work as a consulting forester and game manager shifted his worldview. No longer was his vantage point that of the scientifically enlightened baron of federal land management. He was joining the ranks of stewards, humbled by his ignorance rather than buoyed by his intelligence. Even as he temporarily returned to government service, directing soil erosion programs for the Civilian Conservation Corps (CCC) in New Mexico, he was confronting the limitations of government thinking at the time about conservation. There he saw one agency straightening rivers to accelerate spring runoff while another was teaching farmers to contour their hillsides to slow it down. In response to Silcox and Marshall's campaign for nationalizing cut-over forests, Leopold wrote in his essay "Conservation Economics" that such a move would have limited benefits. "Will it assure the physical integrity of America in A.D. 2000, or even A.D. 1950?" he asked rhetorically. "Most assuredly not. . . . The only cure is the universal reformation of land use, and the longer we dabble with palliatives; the more gigantic grows the job of restoration."[11]

In 1933, now a national conservation leader, Leopold was asked to present the fourth annual John Wesley Powell Lecture to the southwestern division of the American Association for the Advancement of Science in Las Cruces, New Mexico. The speech, entitled "The Conservation Ethic," was his first attempt at linking ecology to philosophy. In it were the basic building blocks of "The Land Ethic," the seminal essay of his greatest work, *A Sand County Almanac*. Leopold told the story of Odysseus killing his wife's slaves for misbehavior upon his return from the Trojan War. "The hanging involved no question of propriety, much less of justice," Leopold said. "The girls were property. The disposal of property was then, as now, a matter of expediency, not of right or wrong."[12]

Over the 3,000 years following the Trojan War humans had extended ethics to many fields of conduct, Leopold said, but not to humans' relationship with the land, animals, and plants. Individuals since biblical times had argued that damaging the land was wrong. "Society, however, had not yet affirmed their belief."[13]

In the "Land Ethic," written fifteen years later, Leopold put the argument into the ecological framework of community. Ethics rests, he said, on the premise that the individual is a member of a community of interdependent parts. Our instincts prompt us to compete for our place in the community, but our ethics prompt us to cooperate. Leopold enlarged the community in which we should consider ourselves to include soils, water, plants, and animals—the whole life community. They required land managers to think beyond the people they served or even the resources directly within their authority to the larger communities that were all interrelated.

In the years preceding publication of that essay, Leopold had broadened his own attention in the life community. In 1933, the University of Wisconsin offered him the job of teaching game management to graduate students. In addition to teaching, the university wanted him to start and oversee soil conservation and game habitat development projects. He was to go on the radio and give farmers tips on how they could increase wildlife on their land. That news was big enough to make the *New York Times*.

Leopold's ideas were attractive enough to Wisconsin farmers that a number were willing to turn their lands into laboratories for game management research. The most significant was the five-year Coon Valley project in southwestern Wisconsin. Leopold convinced half the farmers in the watershed, 315, to participate with federal funding as part of the incentive. The plan was based on a simple concept: remove cattle and crops from the steep slopes and leave them to wildlife and timber. Make up for the lost farmland with more intensive cropping on the flatlands. Success wasn't easy. Drought in 1934 killed many of the trees farmers planted, and a blizzard flattened the sorghum, millet, and sunflower patches planted to feed birds. But over time the program protected the soil, reduced flood damage, and increased wildlife populations. For Leopold the most powerful Coon Valley lesson came from the farmers themselves. "What matter, though, these temporary growing pains when one can cast his eyes upon the hills and see hardboiled farmers who have spent their lives destroying land now carrying water by hand to their new plantations?" Leopold wrote.[14]

In 1934, Leopold and a faculty committee selected a 245-acre farm near the south shore of Madison's Lake Wingra as the site of an arboretum. Their plan was to restore the tallgrass prairie, marshes, and pine forests that had been nearly lost after more than a century of civilization. This restoration work would come to have a direct bearing on shifting ideas on the role of fire in national parks and elsewhere two decades later. He wanted to show Wisconsin that the landscape, destroyed by human-caused fires in the north and human-caused erosion in the south, could be restored. The prairie project was to yield another one of Leopold's major insights. The old farm was plowed and the seeds of native plants were collected from around the area. Leopold and his students and crews of CCC workers hand-watered the struggling plants through drought and wind until they took hold. Leopold had hoped that once the native crop was planted he could walk away and the prairie would reappear.

He soon discovered that nonnative plants, weeds that had hitched a ride with civilization, were prospering along with his native plants. He tried thinning out the competitors by hand. A decade later he realized something had been missing from the prairie since the time of European arrival. It was fire.

In the 1940s, Leopold began burning his new prairie, triggering the rebirth of the wildland of his dream. The fire opened native seeds, unleashing them to grow and thrive. Saplings and other brush that had tenaciously intruded into the area were killed. The invader weeds were brought under control as the almost three hundred species of prairie plants, which had evolved through centuries of frequent fires, took over again. Leopold's prairie fires came at the same time Forest Service scientists in the South were finally convincing the agency of the need for fire to restore the longleaf pine forest. But it would be more than a decade before fire restoration became accepted as more than an oddity in land management.

In 1935, Aldo and Estella purchased forty acres of played-out farmland near Baraboo, Wisconsin, with nothing but a dilapidated chicken coop on it. The farm's sandy soils, created from the washing away of a receding glacier, had never been destined for productive farming. All the timber that had been there was cut and gone. The farmhouse had burned to the ground, and its previous owner had joined the dust bowl migration to California. The Leopolds set out to make the chicken coop habitable, cleaning out manure that was piled waist high. Starker was twenty-one and the rest of the children were all teenagers. Spurred by Estella's enthusiasm, they would drive north on weekends from Madison to build a roof, drill a well, and construct a bunkhouse, turning the coop into "the Shack."

The Shack and the surrounding sandy land would become as important to the history of environmentalism as Walden Pond and Yellowstone. It became the symbol of restoration of the land and the soul. There the Leopold family would heal the land with their own hands. They planted and transplanted native flowers and plants. Each spring they planted pines, hardwoods, and prairie grasses. Some years drought or wind or heat would kill their new crops, just as it had for the farmers who struggled before them. But through the process of restoration and study at the Shack, Nina Leopold Bradley later recalled, she and the rest of her family grew to recognize the interconnectedness of living systems. "As we transformed the land, it transformed us," she wrote.[15]

Leopold himself was continuing his own makeover. His stewardship on those forty acres helped him to appreciate the toil, attention, and care farmers and other landowners assumed if they were to practice conservation on their lands. It would take more than government incentives or profits to get the kind of return on the land Leopold recognized was needed. "When land does well for its owner, and the owner does well by the land; when both end up better by reason of their partnership, we have conservation," Leopold wrote in his 1939 essay "The Farmer as Conservationist." "When one or the other grows poorer, we do not."[16]

In addressing private conservation, Leopold was once again focusing on the limits of government conservation. Simply practicing conservation on public lands was not enough. He didn't want forests to be relegated to huge tracts separated from fields and prairies. Leopold also advocated that private landowners plant forests on steep slopes instead of crops. He saw the need to have trees and other wildlife cover and food interspersed across ownerships and land types. Leopold was moving to a landscape view of conservation. His scale was both large and small. He could look beyond the artificial boundaries of private and public lands, wilderness and developed country to combine the needs of people and the land.

As his trial-and-error experiments on the arboretum and the Shack were teaching him the lessons of the land, his approach to the division between public and private conservation was maturing. The role of ethics he first espoused in 1933 permeated nearly all he wrote. "Conservation is our attempt to put human ecology on a permanent footing," Leopold wrote in "Land-use and Democracy" in *Audubon* in 1942.[17]

This essay, long overlooked by most modern environmentalists, laid out Leopold's strong case for the kind of private, personalized conservation program he believed was necessary for success. He began once again with the limits of government. "Government can't raise crops, maintain small scattered structures, administer small scattered areas, or bring to bear on small local matters that combination of solicitude, foresight, and skill which we call husbandry," Leopold wrote. "Husbandry watches no clock, knows no season of cessation, and for the most part is paid for in love, not dollars. Husbandry of somebody else's land is a contradiction in terms. Husbandry is the heart of conservation."[18]

Pinchot's young man Leopold had now outgrown the worldview that linked Sheridan to Muir to Pinchot and beyond. The firm hand of government could do good things, he acknowledged. But it also did bad things, such as indirectly promote erosion, remove fire from the ecosystem, and spread its mistakes across tens of millions of acres and several generations. Leopold was calling for a more personal view of conservation, one grounded in place and personal responsibility. Writing from a place already settled, he presented an updated vision for conservation not unlike John Wesley Powell's of seventy years earlier. National government played a key role in guiding, funding, educating, and researching. Protecting wilderness and core refuge areas was an especially important job for national government. But these conservation efforts, without the hands that would dig and plant and nurture and cherish the land and all of its ecological cogs and wheels, would be ineffective.

In 1948, Leopold was at the peak of his career. He was elected honorary vice president of the American Forestry Association and president of the Ecological Society of America. The Truman administration asked him to serve as the United States' delegate at an upcoming United Nations conservation conference. The previous year he had finished drafting a book that brought together many of his ideas. Its working title was "Great Possessions." It began with a section called "Sand County Almanac," which included stories of the Leopolds' life at the Shack. The second section, "Sketches Here and There," included "Thinking Like a Mountain" and other essays that told of the lessons he had learned in his forty-year career. The final section included "The Land Ethic" and other philosophical essays. On April 14, he heard from Oxford University Press that they would publish the book.[19]

On Friday, April 16, Aldo, Estella, their daughter Estella, and her boyfriend headed north to the Shack for the annual tree planting trip.

The young man left Sunday. On Tuesday, they planted the trees, bringing the total to more than 30,000 trees since they first began their work
thirteen years before. Leopold, now sixty-one and recovering from the
surgical severing of nerves in his face, was still weak.[20] The next morning, April 21, the Leopolds spotted smoke from a neighbor's farm to the
east of the Shack. A trash fire was burning out of control and heading
downhill toward their beloved trees. The three sprang into action.
Leopold's daughter ran to get the fire pump. His wife gathered buckets.
He picked up a sprinkling can, and they loaded coats, gloves, a gunnysack, a broom, and a shovel into their car.

With buckets filled and dripping, Leopold drove close enough to
see the flames blown by the wind through the native grasses they had
brought back. Estella took the wet gunnysack and broom and captured
embers blowing in the wind as they threatened to cross the road by a
marsh. Leopold and his daughter and other neighbors attacked the
blaze directly. He sent young Estella to a farmer's house to call the fire
department and the Wildlife Conservation Department.

Leopold strapped the water pump on his back and headed into the
marsh to water down the flanks of the fire. Suddenly, Leopold felt a
pain in his chest. He tugged the pump off his back and laid down on
the ground, resting his head on a clump of grass. The old forester folded
his hands over his chest. The massive heart attack killed him quickly.
He died alone, and the fire gently burned over him.

LUNA COMPLETED the editing of his father's work, and "Great Possessions" was published under the title *A Sand County Almanac*. It was
not a big seller. And although Leopold was revered in the conservation
field, he remained largely obscure outside of Wisconsin, wildlife, and
wilderness circles. *A Sand County Almanac* and essays from another
Leopold collection published in 1953, *Round River*, were combined in
1966 and republished just as the modern environmental movement was
beginning to take off. Its ethical and ecological discussions became the
philosophical foundation for much of the movement, and it has since
sold millions of copies worldwide.

Absent from this great work was all but a passing reference to fire.

Leopold mentioned that the tallgrass prairie owed its existence to fire and that bur oak was the only tree that could survive the repeated grass fires. He spoke of the 1871 Peshtigo fire and its destruction of soil. But he left out the lessons he had learned from the juniper and ponderosa in the Southwest. His discussions of the limits of government were carefully worded to ensure that they could not be used as a club to diminish efforts to protect more wilderness or secure additional funding for management and research. So his fire legacy would first be carried out through the example of his son Starker, who became one of the nation's leading wildlife ecologists. Starker's leadership of a National Park Service panel was to lay the groundwork for the natural fire policy in Yellowstone National Park and change forever the federal government's view of fire and nature.

CHAPTER 11

The Face of Conservation

Only You

—Smokey Bear, 1985 (from Forest Service poster)

THROUGH THE MIDDLE of the twentieth century, Aldo Leopold's new ideas about a land ethic and land health had yet to take root in American society or even in Yellowstone. The support for full fire suppression remained a foundation for land managers and a central cog in conservation values. The conservation movement had no obvious leader or national star. As fears surrounding the onset of World War II escalated, it would be the advertising industry, employed by the U.S. government for the purpose, that would step in to give a public face to the idea of conservation for the next twenty years.

It would be a cartoon character, Smokey Bear, that would take center stage. Effective as the symbol of fire prevention, Smokey would come to represent a conservation policy as shallow and thin as Smokey's character—fire exclusion. Yet the bear who grew up with the baby boom generation did more than firmly entrench the Forest Service's fire control policy as the center of the public's image of conservation. Smokey helped alter Americans' relationship to nature. Though his character was weak, his message was strong and survives to this day: Fire destroys what we should value.

As Gifford Pinchot was battling William Greeley for the hearts of foresters in the early 1920s, Aldo Leopold and Robert Marshall were seeking to protect wilderness in the early 1930s, and Elers Koch was urging Gus Silcox to reconsider fire policy in the mid-1930s, most Americans were simply not paying attention. Conservation had not been at the center of American society since the Progressive Era. Outside of foresters and sportsmen, most Americans would have been hard-pressed to name a conservationist in the 1930s. If it was anyone, it was Franklin Delano Roosevelt (FDR), the creator of the Civilian Conservation Corps and the Soil Conservation Service.

Pinchot, who had himself held center stage along with John Muir and Theodore Roosevelt at the beginning of the century, was still around. But the former star no longer played in the limelight of American society. The man whose political skills, energy, and vision had helped create modern America was a footnote even as FDR's New Deal was putting many of his ideas to work. After he completed his final run as Pennsylvania's governor, he made the headlines one last time, at the end of the 1930s, when Harold Ickes, FDR's secretary of the interior, proposed moving the U.S. Forest Service from the Department of Agriculture to the Department of the Interior.

Pinchot's views about forestry had evolved considerably by 1937. He kept up on the works of ecologists and Leopold, who served under him in the early days. The two conservation giants had met first during Leopold's student days and corresponded throughout their lifetimes. In 1927, when Leopold was seeking to restructure Wisconsin's game laws, he convinced Pinchot to come to Madison to give a speech in support of the plan. Pinchot had not only included ecological concepts in his latest edition of *The Training of a Forester*, he had also begun to question the practice of clear-cutting after a tour of western forests that year.[1] Such attitudes should have aligned him with the thinking and philosophy behind the Ickes proposal, which would have kept the agency in the custodial role over forests it had had since Pinchot's day. But Pinchot's greatest moment came in 1905 when he moved the Forest Service from Interior to Agriculture. He balked at the reversal of the bureaucratic fiat he had used so deftly thirty years earlier to put his agency in charge of the national forests.

Pinchot should have been the conservation movement's tribal elder. Instead he was mocked and shunned as a sellout to commercialism. As much as his public fight with Muir over Hetch Hetchy, his last battle with Ickes over moving the Forest Service to Interior tarnished his legacy. Aligned with the timber industry and western congressmen who represented the same interests he had fought so hard at the beginning of the century, he helped to win the battle, and the agency remained under the Department of Agriculture. But Pinchot's position in the debate returned him to the black and white debate between preservation and wise use. Unwittingly, he contributed to that perception when he wrote his own account of his life and work. His autobiography, *Breaking New Ground*, finished just before he died in 1946, ended in 1910, leaving out the accomplishments and wisdom he had added since then. Leopold's respect for Pinchot never waned. When he sent a letter to Pinchot responding to inquiries about the early days of the Forest Service, Leopold started it, "Dear Chief."[2]

In any event, Pinchot was the old face of conservation. Leopold, arguably the new face by the 1940s, and eventually to become an enduring one, was still largely unknown outside of wildlife and forestry circles. Beginning in 1944, the face millions of Americans would instead identify with conservation for the next twenty years was not a man but the bear.

National advertising had become a mainstay of modern society by the early twentieth century, but conservation got little or no attention. Along with the ability to manipulate press coverage, called publicity, advertising was a crucial tool of the new businesses that were pumping cars out of assembly lines, selling food in supermarkets, and converting citizens to consumers. Advertising not only was creating demand and steering customers to products, it was feeding back to a changing audience the cultural expectations and guidelines of the new society. Clean was good. Germs were bad. Smoking was permitted, even by women, and so on.

In the 1930s conservationists didn't have publicity agents, corporations did. Government also was slow to take advantage of the techniques developed to create conformity and steer the masses to act. The one exception was the National Park Service created in 1916. Its founder, Stephen Mather, had made a fortune using the twenty-mule-team logo to sell borax for cleaning. He and his assistant at the Park Service, Horace Albright, had used the same public relations savvy to sell Congress on the need to replace the army in management of the national parks. Mather and Albright, who eventually succeeded Mather, kept promoting the parks through advertising and public relations, working with concessionaires and other businesses to attract people to visit so they would build public support for expansion and funding for their agency. Both tied the national parks to the preservationist goals of Muir, a friend of Mather's. But promotion of preservation took a clear second to the goal of making the parks attractive to visitors. Both men, it turned out, were critical to the development of the professionalism and success of the National Park Service, and both men played pivotal roles in the conservation movement of their times. Though they would find a place in the history books, neither became a national spokesman for the conservation movement.

FDR was developing a conservation legacy, but unlike his cousin Theodore Roosevelt, it was not a personal crusade. It necessarily was obscured by his larger agenda for economic recovery, by the massive scope of government's growth, and then by World War II. After his election in 1932, FDR did successfully begin to use advertising and publicity to promote his programs for recovery and to speak directly to the nation on the radio in his Fireside Chats. In 1936, even the Forest Service began to explore the use of advertising as a part of its fire prevention campaign. The following year it hired James Montgomery Flagg, the artist of the most popular World War I recruitment posters, to paint a series of posters on fire. Dressed in ranger uniform and wearing a fedora, one of the posters had an Uncle Sam character pointing at a forest on fire with the message, "Your Forests, Your Fault, Your Loss." The program had little or no impact.

FDR was the first president to recognize the potential power of advertising. And if many reformers were challenging the very basis for advertising, FDR was integrating it into his programs, and the advertising industry responded warmly. The Depression and the changing world scene had knocked it for a loop in the 1930s. Consumer groups had challenged the rosy pictures of American life it portrayed when many Americans were starving and barely hanging on. The use of the same advertising and public relations tactics that had become so effective for business by the Nazis and Joseph Stalin also clouded the advertising industry's own image. Critics were apt to equate publicity with propaganda, but Roosevelt's support offered executives welcome cover.

In November 1941, as a fleet of Japanese aircraft carriers were steaming east toward Pearl Harbor, the nation's advertisers were meeting at Hot Springs, Arkansas, for the annual convention of the Association of National Advertisers. There industry leaders and Roosevelt administration officials met and found a common need to cooperate. From this meeting the Advertising Council was born to study the government's defense needs and to determine where the advertising industry could help.

Soon after Japan attacked Pearl Harbor and war was declared, the council name was changed to the War Advertising Council. It included representatives from ad agencies, their clients, and the media. It had two primary goals: meet the federal government's wartime advertising needs, and make the advertising industry and its clients look patriotic. Selling took a back seat to saying how great America was and how Americans could help win the war and make the nation even greater.

On February 28, 1942, a Japanese submarine surfaced off Santa Barbara, California, and shelled a pier adjacent to the strategic oil fields there. Only miles from the tinder-dry Los Padres National Forest, the attack sent chills through the Forest Service. Agency leaders feared the forests that would supply gun stocks and packing boxes and building materials would become targets. "The British Royal Air Force found it worthwhile to start great fires in the forests of Germany," said Secretary of Agriculture Claude R. Wichard in May 1942. "Every fire in our fields or forests this year is an enemy fire."[3] Wichard's message, that fire was the enemy, had been the Forest Service's fundamental message since 1910. But Walt Disney Studios delivered the message more forcefully than any forest ranger could through the movie *Bambi*, which was released in 1942.

The main character of the movie, Bambi, a young deer, loses his mother to a great forest fire in an emotional scene that was to stick in the minds of children for the rest of the twentieth century. Later, hunters set yet another forest fire that destroys the forest and kills more of Bambi's wild friends. The advertising firm of Foote, Cone, and Belding, hired by the Forest Service for its fire prevention campaign, recognized Bambi's power and used the deer and his friends in the War Advertising Council's ads. It also convinced Disney to produce a Bambi fire prevention poster.

Later that year a Japanese floatplane flew two missions over Oregon, dropping incendiary bombs on national forests, an apparent attempt to carry out the Forest Service's worst fears. And before the war was over, the Japanese had launched more than nine thousand incendiary balloons that were designed to be carried by the newly discovered jet stream to the United States. About a thousand balloons crossed U.S. boundaries, but they caused little damage. The main reason: the balloons were released in the fall after the fire season was past. Despite the large number of balloons reaching the United States, only one caused any casualties. On May 5, 1945, a balloon bomb killed a woman and her five children near Lakeview, Oregon, when it exploded as they dragged it from the woods.

Bambi ads were very effective in raising fire awareness. Thousands of posters were sent to elementary schools and libraries. Gas stations and factories displayed the popular cartoon character on their walls. But Disney was unwilling to give up a profitable icon of its studio for the long term. It would loan Bambi to the government, but only on its own terms. The Forest Service considered other characters. Southern regional officials came up with a dour-faced old ranger named Jim, who admonished people for acting carelessly in the forest. He may have been the agency's idea of itself, but he wasn't the kind of guy the public wanted to meet in the woods. He looked like he was just waiting to hand out tickets because campers hadn't adequately doused their fires.

The fact was that Bambi was the perfect messenger, but he was already taken. Bambi was especially popular with schoolchildren, a major target of the fire prevention campaign. The advertising executives knew they needed an animal of their own. Today, no one really knows who came up with the idea for a bear. Foote, Cone, and Belding and the Ad Council get the official credit from the Forest Service. They hired artist Albert Staehle to draw fire prevention posters with several animals. He returned with posters using an owl, a squirrel, a chipmunk, and a bear. A committee chose the bear and the squirrel for the 1944 campaign. Staehle's bear, without a hat or pants, was too cute and too naked for some of the campaign managers. But the squirrel, popular with kids, was considered a nuisance and a pest to farmers and other rural residents. He was sent to the same place as Ranger Jim. Staehle put a hat and pants on his bear, and the Forest Service gave him the name Smokey. He was officially born in a memo on August 9, 1944, calling for art for the fire prevention campaign. The Forest Service called for a bear cub in a green pine forest setting, "Nose short (Panda type), color black or brown; expression appealing, knowledgeable, quizzical; wearing a campaign (or Boy Scout) hat that typifies the outdoors and the woods."[4]

Smokey didn't show up publicly until 1945, but then he was an immediate hit. Demand for posters and school kits soared. Children began writing the bear like he was Santa Claus. In 1947 his motto, "Only You Can Prevent Forest Fires," was added. The imaginary bear, who still receives up to one thousand letters a day, even was issued his own zip code by the U.S. Postal Service in 1964. For better or worse Smokey became a symbol of the Forest Service. Smokey elevated its role as the firefighting agency, obscuring its other duties and initiatives. But his success was intoxicating. By 1950 the agency could report 20,000 fewer forest fires since 1944. And the popular bear, who showed up on lunch boxes, pajamas, watches, and plastic jeeps, was bringing the Forest Service $172, 000 a year in licensing fees.

Smokey's agency and advertising handlers were slowly changing Smokey's message in ways they didn't even recognize, however. Smokey's early ads and posters portrayed a brown bear complete with paws even though he wore the obligatory hat and jeans. He was usually in the forest and often surrounded by other forest creatures. Sometimes the forest was green, and other times it was red and yellow with flames. But Smokey was clearly a bear and his home was a forest. When a small black bear cub was discovered in a forest fire in New Mexico in 1950, Smokey came to life and moved to the National Zoo in Washington,

D.C. The live Smokey increased his popularity and publicity, but it took Smokey physically out of the forest. The advertising campaign did as well. Smokey became more human. He prayed. He grew hands and a muscular build that would make any National Football League line-backer proud.

The Forest Service was changing too. The postwar building boom came as the harvest on private forestlands in the United States was peaking. The timber market was still largely a domestic market, and the timber industry gladly moved to national forestlands to pick up the dif-ference with steadily reduced supplies on private forests. Working closely with Congress, the Forest Service developed a system through which it could use revenues from timber sales for reforestation, wildlife enhancement, road building, and a steadily increasing blend of activi-ties. Like Pinchot's emergency fire fund of 1909 this new budgeting device gave the agency even more money and control over its own des-tiny. All it had to do was keep giving concessions to cut more and more trees. Now the agency had many of the same fiscal concerns that indus-trial foresters had. Fire prevention was critical not only to protecting the forest but also to its year-to-year budget.

Smokey joined this campaign, scolding Americans for wasting valu-able timber in a 1951 poster.[5] At this moment, when the Forest Service was beginning its massive campaign to harvest millions of acres of national forest, Smokey was telling Americans to protect the trees so the Forest Service could sell them to timber companies to cut them down. Before this massive logging campaign was to end forty years later in 1990, millions of acres of forest were clear-cut and 444,000 miles of roads were built, enough to circle the globe at the equator seventeen times, and nearly ten times the total miles of the U.S. interstate system.

What mattered to the Forest Service and its advertising partners is that they believed Smokey worked. In 1940, nearly 26 million acres of forest burned, still half of the 52 million acres that burned in 1930. By 1950 the number of acres dropped to 15 million, and by 1960 the burned acres dropped to less than 5 million. The number of fires dropped from 195 in 1940 to 103 by 1960.[6] The Forest Service and its federal partners in the National Park Service and other agencies and the states had finally carried out Greeley's dream. Advanced meteorology techniques, a fleet of military surplus bombers to drop chemical retardants, bulldozers and smokejumpers who arrived on fires within hours, and an unusually long period of wet years all helped the Forest Service bring the fire beast to heel.

The success of Smokey and the fire bureaucracy wasn't cheap. From 1965 to 1975 the cost of fire suppression and "pre-suppression activities" increased tenfold.[7] Fire control was saving trees, but it wasn't saving money. Even the agency's more ardent fire control advocates could see that the program was not economically sustainable. The logging and road-building program cost more than it was returning.

Meanwhile, pioneers in the agency, notably Harold Biswell in California, had been quietly and carefully making a strong case for the wisdom of restoring fire to some forests. Spurned in his early years just as the light burning advocates had been thirty years earlier, Biswell's ideas about what he called prescribed burning were finally getting attention. Biswell was rediscovering light burning, but he gave it a new name. Prescribed burning became more and more accepted as a forestry tool as its utility was recognized in the 1960s and 1970s. After the passage of the Wilderness Act in 1964, the Forest Service cautiously instituted plans to allow wilderness fires to burn under very controlled conditions.

But by this time, fire control, the Forest Service, and Smokey were inexorably tied. Smokey came to represent more than just his fire prevention message. Forest rangers and other Forest Service employees became known to many in the public as "Smokeys." In the 1970s, when citizens band (CB) radios created their own lingo among the nation of truck drivers who used them to communicate on the road, Smokey was the nickname for the police. Smokey Bear, the face of conservation from the 1940s to the 1960s, was transformed into the face of the enforcers.

A new face was soon to come along that would put Smokey in the shadows, however. Mass society had produced more than the need for the kind of conformity advertising provided. It also created huge amounts of waste. After World War II, as the nation's economy was growing at a breakneck pace, so was its production of garbage, air pollution, and water pollution. The world's technological genius also had produced hundreds of new chemicals it applied generously throughout the environment. By the 1950s pollution was a problem recognized by most everyone in places such as Los Angeles, where the combination of weather and geography held the smog over its growing population.

The publication in 1962 of Rachel Carson's environmental classic *Silent Spring*, which told how pesticides such as DDT were killing songbirds and threatening the life support system on which all of life on earth depends, changed the public understanding of the world in a moment. No longer was conservation a subject that concerned only sportsmen, preservationists, foresters, and nature lovers. The new term describing the increased interest was "environment," once only used to describe a person's surroundings and home. It now meant the larger ecological, economic, and social world humans shared with the rest of nature.

Madison Avenue quickly caught up with this changing attitude. It gave the environment a face just as it had conservation twenty years earlier. The face belonged to Iron Eyes Cody, a Cree Cherokee Indian who had appeared in more than two hundred movies before the Ad Council pegged him to become the leading character for a series of ads aimed at preventing littering. In a television commercial that first ran in 1971, the pigtailed American Indian paddled his canoe up a polluted stream past a belching smokestack, then walked to the edge of a busy highway strewn with trash. In one of the most powerful scenes in television history the camera moved in for a close-up as a single tear rolled down Cody's cheek. "People start pollution," said the narrator's voice, "people can stop it."

In many ways, the "Crying Indian" campaign was similar to Smokey Bear's. Both had a simple message urging people to stop doing something within their power. People could quit starting forest fires, and they also could stop littering. Both campaigns had power and impact beyond their direct goals. Smokey became both conservation and the Forest Service's icon. Iron Eyes Cody helped develop an environmental ethic—a simple message similar to the one espoused by Leopold in *A Sand County Almanac*—for an entire generation. Cody's ads also helped project the image that American Indians had a special relationship with nature. The term "Paiute forestry" had been all but lost to the fire debate, but in the 1970s it could have been used only as a positive term instead of pejoratively, as Greeley used it fifty years earlier.

In fact, the two commercial images, Smokey and Iron Eyes Cody, did not conflict or clash. They worked alongside each other effectively as the Forest Service kept evolving the image of their favorite bear. As environmental awareness grew, Smokey's creators surrounded him with bunnies, fawns, and baby squirrels, suggesting that he was the protector of his little friends in the forest. But Smokey, no longer viewed simply as a bear, was an anthropomorphized version of the Forest Service, protecting nature for its own sake.

Even as the Forest Service was making slow but steady efforts to restore fire to wilderness areas and to increase its use of prescribed fire in the 1970s and 1980s, it was hesitant to rewire its messenger born out of its policy of fire exclusion. Long after its scientists had resolved the debate over fire's role in the forest ecosystems of the United States, Smokey was still demonizing fire. University of New Mexico researcher Melanie Armstrong wrote in 2004 that Smokey's message, shifting from economic to spiritual and utilitarian appeals, ultimately has simplified the complex ecological issues surrounding fire into "an intangible message about blame and responsibility for an often natural process."[8] Overcoming more than sixty years of that simple message has turned out to be incredibly challenging.

Yellowstone itself was also caught unwittingly in a mass image that was to shape the public's view. Once again it was a bear that captured the nation's attention. His name was Yogi Bear, the creation of cartoonists William Hanna and Joseph Barbera. Introduced in 1958, Yogi Bear became one of the most popular cartoon characters on television. His home was Jellystone Park, a clear reference to Yellowstone. He made his living stealing picnic baskets and breaking park rules along with his loveable sidekick, Boo-Boo. His foil was Ranger Smith, also known as Mr. Ranger, who never could outsmart the sarcastic and savvy bear.

To baby boomers growing up in a time of rebellion, forest rangers were saddled with the nickname and image of "Smokeys," which suggested a heavy-handed policing attitude toward enforcement. But park rangers now had to overcome an even more discouraging image: that of the hapless Mr. Ranger.

Yet as the new environmental movement was taking off in the 1960s, the images of the two agencies, the U.S. Forest Service and the National Park Service, were to be dramatically transformed. The Forest Service's postwar mission to meet the lumber needs of a growing nation had surpassed even fire fighting as a priority of the agency. Millions of acres of national forests were clear-cut, an accepted forestry practice that was greeted with almost as much dismay as forest fires were. By the 1970s the agency was fast losing its leadership role as conservation was replaced by environmentalism.

The National Park Service, thanks to Mather always tied to its preservationist roots, was in a position to become the government's face of environmentalism. But its programs didn't fit either. Rangers were killing thousands of elk in Yellowstone to protect the rangelands, an ambitious master plan called for building miles of new roads and guest facilities, and the agency remained a strong proponent for fighting all fires.

It would take another Leopold—Aldo Starker Leopold—to set in motion events that would turn the Park Service back to nature and set the stage for the next Yellowstone fires that would change America once again.

CHAPTER 12

The Natural Revolution

> A reasonable illusion of primitive America could be recreated, using the utmost in skill, judgment, and ecologic sensitivity. This in our opinion should be the objective of every national park and monument.
>
> —Leopold Report, 1963

ASK MANY ENGINEERS where their interest in the profession began and they will point back to childhood play in mud puddles. There they would build their first dams and canals, bridges and reservoirs. Fire ecologist Don Despain tracks his interest back to youthful experience as well. Only Despain didn't play in mud puddles. He played with matches.

Despain was a Boy Scout, eleven years old, growing up in Lovell, Wyoming, near the Bighorn Mountains east of Yellowstone. It was 1952, and he was on his first hike with his scout troop, and Despain intended to use the occasion to rise from a tenderfoot to a second-class scout. One of the requirements was to start a fire with two matches. It was cold and rainy that spring day as the youngster attempted to arrange tinder and sticks in a manner that would ignite and kindle with the very first match. He tried once; the match went out without a fire. He tried again. No go. Looking back, the scientist can't help but correct in his mind's eye how he had arranged the mass and volume of wood. "It's called fuel bulk density," Despain said. "That's where I began learning about fire." [1]

Despain would grow up to become one of the leading scientists in the field of fire ecology, a discipline he and others would pioneer as the modern environmental movement was dawning in the 1970s. His research would be the basis on which Yellowstone National Park would develop the fire policy it had in place in 1988. And that policy could be traced back to a remarkable report by a federal panel headed by Starker Leopold. The National Park Service's policy was nearly a mirror image of the fire exclusion policy that had been created by the army in Yellowstone National Park in 1886. When the fires of 1988 appeared like a national disaster, Despain and his boss, Robert Barbee, Yellowstone's superintendent, would be the primary scapegoats.

The young Don Despain eventually passed his 1950s trial by fire and soon mastered the act of creating fire from flint and steel. His fascination with fire would never end. As a sixteen-year-old, big for his age, Despain joined a crew fighting fires in the nearby Bighorn National Forest. In 1959 he entered the University of Wyoming.

While Despain was anchored in rural Wyoming, young Robert Barbee was moving around the West. He lived for a time with his grandparents on a ranch in Colorado and in Oregon and had developed a serious interest in mountaineering even before graduating from high school in Albuquerque, New Mexico. At Colorado State University he took a recreation and conservation class from J. V. K. Wagar, who introduced him to *A Sand County Almanac*. It was 1955 and few but dedicated wildlife biologists and others in similar fields had read the book.

"Leopold's *Sand County Almanac* was Wagar's bible," Barbee said. "I was greatly influenced by him."[2] Barbee didn't know then that it would be the work of another Leopold who would leave a greater mark on his life and future career in the National Park Service.

Aldo Starker Leopold, the oldest of Aldo Leopold's children, was already building his own reputation in wildlife management even before his famous father died. He was a slow starter, flunking out of the University of Wisconsin in 1931, due in part to his partying as a freshman. But even away from college Starker Leopold dedicated himself to wildlife, working at a state game farm in Poyette, Wisconsin, and as an apprentice biologist for the Soil Conservation Service in LaCrosse, Wisconsin. He went back to the university in 1934 after "[finding] out how much [he] didn't know," and graduated with a degree in soils and agronomy in 1936.3 He went to Yale's forestry school in 1936, but left when he chose to stay in wildlife biology. He then moved west to Berkeley and the University of California.

At Berkeley he went on a hunting trip to Mexico that was to have as transforming an effect on the young Leopold as his father's 1936 Mexican trip had on him. For a month Starker, his father, his uncle Carl, and two of his father's friends hunted deer with bow and arrow in the wilderness of the Rio Gavilan region. Aldo Leopold had passed on to Starker his own great powers of observation. As they stalked deer through canyons and up through the tall grasses and forests, Starker was getting to see something few of his generation would be able to share: a native ecosystem nearly untouched by livestock or people. He was also learning what his father had first suggested in the 1920s and what he had confirmed on his trips to Mexico. "It began to dawn on me that fire was a perfectly normal part of that sort of semi-arid country, and might even be an essential part of it," Starker told an interviewer.4

In the years that followed, Starker developed his own views about fire management based on those earlier observations in Rio Gavilan. As a wildlife biologist, he was looking at the problem in terms of habitat. While studying turkeys in Missouri he viewed fire as a destroyer of habitat. But California, where he gained a Berkeley professorship, was showing him a different story. "I started looking around California at some of the situations that you could see right from the highway—including our own national parks, Yosemite," Leopold said. "I was struck with how prevention of fire was creating tremendous fire hazards in the thick growth of white fir and incense cedar and other stuff."5

Leopold was a scientist, but he was always interested in management as much as research. He integrated his thinking on fire into his studies of deer in California. In 1949, at the United Nations Scientific Conference on the Conservation and Utilization of Resources, he first presented his ideas that fire actually increased the habitat for deer and many other species that thrived on disturbed forest communities. "Fire, which is devastation when out of control, still may be one of the most useful tools in managing key areas of deer range," Leopold said.6

His views were not a part of mainstream thought among land

managers at the time. But the situation was beginning to change. The U.S. Forest Service had ended its complete ban on the use of fire in 1943 largely based on the research of H. H. Chapman, who showed that fire was critical to the regeneration of longleaf pine in the south. H. L. Stoddard, a friend and associate of Aldo Leopold, also had demonstrated the key role fire played in natural communities, especially those of bobwhite quail.

But the Forest Service remained skeptical about the use of fire in the West. In the 1950s the National Park Service was even more trapped in the fire exclusion paradigm. "Prior to 1968 the standing directive for the national parks was that firefighting took precedence over all other activities except the safeguarding of human life," wrote fire historian Stephen Pyne.7

Starker Leopold took it upon himself to challenge the idea that still had support among not only the federal land managers but also leaders of most of the major conservation groups, including the Sierra Club, the Wilderness Society, and others. At the fifth Biennial Wilderness Conference in 1957, his paper "Wilderness and Culture" urged federal agencies to reconsider the role of fire in wilderness areas and national parks. "There is still one striking exception in the trend toward natural-ness in park preservation, the complete exclusion of fire from all areas, even those that burned naturally every year or two before becoming parks" Leopold remarked.8

He predicted that the National Park Service would eventually restore fire to its lands. "I'm convinced that ground fires some day will be reinstated in the regimen of natural factors permitted to maintain the parks in something resembling a virgin state," he told the crowd. "Both esthetic considerations of open airy forest versus dense brush and assurance of safety from conflagration of accumulated fuel will force this issue sooner or later."9

For the old guard of the Park Service, Starker's comments were fighting words. Harold Bryant, a protégé of Park Service founder Stephen Mather and one of the principal architects of interpretation in the national parks, stood up shaking he was so mad, Leopold later said. "And he made me mad when he started out and said 'I am amazed that the son of Aldo Leopold . . .' And boy, that really set me off," Leopold said. "So we had a hell of a good little debate there. My wife claims that two of my students were holding me back!"[10]

When Starker Leopold placed himself in the vanguard of the debate over fire in national parks, he didn't base his position on original research or even his own studies of deer and habitat. He was consciously and voluntarily stepping into the political arena of conservation politics. It was ground his father had plowed in his early days pushing for wildlife management in the Southwest and wilderness management within the U.S. Forest Service.

The Park Service had been through some hard times since the beginning of World War II. Its budget had been cut to the bone and its infrastructure remained outdated and overused. The postwar boom had prompted a huge rise in visitations, and many parks had neither the roads nor the sanitation facilities necessary to handle the crowds. Historian Bernard DeVoto compared employee housing to the shacks of Hooverville hastily erected in downtown Washington, D.C., during the Depression by protesting veterans.[11] The Harvard scholar and former westerner suggested Congress close the parks if it wasn't going to fund them properly. "Let us, as a beginning, close Yellowstone, Yosemite, Rocky Mountain, and Grand Canyon National Parks—close and seal them, assign the Army to patrol them, and so hold them secure till they can be reopened," DeVoto wrote.[12]

That hard time came to an end in the late 1950s. Congress approved the Park Service's ambitious "Mission 66" program, intended to develop new roads, visitor centers, and interpretive programs across the National Park system by 1966. However, the program, in responding to the national concern about the quality of the parks, did not address its shortcomings in research in managing and protecting its natural treasures.

AS THE 1960S BEGAN, Yellowstone National Park once again stepped on to the national stage. The subject was the vast elk herd of the park's northern range. The herd had recovered at the turn of the century after the army, with support from Congress, was able to bringing poaching under control. The massive campaign to eliminate wolves removed the elk's primary predator, and the elk population ballooned to more than 35,000 by 1914. When it crashed after the severe winter of 1919–1920, the Park Service had regularly reduced the population when it rose to levels biologists said were unsustainable by the forage and range. Between 1935 and 1961 more than 58,000 elk were removed or killed.[13]

Despite this cropping, the herd remained at around ten thousand, a population park officials considered too high. In 1961 Yellowstone's managers decided to cut the herd in half. Rangers rounded up thousands of elk in corrals during the winter of 1961–1962. The killing, often brutal, always bloody, and sometimes done in plain sight of visitors from the road, prompted a national controversy. Urban Americans were offended by the carnage. Hunters wanted to kill the elk themselves. Secretary of the Interior Stewart Udall decided he needed to go outside of the Park Service to find new ideas.

He appointed the Advisory Board for Wildlife Management to evaluate the parks' wildlife programs, with A. Starker Leopold as chairman. The committee's debate largely focused on the center of controversy in Yellowstone, specifically on whether to allow public hunting in the parks or not. All of its members accepted the elk reduction thesis at the time. But Leopold in particular saw the opportunity to step beyond the immediate controversy. He and his colleagues developed a completely new vision in their report, "Wildlife Management in the National Parks": "As a primary goal, we would recommend that the biotic associations within each park be maintained, or where necessary recreated, as nearly as possible in the condition that prevailed when the area was first visited by the white man. A national park should represent a vignette of primitive America."[14]

The parks had gone through periods of indiscriminate logging, burning, grazing, and hunting even before they were protected as parks, the committee said. "Then they entered the park system and shifted abruptly to a regime of equally unnatural protection from lightning fires, from insect outbreaks, absence of natural controls of ungulates, and in some areas elimination of normal fluctuations in water levels."[15]

The panel recognized how hard it would be to change management philosophies both institutionally and ecologically. To start, the most important requirement was scientific information. No one truly understood the complexities of the ecosystems on which such new programs would depend, and they urged an expanded scientific program aimed at management rather than interpretation.

A program to re-create a "reasonable illusion" of primitive America would require active management. The panel accepted the need for bulldozing habitat, reintroduction of native species, population reductions, and even elimination of exotic species. Their tool of choice was fire: "Of the various methods of manipulating vegetation, the controlled use of fire is the most 'natural' and much the cheapest and easiest to apply."[16]

The report was forever after known as the Leopold Report. It became itself one of the milestones of the modern environmental movement. Its call for ecosystem management and its vision of restoring naturalness to wildlands became a model for the world. Later critics would argue that its goals were unrealistic and that it did not properly recognize the role of pre-Columbian humans in the ecosystem. Yet for the next two generations of land managers, not only in Yellowstone and other national parks, but on other state and federal lands, the Leopold Report provided guidance that was to be carried out with dramatic results.

Leopold didn't know it at the time, but the report would be the blueprint that placed the National Park Service itself at the vanguard of environmental thinking in the federal government. Once embraced, the Leopold Report springboarded the Park Service past the U.S. Forest Service as the agency to carry the mantle of the values of Aldo Leopold and the new, more ecological view. Robert Barbee remembered talking to Starker Leopold years later about his choice of words in the report. "He told me: 'We had no idea it would be viewed as some kind of manifesto,'" Barbee recalled. "'Had we known that, we would have taken more care with some of the things said.'"[17]

BARBEE SERVED A STINT as a lieutenant in the U.S. Army before joining the Park Service himself as a seasonal ranger while attending graduate school. As a young interpreter in Rocky Mountain National

Park he began to see some of the hypocrisy and inconsistency of park policy that the Leopold Report addressed. He remembered looking at the slopes of Long Mountain in Rocky Mountain where a forest fire in the early 1900s had prompted a regeneration of the forest. "There was a period of time when the Park Service did not react positively to [fire] at all," Barbee said in an interview.[18]

Barbee caught the attention of new Park Service leaders who were seeking a cadre of young managers who could put the recommendations of the Leopold Report into action. He was sent back to graduate school once again at Colorado State. In 1968, the National Park Service approved new policies that put in place the report's recommendations, recognizing ecosystems as a composite whole. "Management will minimize, give direction to, or control those changes in the native environment and scenic landscape resulting from human influences on natural processes of ecological succession," the NPS said in its new policy.[19]

When Barbee completed his master's, he was sent to Yosemite in 1968 with the clear mandate to begin restoring the preexisting condition of John Muir's favorite place. When Barbee arrived, the new resource management specialist, as he was now called, was received with ambivalence. They didn't give him an office, instead placing him in the library at John Muir's old desk. "The park service didn't know how to deal with the Leopold Report or me," Barbee said. "The thing was you had an entrenched bureaucracy that had its own way of doing business."[20]

Barbee's job was to write a new resource management plan. But he wanted to do more than just push paper. Yosemite managers were still spraying DDT in massive amounts to control mosquitoes. Herbicides were used to kill brush. Fire had been suppressed since the army had patrolled the park, and thick patches of white fir now crowded the giant sequoia of the park's cherished Mariposa Grove, which Barbee proposed burning. He also proposed restoring meadows by clipping and later burning the pines that had encroached on them since fires had been suppressed. He convinced his bosses to let him do test burns in the El Capitan meadows.

Sequoia National Park and the Everglades had already begun burning programs to reduce the dense growth that threatened those ecosystems. Barbee looked to them for guidance as well as to Harold Biswell, the legendary fire researcher from the U.S. Forest Service. Biswell, derisively called "Harry the Torch" by his old forester colleagues, offered his expertise to the young park manager as they carefully and slowly increased the controlled burning program in Yosemite.

Even though Yellowstone had prompted the Leopold Report, management there did not change until 1967. Yet another controversy over elk killing had landed Jack Anderson, superintendent from Grand Teton National Park, in Yellowstone. Anderson brought in Glen Cole as supervisory research biologist. Cole's charge was to put into place the kind of research program that would allow Yellowstone to begin the ecosystem management envisioned by the Leopold Report. Thus began the most exciting and controversial period of science and management in the history of the park. Yellowstone was to ecology in the 1960s and 1970s what Paris was to art and literature in the 1920s.

It began with the remarkable twin biologists, Frank and John Craighead. From 1959 through the late 1960s they followed radio-collared grizzly bears in and around the park and quickly recognized that the population, which was isolated from the others in the West by human settlement, depended on habitat that went beyond the park's boundaries. The twin biologists embraced the Leopold Report's call for additional research and its endorsement of active management of wildlife populations. But their approach clashed with the new programs of Anderson and Cole, especially the plan to wean the park's bears off of garbage. To separate bears from garbage meant that many bears, accustomed to eating the easy food, had to be killed because of their threat to people in campgrounds. Although the Craigheads eventually accepted the wisdom of separating bears and garbage, they sharply criticized the park for decimating the grizzly population in its rapid and aggressive program. Their debate became one of the most famous of biological debates and brought great attention to Yellowstone's Leopold-based research and management.

Cole's approach to the elk was also controversial. Politically, killing the elk in the park was quickly becoming untenable. Research by wildlife biologist Douglas Houston challenged the prevalent view that the elk were destroying Yellowstone's northern range. He and biologist Mary Meagher, who was studying Yellowstone's bison, argued that large grazing animals and their range were largely naturally regulated when left alone.

Meagher, a student of Starker's, went fishing with him when he would make almost annual visits to Yellowstone. She described Leopold the teacher as detached, but viewed him as a skilled conservation politician. "If I was smart enough to ask the right questions, he'd give me the answers," she recalled.[21]

WHILE YELLOWSTONE'S elk controversies were swirling only a few hundred miles away, young Don Despain was leaving Wyoming for the first time to serve on a mission for his church in Germany. He returned and eventually was award a doctoral degree in ecology from the University of Illinois. In 1971 he got the opportunity to join Cole, Houston, and Meagher in Yellowstone as a plant ecologist. There, the new National Park Service–wide fire policy, released in 1970, would especially direct his attention and work. It was a policy that Barbee's work at Yosemite had helped shape. "The presence or absence of natural fire within a given habitat is recognized as one of the ecological factors contributing to the perpetuation of plants and animals native to that habitat. Fires in vegetation resulting from natural causes are recognized as natural phenomena and may be allowed to run their course when such burning will contribute to the accomplishment of approved vegetation and/or wildlife management objectives."[22]

Yet the program had an underlying philosophy that went far beyond the early controlled burning in the parks or the programs advocated by Biswell and others in the U.S. Forest Service. The decision about where fire was to start was zoned with the designation of natural fire areas, but was not solely a human decision. Managers let lightning decide where the blazes would begin. Humbled by more than a century of human control over fires on wildlands, the Park Service's leaders wanted to restore ignition to nature. They were seeking to find the line between the fires that Muir and Pinchot suggested had shaped and painted the landscape naturally, and those that European settlers had carelessly carried with them along with roads, logging, mining, and development. Not only were park managers seeking to restore the "reasonable illusion" to the landscape, they sought to place the nebulous goal into the decision-making process.

When Despain arrived in Yellowstone, twelve national parks allowed at least some lightning-ignited fires to burn. But if a careless camper threw a match in the same area at the same time, park managers had decided the fire must be fought with the same ferocity as the 1910 fires. In the spring of 1972 Yellowstone embarked on its own natural fire policy, allowing naturally occurring fires to run their course over 340,000 acres of the park, about fifteen percent of its total land area. The plan required that natural fires that started in these specially designated areas must not pose an immediate threat to visitor-use areas such as Old Faithful; human life could not be endangered, and lands managed by other agencies, such as surrounding national forests, had to be protected. The areas were located northeast and east of visitor centers because a history of larger fires in the park indicated that the dominant direction of travel was to the northeast and wind was necessary for large fires to develop, Despain wrote in a paper he coauthored.[23] That insight into Yellowstone fire behavior was confirmed in August 1988.

In 1974, upon Despain's recommendation, Yellowstone officials began work to expand the natural fire area to include all portions of the park managed as wilderness—about 1.7 million acres of the 2.2-million-acre park. Final approval of the plan was given in early spring 1976. Then Yellowstone officials negotiated a cooperative agreement with the U.S. Forest Service in the Bridger-Teton National Forest to the south. The agreement allowed natural fires to burn across the common boundary between the park and the Teton Wilderness, which had a similar plan. Yellowstone had tough fire years in past dry spells, but the largest fire in the history of the park to that point was still the fire that Moses Harris saw when he led the cavalry into the park in 1886. It burned only 25,000 acres. Between 1972 and 1987, lightning started 235 natural fires, which burned only 34,000 acres in Yellowstone. The 1981 fire season was the most severe under the natural burning program before 1988. It included fifty-seven fires caused by lightning, one short of the highest number of fires in fifty years. Twenty-eight were allowed to burn themselves out. Fifteen remained less than an acre in size, and a total of 20,240 acres burned.

As a forest grows from scratch, such as after a major fire, it goes through several stages of succession. In Yellowstone succession begins with pioneer species such as lodgepole pine and aspen. Then slowly the species composition, if left undisturbed, becomes dominated by such species as alpine fir. These climax forests are generally more diverse. Before 1988, Despain had observed that most large crown fires started in older stands of lodgepole pines or in climax, old-growth forests. When these fires reached younger forests, he reported in 1977, the flames would drop out of the canopy and creep slowly across the ground for a short distance. Then they would either burn around the younger trees or go out.

Despain knew that some fires in Yellowstone had exceeded 50,000 acres in size in the past. His studies of natural fire through 1987 had built a solid basis on which to measure the coming events, he believed. Yet like so many management decisions based on our relatively short experience, his knowledge turned out to fall far short of reality.

Today, Despain acknowledges he had not fully studied or understood the park's fire history before 1988. For instance, a large stand of even-aged lodgepole pine stretching from the Norris Geyser basin area to Yellowstone Lake now is recognized as the site of a huge burn in the 1860s.

Yellowstone's natural fire policy was very popular in the 1970s among the swelling ranks of the rejuvenated environmental movement. It carried none of the controversy over competing values that typified the grizzly bear and elk programs. It fit the belief system of many wilderness and wildlife advocates, which was to leave the land to its natural processes and allow it to take care of itself.

In 1978, the U.S. Forest Service followed the Park Service in expanding the place for fire across its 191 million acres. The same initiatives that came in response to the public's opposition to clear-cutting reshaped fire policy. Fire management became tied to land management. Prescribed burning was incorporated into the plans that staff at each national forest were required to complete. These arcane and detailed plans went beyond those Barbee and others had pioneered in the National Park Service. Eventually they would dictate where and when fires could burn. Wilderness areas were the first test sites, and the Frank Church–River of No Return and the Selway-Bitterroot wildernesses in Idaho, the place where Elers Koch had recommended letting fires burn, were among the first places chosen The 10 a.m. policy also was scrapped, and fire bosses were required to evaluate each fire after initial attack to determine how hard to fight a fire and how much money should be spent. Congress also had eliminated the blank check for firefighting. Fire control was now part of the budget.

The political realities made the changes hardly noticeable. No fire boss or land manager could survive if he made the decision to allow a fire to burn that later grew out of control and destroyed homes or commercial timber. The same was true in the Park Service, though it was easier politically to allow fires to burn there because of the Leopold Report. Leopold's student Mary Meagher replaced Glen Cole as Yellowstone's head of research in 1976. She continued what Yellowstone managers were beginning to describe as "the great experiment"— management of the park's biological resources based on the theory of natural regulation.

Controversy grew along with the park's elk and bison herds. New concern over the spread of brucellosis, an exotic disease threatening cattle, which occurs in the park's bison herd, prompted even more conflict with officials in surrounding states. The disease, which causes cows to abort their young, had been eliminated in all but the states surrounding Yellowstone. That made it harder for the cattlemen to sell their herds without expensive testing. The cattlemen wanted the park's bison herd vaccinated or quarantined.

Earlier, the passage of the Endangered Species Act in 1973 seemed to move Aldo Leopold's philosophy of protection of biodiversity to the top of government priorities. But when Yellowstone's grizzly bear was placed on the endangered species list, in part because of the many killings by rangers in the wake of the dump closings and garbage-weaning program, Yellowstone's management was coming under increasing fire. Critics wanted more hands-on management, such as bear feeding programs. However, the park's natural fire program remained largely ignored.

Starker Leopold remained a supporter of the natural regulation program that had become the most prominent result of his famous report. "He was really behind the experiment, but he brought with him all the baggage and all the wisdom of those earlier generations," commented historian Paul Schullery, after speaking with him.[24] In other words, Starker Leopold, like many biologists, had no problem supporting the intervention of human management to reach natural management goals. He thought that leaving ecosystems alone was not inherently the way to reach the "reasonable illusion" he had sought as a goal for wildlands management. He supported hunting and recognized the importance of building political support for wildlife management.

Robert Barbee shared Starker Leopold's clear-eyed vision for integrating political reality into biological understanding. In graduate school, he had taken a class with Philip Foss in political science. Foss taught his students to study an issue, debate, or controversy not by becoming an advocate for either side but by looking at the forces and ideas that strengthen conflicting views. "He taught me not to take these conflicts personally," Barbee said of Foss. "That doesn't mean you take some kind of clinical stance. You can't divorce yourself from your values and you shouldn't. But if I was going to be a success I needed to learn how to win."[25]

Barbee's success in Yosemite earned him his first appointment as a superintendent at Cape Lookout National Seashore in Virginia. After several other posts, he landed at the new Redwoods National Park, where he found huge eroding slopes and three thousand miles of skid trails from a century of logging. His job was to begin the restoration effort. Simply leaving the land alone would have left the streams filled with mud, the hillsides eroding away, and little of the beauty people expected from a park. He put to work many of the heavy equipment operators and loggers who had caused the land destruction in the first place. Today Redwood Creek runs clear and the park has become a model for restoration. After the Redwoods success, Barbee was sent to

Yellowstone in 1983, to take on the most prestigious and visible job in the National Park Service.

By then, the political winds had changed once again. Ronald Reagan was president and his secretary of the interior, James Watt, was reviled in environmental circles for his support of rolling back many of the environmental victories they had won in the 1970s. Starker Leopold shared environmentalists' disgust and in retirement came to the same reservations about government conservation that his father had expressed forty years earlier. Aldo Leopold's views on the limits of government conservation came from watching the excesses of the New Deal's ambitious conservation agenda. Starker Leopold's came during the Reagan era as programs and management schemes he advocated were reversed. When he considered a location for a museum adjacent to San Francisco's marshlands to help educate the public of their value, he rejected placing it on state or federal land.

"You can't trust them," he told a Sierra Club interviewer in 1983. "Twenty years from now, all of a sudden you get somebody in there as head of fish and game or head of some government agency and he's not the least interested in this."[26] In a response to a question about what organizations had been the most effective in environmental protection, his view was clear. "I would say that the government agencies, generally speaking, I'd put toward the bottom of the list, in terms of real performing and producing over a continuing period of time," Leopold said. "You can't really depend on the state or the federal government."[27]

Like his father, Starker suffered from heart problems. He had a heart attack in July 1983 and died on August 23, after a second attack. But his ideas and those of his father would soon be amplified by people and events in Yellowstone. Starker Leopold had led the natural revolution that changed the way national parks were seen, managed, and enjoyed. Now it was up to Barbee, Despain, and their peers to carry the revolution through.

CHAPTER 13

Greater Yellowstone Rediscovered

> We were talking about the Yellowstone ecosystem as early as
> 1959. I don't know if we just tacked greater on to it. That just
> kind of evolved.
>
> —John Craighead, 1986

WHEN STARKER LEOPOLD DIED, General Phil Sheridan's vision of a Greater Yellowstone was under assault. Six national forests, a national wildlife refuge, and Teton National Park surrounded Yellowstone National Park, representing 11 million acres of lands under federal control. Most of these lands were set aside as a direct result of Sheridan's decision to send in the army to save Yellowstone a century earlier. The success of Moses Harris, the Medal of Honor winner who began the federal government's involvement in firefighting in Yellowstone, and his successors to limit fire provided both the pretext and political case for federal conservation. Theodore Roosevelt, his cousin Franklin Delano Roosevelt, and presidents of both parties through Jimmy Carter had accepted the basic wisdom of those earlier decisions without challenge.

Yet the federal conservation bureaucracy was only selectively protecting the Greater Yellowstone that Sheridan had grown to love. Fire was replaced as the greatest menace to Yellowstone by a growing list of largely external threats. The Forest Service had clear-cut a swath of the Targhee National Forest so wide and straight that the eastern boundary with Yellowstone National Park could be seen from space. Nearly every timber sale in the Greater Yellowstone region cost the government more than it made and forced hundreds of miles of new roads to fragment the remaining wild habitat. Grizzly bears, now dependent on natural food sources rather than park garbage, were roaming widely out-side the park and disappearing into what biologists called "black holes," where they were killed by sheepherders, lured into garbage dumps and killed because of their threat to residents, or poached by hunters. Oil and gas exploration was creeping to the edge of Yellowstone's bound-aries. Rapid population growth from former urban residents lured by the region's beauty was crowding wildlife habitat on private lands sur-rounding the park. Western states and local governments had few laws and ordinances to control these growing problems.

These threats appeared even more ominous to a new generation of environmentalists because of attitudes expressed by the Reagan admin-istration. Ronald Reagan's own rhetoric supporting what was called the Sagebrush Rebellion, a band of western ranchers, miners, and loggers who wanted federal land policy moved back to state control, or no con-trol, swelled the membership of organizations such as the Wilderness Society and the Sierra Club. His appointment of James Watt, a Wyoming lawyer for a law firm that challenged environmental public land initiatives, as secretary of the interior further worried environmen-talists. Even though Sheridan's conservation efforts led to both the U.S. Forest Service and the National Park Service, his concept of a Greater Yellowstone was largely lost until the 1970s. Each unit of federal land was managed separately with little coordination or recognition of their common value as one place. There was no formal process in federal or state governments to cope with the threats in a coordinated manner. Sheridan's vision was simply to expand the park, but one hundred years later the land was a convoluted mosaic of ownerships with often clash-ing goals.

Greater Yellowstone was rediscovered by John and Frank Craighead, the twin biologists who had conducted the landmark research on grizzly bears. As they followed the bears through their lives, they regularly crossed in and out of Yellowstone. Mapping the habitat critical to bears' survival, the brothers had identified a "Yellowstone ecosystem" for griz-zly bears. During congressional hearings in 1977 the Craigheads had added the word "greater" to their Yellowstone ecosystem map, and when

Frank wrote *Track of the Grizzly* in 1979, he again referred to a greater Yellowstone ecosystem.[1] Several national park officials and environmental activists, such as Rick Reese in *Greater Yellowstone: The National Park and Adjacent Wildlands*, took hold of the idea.[2] Ralph Maughan, a professor of political science at Idaho State University, said even as a child growing up in Rexburg, Idaho, he recognized Yellowstone as a place larger than the park. His family would take day trips north into the park by car, leaving their home on the sagebrush-covered Snake River plain. At Ashton, the road climbed up the Island Park plateau, which was formed by an ancient volcano. There the landscape changed to the expansive lodgepole pine forest that covers the adjacent plateaus ranging through the park and out to the surrounding national forests.

In 1980, Maughan took a sabbatical from his teaching to write a book about the Greater Yellowstone ecosystem. As he traveled around the region through Wyoming and Montana talking to other environmental activists he found they shared similar stories of conflicts over logging, development, and wildlife protection with the U.S. Forest Service and other federal agencies. With the election of Ronald Reagan, Maughan's goal shifted from writing a book to forming an organization to advocate a single management vision for Greater Yellowstone. "Reagan scared me into action," Maughan said. "I just felt sick. I still remember hearing him talk about the Sagebrush Rebellion and how he wanted to turn public lands over to the states."[3]

Over the next three years Maughan and others, including Reese, a former park ranger, and Phil Hocker, an architect from Jackson, Wyoming, and a national Sierra Club board member, began organizing the Greater Yellowstone Alliance. In 1983, the new organization was officially established by several dozen environmentalists at the Teton Science School in Moose, Wyoming. It was called the Greater Yellowstone Coalition, and it quickly grew to represent thirty-five local groups, twelve national environmental groups, and more than 1,500 individuals. Its goal: "to promote the scientific concept of the Greater Yellowstone Ecosystem; to create a national public awareness of issues and threats" and to "utilize the combined effectiveness of the coalition's constituent organizations and individuals to preserve the ecosystem intact."[4]

In less than five years after Maughan began his journey, the coalition had wildly succeeded. The concept of a Greater Yellowstone ecosystem had entered the vernacular of the environmental movement not just in Yellowstone but far beyond. Congress had held hearings on the threats to the ecosystem. Virtually every activity that took place in the 20-million-acre circle surrounding Yellowstone was now scrutinized for its effects on the entire ecosystem. The Greater Yellowstone Coalition had tied together the strands of ideas of Sheridan, Aldo Leopold, Starker Leopold, and the Craigheads into a powerful vision that would spread from Yellowstone to the world. They were prodding land managers to look past jurisdictional boundaries to the ways in which landforms vary and plants and animals are deployed across a landscape.

The hearings demonstrated the ways in which federal agencies that controlled the federal land within the region were not doing a good job of coordination. This in turn triggered a response from the federal agencies, which was called the "Yellowstone Blueprint" process, wherein all of the national forests, the two national parks, and the two national wildlife refuges in the region aggregated all of their management plans. In 1987, the federal agencies produced a document called "The Greater Yellowstone Area" (Forest Service officials still did not like the politically charged word "ecosystem"). It didn't change much, but it did allow the managers to see where their management conflicts were greatest. It also showed where they had opportunities for coordination. A committee of the land managers of the all of the forests, parks, and refuges was elevated in emphasis to the Greater Yellowstone Coordinating Committee, with staff. Their charge was to develop a plan that would address the coordination problems without limiting the multiple use mission of the Forest Service, through which logging, grazing, and oil and gas development was allowed, or the National Park Service's mandate for preservation and visitor services.

None of this happened in a vacuum. Reagan's election quieted the extreme edges of the Sagebrush Rebellion's efforts to wrestle power from the federal government. But the loggers, ranchers, miners, and even tourism promoters in the small towns around Yellowstone viewed the Greater Yellowstone movement as an attack on their values. They worried, with some justification, that logging, grazing, and energy exploration would be further curtailed if environmentalists got their way. History was repeating itself. When Sheridan and George Bird Grinnell were promoting a Greater Yellowstone one hundred years before, local residents, few though they were, were equally opposed. One Montana editor said the park was already "too huge a joke for them [easterners] to comprehend."⁵

The Wyoming legislature tried but failed to stop the Greater Yellowstone effort. Fremont County, Idaho, which included the area west of Yellowstone, passed a resolution expressing opposition to any management changes. "We strongly oppose the concept of allowing one federal agency to regulate or have jurisdiction over the mission or activities of another agency, as that has proved to be wasteful duplication in the extreme, and costly to the citizens of our county," the commissioners wrote.⁶ Ironically, a major reason the Greater Yellowstone ecosystem concept grew was because it was embraced by a new National Park Service director appointed in 1985 by Reagan. William Penn Mott had been Reagan's parks director in California and was a friend of the affable president. This friendship gave him surprisingly wide latitude to press his own ambitious environmental agenda as Park Service director. His support for reintroduction of wolves into Yellowstone, for example, placed him squarely in opposition to Republican congressmen in Wyoming, Montana, and Idaho, as well as to his bosses in the Department of the Interior.

Mott defended the park's natural regulation program, its fire policy, and the other research-based programs that were tied together as ecosystem management. But for Mott, Yellowstone's superintendent Robert Barbee, and others, the challenge was sifting out the science of ecosystem management from the related ethical values of Leopold. U.S. Representative Larry Craig, a Republican representing Idaho, teased out the problem during cross-examination of Barbee and Mott during the Greater Yellowstone hearings in 1985. Craig asked them if an ecosystem was in the eye of a beholder. Barbee agreed and Mott too conceded.

"Technically, it seems to me we have to recognize that in applying the word 'ecosystem' it should be applied to a single subject," Mott said. "We know what the ecosystem is of the grizzly, for example. We can define that. But when we use it as a general term as I indicated, we are using it incorrectly scientifically. We should call it a biogeographical . . . "

Craig interrupted him: "But that might not get people's emotions flying."

"That's right," Mott replied.7

Craig was one of the typical western Republicans who were moving to dominate politics in the states surrounding Yellowstone in the wake of Reagan's election. He was a strong supporter of the timber industry and ranchers—he grew up on a ranch himself in Midvale, Idaho. His crusade was to get an amendment to the Constitution passed to balance the federal budget. Yet he was a strong supporter of the Forest Service's budget for firefighting, logging, grazing, and recreation.

One of the Greater Yellowstone Coalition's strongest pieces of research was a study it funded of the economics of the Forest Service's budgets for the forests surrounding Yellowstone. The group hired a young Oregon economist, Randal O'Toole, to prepare the report. O'Toole showed that all seven of the national forests around Yellowstone were operating inefficiently. The major revenue source for the forests was timber cutting, so managers were cutting as much timber as they could, because the more they cut, the more the agency's system rewarded them with money for other programs. It didn't matter that the timber program was forcing the agency to cut new roads into wildlife habitat and to clear-cut some of the last best places for grizzly bears and other endangered animals. O'Toole, a ponytailed libertarian, urged the agency to charge recreation fees just as the national parks did, which would give managers an incentive to protect the scenic beauty of the forests rather than simply incentives to destroy habitat.8

O'Toole, and others who called themselves the new resource economists, pressed environmentalists to consider free-market alternatives to government regulations for protecting natural values and ecosystems. They didn't know it yet, but they were treading ground already explored by Aldo Leopold.

O'Toole's findings in 1987 and his economic approach to environmental issues in forests across the West connected the Greater Yellowstone Coalition to the same Leopold approach that had been largely lost among environmentalists until the 1980s. Providing incentives to do good work and encouraging personal responsibility among users and managers of the public land was as important as politics and regulatory approaches, this view suggested. Ironically, this fundamentally Republican approach was most spiritedly opposed by western Republicans such as Craig and Wyoming senators Alan Simpson and Malcolm Wallop. They accurately saw it as an attack on traditional uses of the land and a threat to one of their best methods of bringing federal dollars to their states by subsidizing resource extraction. However, O'Toole's approach was embraced by mainstream environmental groups only because it presented a strong economic argument against logging and road building. The goal of the Greater Yellowstone Coalition remained to give the federal government more power, not less, using the Endangered Species Act and other laws to limit development around Yellowstone.

At the same time as the Greater Yellowstone movement was gaining momentum by focusing on external threats, the debate over natural regulation of the landscape was revived in a 1986 best-selling book, *Playing God in Yellowstone*, written by a retired philosophy professor, Alston Chase. It was the Park Service itself, Chase said, that was threatening Yellowstone with "benign neglect." He resurrected the debate between park biologists and the Craigheads over grizzly bears and attacked the elk and bison programs for destroying the rangelands. "Why should we believe that some invisible hand always guarantees that natural systems, if left undisturbed, will despite continual fluctuation, remain roughly stable?" he wrote.[9]

Chase was challenging one of the underlying philosophies of the environmental movement—that nature knows best. Though viewed as an attack on Starker Leopold's findings, Chase's attack actually encouraged many of the recommendations of the Leopold Report. Chase supported active management to restore the national parks by eliminating exotic species, for example. He supported prescribed burning. But Chase devoted an entire chapter to criticizing the park's natural fire program.

The program was based on the false notion that humans had no impact on the park prior to 1872, he said. With the zeal of John Wesley Powell, Chase showed how American Indians had regularly burned the area prior to European settlement. Chase advocated for Yellowstone the same prescription as did Powell—controlled burning to reduce the fuels and improve wildlife habitat.

Since Barbee and the Park Service both had embraced controlled burning in Sequoia, Yosemite, and the Everglades, there was no institutional opposition to Chase's fire position. For Chase it was not so much a plan as another way of showing how Yellowstone's scientists had ignored science and history in developing their own natural regulation management plan. Chase thought that the idea of leaving the timing and placement of fire ignitions to lightning ignored the role of American Indians in starting fires historically. He instead wanted managers to set the fires when and where they considered them necessary.

Don Despain, now recognized as the chief architect of the Yellowstone fire plan, never challenged the idea that American Indians regularly burned in Yellowstone before 1872. But his research suggested that they had little impact on the dominating lodgepole pine forest or the rangelands. Their experience, he suggested, offered some guidance as to why an aggressive controlled burning program would have little effect on the forests of the park. Fires in the high-elevation lodgepole pine forest are difficult to get started and quickly go out in all but extremely dry years, Despain showed. Yellowstone was therefore the perfect place to experiment with natural fire, allowing lightning to determine the starting point, and weather, climate, insects, and forest succession to prepare the fuel.

What Chase and Despain really disagreed about was how fires in Yellowstone should get started. Chase wanted prescribed fires set by people under controlled conditions. Despain wanted lightning because that was the policy. Ultimately, Despain just wanted fire when natural conditions allowed it, no matter how it started.

In the surrounding national forests, fire continued to be viewed as a threat to timber resources, visitors, and residents. Despite the official recognition that a century of fire suppression had made forests more flammable, not less, suppression remained the tool of choice. Still, at least in the high-elevation lodgepole pine forests, Despain's research suggested that fire suppression had made little or no difference in the forest.

But by the late 1980s, managers had become more flexible about how they fought fire, instituting a confinement strategy—essentially circling the fire and letting it burn—when they were confident they could keep it under control. In wilderness areas across the West the Forest Service also was experimenting with a natural fire policy similar to Yellowstone's.

The consensus on fire exclusion, begun with John Muir and Gifford Pinchot, had survived without public challenge until Aldo Leopold's work on land health and the Leopold Report offered a competing vision. Despite the new Park Service natural fire policy and the Forest Service's own prescribed burning program, most managers and the public remained skeptical and careful about letting fires burn. Fire suppression, still strongly promoted through the Smokey Bear advertising campaign, had strong public support.

The 1987 "Greater Yellowstone Area" report showed that more than fifty percent of the 11 million acres of federal land within the region had a moderate to high probability of high-intensity fire. Still, Yellowstone's program, based on Don Despain's research, allowed lightning-caused fires to burn in all but a few areas around the park's lodges and developments. Despain's work in Yellowstone gave his managers an increasing comfort level with fire. The result of Greater Yellowstone hearings and the success of Chase's book was that Yellowstone was back at the center of national and international debates on the environment. At the same time that Mott and others were warning of such external threats to the park as unchecked development and road building, they were defending themselves from Chase and others' attacks on the Greater Yellowstone Coalition's version of scientific management—ecosystem management. In May 1987, Mott addressed the Greater Yellowstone Coalition at a meeting at the Lake Lodge along Yellowstone Lake. He shared with them his optimistic, positive view of the state of what was once again recognized as the world's leading environmental landscape.

"I submit that, without question, this grand and precious Yellow-stone ecosystem is healthy, strong and vigorous," Mott said. "I would further suggest that it is growing healthier all the while."[10]

CHAPTER 14

———————

Calm before the Storm

I told Dan Sholly when the Fan fire started in June we may
actually get a little burned acreage this summer.

—Robert Barbee, 2003

T HERE WAS NOTHING in the winter and spring of 1988 that
prepared Don Despain or others in Yellowstone for the events that
were to come in July and August. Moisture that spring was above
average—eighty-one percent above at Mammoth Hot Springs in May.
Despain, now forty-seven, tall, dark-haired and brawny, had become a
part of the landscape himself. Like old farmers, commercial fishermen,
or the American Indians who had lived in the park before 1872, Despain
could tell how far the seasons had advanced by the timing of flower
blossoms, the return of migrating birds, or the behavior of elk and
bison.

He also had noticed a shift in the climate from his earliest days in
the park and even his youth. Since 1979 the winters had been getting
drier and the springs and the summers wetter. The unusually wet spring
would be followed by a wetter summer, Despain surmised. In other
years with dry winters, rains would come in July, making it difficult for
a fire to get a start in the pines.

The conditions looked dramatically different to the residents of the
surrounding communities several thousand feet below Yellowstone.
The West was suffering through its second year of drought. A dry winter meant a low snowpack, and farmers in Idaho, Montana, and
Wyoming depended on the melting snows to fill their reservoirs, canals,
and ditches to water potato fields, wheat crops, and pasture. Reservoirs

were not full when irrigation season began in April. Many farmers prepared to run out of water early.

Robert Barbee was looking forward to the first National Park Service superintendents' conference in fifteen years, scheduled for early
June. Organized by William Penn Mott, the $600,000 weeklong con-
clave at Jackson Lake Lodge in Grand Teton National Park was to be
as much a celebration as a chance for the agency's leaders to compare
notes. Barbee was the cohost, and it was a chance for him and the Yellowstone park staff to show off what they had done in the five years
since he had arrived. The park had shrugged off the criticism prompted
by Chase's book thanks to the political acumen of its superintendent.
Barbee had deftly handled the elk and grizzly bear controversies, allowing elk numbers to rise and reducing the number of bears that were
killed in the park. He was restoring the Park Service's environmental
leadership by taking a strong stand against threats to the park's iconic
geothermal resources from development north and west of the park
boundaries.

Despain had just completed four years of extensive on-the-ground
research of the fire history of a large chunk of Yellowstone. Teamed with
Bill Romme, a professor at Fort Lewis College in Durango, Colorado,
Despain was seeking to expand his understanding of fire's historic role
in the forests that dominated the park. Romme had worked toward his
doctorate by examining fire scars and tree rings to determine the fire
history of the Little Firehole River watershed, which covered about
18,000 acres in Yellowstone's southwest corner. In the high-elevation
lodgepole pine forest, Romme had shown, fire came infrequently, but
when it did, it was high intensity and burned both the old and young
trees, essentially beginning the forest all over again. Most of the area
had burned in the 1700s and the forest had matured since then.

Despain and Romme decided to expand the area of research to
more than 300,000 acres to see if there might be a more even or propor-
tioned age class. In spring 1988, the two scientists were completing
analysis of the data they had collected over four years. The results, they
hoped, would give them a richer understanding of the fire history over
the entire 2.2-million-acre park. They were scheduled to present their

results at a meeting of the Ecological Society of America in August and hoped to begin writing by early summer.

The fire season began on May 24, 1988, in the Lamar valley on the northeast corner of the park near Rose Creek. A few hours later rain from the thunderstorm that spawned the fire snuffed it out. Up to that moment, it was business as usual for Despain and Yellowstone officials. From then on, however, the forests and rangelands began to dry out uncharacteristically. The Palmer Drought Severity Index, the official formula developed by the National Weather Service to measure burning conditions by fire officials, went from severe to extreme in less than a month. But Yellowstone's fire officials didn't use or look at it.

The superintendents' conference went off without a hitch the first week of June. It brought together 341 park managers from all over the country, and they generally agreed that ecological conditions were improving throughout the 343 parks and historical sites in the system. With grizzly numbers rising and his decision to close the controversial Fishing Bridge Campground in prime grizzly bear habitat, Barbee was able to brag a bit about the state of the system's crown jewel. "I would contend that in Yellowstone we are better off biologically than we were seventy-five years ago," Barbee told his peers.[1] Mott told the attendees to take risks to defend park values and resources: "We must aggressively, with facts, present our case and defend our mission," he said.[2]

Barbee could see that the snow was melting early and the fine fuels were beginning to dry up and turn brown. He told a colleague there could be a lot of fire that summer, he later recalled.

THE FIRST MAJOR FIRE of Yellowstone's 1988 season didn't actually start in the park. On June 14, a lightning strike started a fire on the lower part of the Storm Creek drainage, north of the park in Montana's Custer National Forest. It began in the Absaroka-Beartooth Wilderness, and under rules the U.S. Forest Service had put in place, it was to be treated like a natural fire inside the park. When Custer National Forest officials were notified by outfitters on June 16 of the fire, they thus decided to let it burn. They expected it would burn out over time.

Just over a week later, on June 23, in the southwest corner of

Yellowstone, a lightning strike ignited old lodgepole stands circling Shoshone Lake. The area around the lake was a prime display of the damage that could be done by mountain pine beetle. The beetle bores into the older trees of a stand to leave its larvae. When the trees sustain too much damage, they turn red and then finally gray when they die. This leaves the younger trees to grow up and replace them unless fire interrupts the process. The pale gray trees painted across the hills overlooking the lake interrupted the green forest. Where the beetle had been particularly aggressive, in many areas of the Pitchstone and Madison plateaus, the dead trees dominated the skyline.

Two days later, a dry lightning storm moving through the region ignited two small fires on the Targhee National Forest west of the park in Idaho and another in the northwest corner of the park in the Fan Creek drainage. The fires in the Targhee were quickly extinguished because the area was open to logging and forest managers there remained committed to fire suppression. Park officials allowed the Fan Creek fire to burn, under monitoring.

Billings Gazette reporter Bob Ekey, stationed in Bozeman, saw the Fan fire as a chance to highlight the park's natural fire program for his readers. He contacted Despain, who agreed to meet him on the edge of the fire for a tour. Together they hiked into an old burn where Despain showed him young lodgepoles that had been reseeded by the earlier fire and how the entire area was growing back in predictable stages. He told the familiar stories about the relatively small size of most natural fires and predicted the old burn would slow the growth of the new fire.

Even to Despain it was clear that the summer rains were arriving late. He too was beginning to expect more fire this season. Nationwide, U.S. Forest Service officials were beginning to worry. Fire conditions were beginning to look more ominous than in 1987, one of the worst fire seasons that century. "The conditions we are experiencing now are very similar to what we would expect to be experiencing in August at the height of the fire season," said Paul Weeden, a U.S. Forest Service emergency operations specialist in Washington, D.C., on June 29.3

By June 30, the Fan fire had spread to 35 acres. Gusty winds the next day suddenly swelled it to 145 acres. On that day the Red fire, on the west side of Lewis Lake in the southern side of the park, broke out about four miles from the Shoshone fire. On July 3, the Storm Creek fire north of the park, already grown to 3,000 acres, tossed a spot fire on the west side of Stillwater Creek which, because it was threatening to leave the wilderness, was declared a wildfire and now had to be fought under Forest Service rules. Forest Service officials called in one of the nation's special teams of firefighting managers, called a Class 1 Overhead team. Their job was to stop the fire at the wilderness boundary. By July 9, they had temporarily reached that goal.

The Red and Shoshone fires each still were smaller than 100 acres. A fire started by lightning near Lava Lake east of Mammoth on July 5. The Mist fire started on July 9 northwest of the park's east entrance, and park officials decided to let it burn. But they breathed a sigh of relief when rain cooled the flames the next day, July 10. They didn't know it would be the last rain of any consequence for two months.

Barbee and other fire managers were beginning to feel uneasy. They discussed putting an overhead team on the Fan fire, which had grown to 1,800 acres, but finally agreed to allow it to continue. The politically sensitive Barbee wanted to use the fires as much as possible to restore the ecological health of the park, just as he had pioneered the use of fire in Yosemite. But he knew there was a point after which the fires would begin to become a social and political problem. That point had not been reached yet, though, he felt. But it was already an unusual year to have so many fires burning in so many parts of the park.

John Burns, supervisor of the Targhee National Forest, which borders the park on the west, had a completely different perspective. The longtime Forest Service veteran was also a politically astute manager who had learned to work with the unusually conservative and resource-driven congressional delegation in Idaho. About the same time Barbee came to Yellowstone, Burns had taken over the Targhee when it was in the middle of a massive clear-cutting campaign. Targhee officials were attempting to cut down as much lodgepole pine as possible to salvage it before the mountain pine beetle killed it. They considered the practice good forestry, essentially mimicking the effects of a major forest fire. The linear clear-cuts along Yellowstone's boundary had been made prior to Burns's time and he considered it regrettable from an aesthetic standpoint. He and Barbee got along well and annually got together with other managers on weeklong retreats on horseback through the backcountry.

Burns lived in St. Anthony, a thousand feet in elevation below Mammoth Hot Springs, where Yellowstone park officials resided. Even though portions of the Targhee had received some early spring rain, St. Anthony, like most of the Snake River valley, was deep in the throes of a long drought. On July 12, clearly concerned about dry forest conditions, Burns wrote to Barbee, saying that the Targhee would not officially accept any lightning-ignited fires that started in Yellowstone and had purposely been let burn. That meant he expected the Park Service to begin fighting any fires headed his way.

"Our burning conditions are at a point that risks are too great for us to do so this season," Burns wrote. "Other national forests within our region are also experiencing similar conditions . . . our resources for controlling fires are in heavy demand at this time and are expected to be committed throughout this season."4 But not all Forest Service managers shared Burns's uneasiness. On July 11, lightning ignited brush in the Mink Creek drainage in the Bridger-Teton National Forest south of Yellowstone. The fire grew to 50 acres in twenty-four hours and was moving toward a 15,000-acre blowdown caused by a rare high-altitude tornado in 1987. Brian Stout, supervisor of the Bridger-Teton National Forest in Wyoming, was already fighting one blaze in that state's Gros Ventre Wilderness and decided to let the Mink Creek fire burn. "This is a natural fire, something which would naturally occur in the wilderness if man were not intervening," Fred Kingwill, Stout's spokesman, told reporters. "This is the kind of weather pattern that created the wilderness we know today."5

About forty miles north in the same storm, lightning ignited the Clover fire south of Cooke City, Montana. Barbee let it burn.

As the fires ebbed and flowed from smoldering embers to wind-driven crown fires and back, Despain and Romme were coming to some conclusions about the fire history of the 300,000-acre swath of park—fifteen percent of the total—they had studied for four years. Most of the area burned in several large fires between 1690 and 1710 and then again between 1730 and 1750, Romme said.[6] There had been no large fire since. The results were the first indication that fires larger than 50,000 acres in size might once have burned in the park.

But their analysis was in its preliminary stages. Despain had watched fire burn in Yellowstone for seventeen years and nothing remotely that large had occurred. This season was providing him a wonderful new data set to examine the role of fire. The idea that fires like those that burned in the 1700s might repeat themselves this summer was not yet in his or Romme's head. No one, not even cautious John Burns, could predict what was to come.

CHAPTER 15

The Fires of Summer

I had been struck by how suddenly and thoroughly it had attacked the trees. It was as if they had been primed and waiting for the fire to happen.

—Dan Sholly, *Guardians of Yellowstone*, 1991

D AN SHOLLY WAS the kind of man General Phil Sheridan would have appreciated. He was the consummate man of action. Yellowstone's chief ranger in 1988 three years earlier had given up the job as the top ranger of the entire National Park Service in Washington, D.C., even taking a pay cut, to take command of the ranger force of its crown jewel. Sholly had inherited his devotion to the national parks from his father, who had been a chief ranger at Big Bend National Park in Texas. The same commitment took him to the U.S. Marine Corps and the Vietnam War. He returned with a glass eye that, along with his deeply cleft chin, gave him a look of strength and intensity. His admirers and detractors both called him "Danbo," a reference to the Sylvester Stallone movie character "Rambo," who would take on anyone who challenged him.

Except for Barbee himself, Sholly was the main man who decided when and how to fight fire in Yellowstone or to let it burn. Sholly didn't let anything happen. He made things happen. His years of experience made fighting fire come naturally. He considered himself an expert. But he was also a true believer in Yellowstone's natural fire program. Yellowstone's forests needed a healthy dose of fire, and he was willing to take legitimate risks to make that happen. He was the general of the day-to-day ecosystem management operation, and in his view lightning-caused fire was just a part of his toolbox.

Like Sheridan and Elers Koch, Sholly preferred to lead from the front. His steed was a helicopter, dubbed "Sholly's Trolly" by park employees. It gave him a bird's-eye view of both the typical daily conflicts between tourists and nature and the eight fires that were burning around the 3,400-square-mile park on July 14, 1988. That day Sholly had another more sensitive guest to consider. George H. W. Bush, vice president of the United States and recently nominated Republican candidate for president, was soon to arrive on a vacation. There was no press, and Bush, accompanied by his close friend Wyoming Republican senator Alan Simpson and James Baker, his campaign chief, was hoping to get some backcountry fishing in under the radar. Sholly had a maintenance crew replace a shed roof, paint the floor, and build a food storage cabinet that would hold up to grizzly bears at an old patrol cabin on Cold Creek for the vice president. His entourage was scheduled to arrive the next day, and Sholly and Barbee were to escort them to their Yellowstone hideaway.

But as Sholly flew over the Clover fire that afternoon, it was quickly apparent that a change of plans was in order. The 300-acre fire that had been quiet the day before had been whipped into a running crown fire of 4,700 acres in just one day. Pine trees were exploding all over the place, torching out as if they were covered with napalm. Sholly briefly imagined he was back in Vietnam.[1]

These were the moments for which he was trained. His thoughts shifted from warning tourists at a nearby outfitter's camp to protecting a historic patrol cabin on Calfee Creek directly in the path of the fire. Like most of Yellowstone's buildings it had never been prepared for fire. Park officials had readied themselves for dealing with lightning, but they had done no landscaping or fireproofing to the park's multimillion-dollar developments or backwoods buildings. Trees grew right up to the Calfee Creek cabin's edge and a pile of firewood was neatly stacked against its log walls. Sholly picked up a crew that had been clearing trail nearby in anticipation of Bush's visit, to help. But when they arrived at the cabin high winds buffeted the helicopter and made it too hard to control with the full load.

When they finally managed to return to the cabin, they quickly began fireproofing it by throwing the firewood away and burning piles of pine needles against nearby trees to starve the fire of fuel near the cabin. By now, hot embers were beginning to drop from the sky.

Curt Wainwright, the Vietnam veteran helicopter pilot, stayed on the ground at a nearby gravel bar despite the swirling winds and heavy smoke generated by the fire's own cauldron. He got a call that the fire had crossed the river and was heading straight for them. "The trees began to shake around me," Wainwright said. "I cut the frequency and told Sholly I'd have to leave in sixty seconds. Did he want me to pull them out?"

"Negative," Sholly answered.[2]

Sholly had sized up the situation like this: If they left, the smoke would be too thick to allow them to land after the fire front passed. The only way to save the cabin was to stay. But to stay meant that the three would have to go to a nearby wet meadow to ride out the fire. They would essentially allow the fire to burn over them. To do that, they would hide under fire shelters, specially designed aluminum tents. The shelters would provide them with a pocket of oxygen to breathe and shield them from temperatures up to 1,400 degrees Fahrenheit—if they worked as intended. They were never to be deployed unless the only alternative was death.

Twice more Wainwright asked Sholly if he wanted a ride and twice more he refused. Sholly and the two others ran for the safety zone as the fire raced through the branches of the pines surrounding the cabin. John Dunfee, from the trail crew, dropped to the ground and covered himself with the shelter, holding down the end with his boots and the sides with his leather gloved hands. Sholly and Janice Cowan climbed under the only other shelter they had with them. When nothing happened, they climbed out to see what was up. Suddenly the fire roared like a jet engine and the wind began blowing toward the fire as it sucked the oxygen from the air. They covered themselves again and rode out the firestorm, their shelters shaking in the wind and pelted with firebrands.

Up above in an airplane Robert Barbee was watching the situation in horror. The biggest fire he had ever seen was burning over his chief ranger and two other employees. "I thought Sholly was going to die," Barbee said. "I thought I was going to have to do the eulogy."3

When Sholly and the two others emerged from their shelters, they found that the fire had turned the lush wildflower-covered meadow into scorched earth. Smoking black ashen trunks and branches were all that was left of the forest that had been so thick and green only minutes before. Surprisingly, the historic cabin also had survived. Even in the worst firestorm imaginable, fireproofing could save even the most flammable structure if it had a metal roof.

Sholly charged back to Mammoth after his ordeal and called together Yellowstone's fire committee, the team of managers who carried out the park's fire policy. Sholly, the chairman, wanted to begin fighting some of the fires in the park immediately. He wasn't ready to give up on the natural fire program even after nearly becoming its first victim. But he wanted the Shoshone and Red fires that were threatening Grant Village, one of the park's visitor centers on Yellowstone Lake, stopped. He also responded to John Burns's directive from the Targhee and told Barbee to order the two-day-old Falls fire fought before it burned into Idaho. The committee also had at its disposal new information. The National Weather Service issued that day its thirty-day forecast, predicting sixty-five percent chance of hotter than normal temperatures in the Yellowstone area. It also predicted a fifty-five percent chance of less than normal rain.

Sholly was not ready to give up on the Clover fire. Initial analysis suggested that the fire would not exceed 25,000 acres, which still would have made it the largest fire in the park since 1886. But it had not been expected to leave Yellowstone. Now, however, it had grown so big so fast that there was a chance it might burn into the adjacent Shoshone National Forest on Yellowstone's eastern boundary in Wyoming. But he was still convinced it would burn itself out.

Barbee was earning his keep that day. He had already called Steve Mealey, the supervisor of the Shoshone National Forest, and told him to cancel the Yellowstone trip for Bush. Now he was being asked by firefighters and forest supervisors to end the natural fire program for the first time since he arrived. He would also have to ask the National

Interagency Fire Center to send in one of its crack Class 1 Overhead teams to lead the Shoshone and Red firefights, the first time Yellowstone had been forced to get extra help for years. Barbee would also have to go back to the Shoshone National Forest and ask them whether they would accept the Clover fire—allow him to let it burn into the forest's wilderness areas—if it were to make the unlikely climb over the nine-thousand-foot Absaroka Range ridge out of the park. But Mealey was now away, having decided he would guide the vice president himself, taking his group to a tent camp on the North Fork of the Shoshone River by outfitter and horses.

With Mealey away, the decision on accepting or turning away the fire fell to Mealey's assistant, Jim Fischer. The exchange was ecosystem management in action. Most of the land in the Shoshone eighteen miles away was wilderness anyway and burning there also would be beneficial, both managers surmised. And the chances of it really getting there were small. What Barbee didn't tell Fischer, however, was that he and Sholly were taking extraordinary steps to keep the Clover fire burning. Under Yellowstone's own fire plan, managers were supposed to begin fighting a fire when a structure had been directly threatened or when people had been threatened. Sholly's ordeal at the cabin fit the rules, even if only technically. Fuel and weather conditions also warranted Fischer to reject the fire and require Yellowstone to begin fighting it aggressively.

The most emphatic voice on the Fire Committee for allowing the fires to continue was Don Despain. His expertise in fuels and fire behavior made him a critical voice. His leading role in developing the natural fire policy gave him a transparent bias that Barbee always took into account. Barbee decided to start fighting the Shoshone and Red fires, the Falls fire, the Fan fire (which had grown to 2,900 acres), and the two-acre Lava fire on the Blacktail Plateau seven miles southeast of Mammoth. The Clover and Mist fires would remain natural.

Today Barbee isn't afraid to say, had he had the chance to make his decisions over again, that he would have started fighting the Fan fire weeks earlier, in June, and the Clover fire that day, July 14. How much difference such actions might have made remains arguable and largely unanswerable. The interagency review team, which examined fire decisions later that year, concluded the Clover and Mist fires could have been controlled if they had been attacked in the five days preceding July 14. After that it was a crapshoot.

Barbee's decisions that day were not popular at the time among many of Yellowstone's employees for the opposite reason, however. They believed in the natural fire program. They especially opposed the decision to fight the little Lava fire. A group of Yellowstone employees decided to protest by wearing T-shirts saying "Let Lava Live." Despain was among them; he truly was disappointed when the decision was made to put it out.

He wasn't alone. No firefighter living had seen the kind of fires that had chased Ed Pulaski down into the War Eagle Mine in 1910. The only firestorm equal to the Clover fire since then may have been the Sundance fire in northern Idaho in 1967. Its firestorm characteristics made it the subject of research and firefighter awe for a generation.

A big fire in Yellowstone was expected to peak at 40,000–50,000 acres. With hundreds of thousands of acres of wilderness backcountry in Yellowstone and surrounding national forests, where else could scientists really see how a natural fire burned?

In the Bridger-Teton, the Mink Creek fire jumped from 1,000 acres to 3,000 acres in less than twenty-four hours and began threatening outfitter camps. By exceeding 1,000 acres, the Mink Creek fire went over the limit for prescription burns in the Bridger-Teton National Forest. On the evening of July 15, Bridger-Teton supervisor Brian Stout declared it a wildfire, and five hundred firefighters were sent to battle the blaze's southern front, which threatened ranches in Buffalo valley. By July 18, it had grown to 13,500 acres. Bridger-Teton officials allowed it to burn north toward the Yellowstone boundary, but the following day Stout decided to pull out the stops, initiating a strategy for full containment of the Mink Creek fire and declaring that the forest staff would fight every fire when it started in the Bridger-Teton. The decision brought howls of protest from environmental groups. "Biologically it would be better to let it go," commented the Wilderness Society's Northern Rockies regional director.4

The Greater Yellowstone Coalition's executive director, Ed Lewis, was in Jackson to talk to Stout and other national forest officials when the forest supervisor made his decision. He didn't challenge it, but he told his members in a newsletter soon afterward that there were other more serious issues. "If it ever rains again here, it might take care of Mink Creek and the other fires of '88," Lewis wrote. "But it will be much more difficult to put out the development fires raging around Grand Teton."5

Despite the growth of the fires, they were still mostly regional news. The Democratic National Convention was dominating the airwaves, and Vice President Bush's "secret" fishing trip was getting more attention than the fires themselves. When Mealey returned on July 21, he surveyed the situation and reversed Fischer's call on accepting the Clover fire. The Shoshone National Forest would not accept it, and the Clover-Mist fire, now that the two had burned together, was characterized as a wildfire to be fought.

It really didn't matter much at this point. The weather, the fuel, and mostly the wind were now in control of events in Yellowstone. People could still steer fires and perhaps decide in a general degree where they would go. But from July 14 until September 11, nature was in the driver's seat. It wasn't always managers who would make the decisions. Leland Owens was just about to end his day of wood cutting on the North Fork drainage of Moose Creek in the Targhee National Forest on July 22, only 250 yards from the Yellowstone boundary. He and his buddies sat down to have a beer and smoke. When he was done, he tossed the still-burning butt into the grass and left.

The afternoon breeze brought the flames to life in the dry kindling, and it quickly grew into a crown fire in dead lodgepole pine blown down after pine beetle infestation. A Targhee employee spotted the fire within an hour and called the district ranger, who immediately called in smokejumpers and sent a team to help them. The smokejumpers began fighting the fire at 2:50 p.m., but at seventy-five acres and burning fiercely, it already was too big for them to tackle head-on. By late afternoon hand crews, two bulldozers, and air tankers from West Yellowstone were throwing everything they had at the fire. But already the

North Fork fire was sending huge firebrands into the high winds and causing spot fires a full half-mile ahead of the fire head east into Yellowstone National Park. The district ranger asked West Yellowstone park ranger Joe Evans if the park would allow bulldozers into the park in the evening when the fire could be expected to calm as it cooled.

Park policy allowed bulldozers to be approved by Barbee, but usually they were not used. The dozers cut deep gashes into the earth that often lasted long after other fire scars. Generally Yellowstone allowed bulldozers only when structures or people were threatened, and the Madison Plateau on the park's western side was far from any structure. Evans had already discussed the issue with Sholly and refused any bulldozers in the park.

Without bulldozers firefighters never cut a line around the front of the fire. But even with bulldozers it is questionable whether firefighters would have been ordered to build a line around the front of the fire because of the danger the strong and erratic winds presented. By the next day the fire had grown to five hundred acres. A huge spot fire had shot out about a quarter-mile ahead.

The decision not to use bulldozers became one of the critics' major debate points when they blasted the park's let-burn policy. Some Targhee fire officials were convinced that they could have stopped the North Fork fire if they had been able to use bulldozers during the first crucial hours before the late-morning burning period started on July 23. But Yellowstone officials were as adamant that it could not have been stopped. As proof they pointed to the unusual spotting behavior of the fire as it sent out burning firebrands that started dozens of spot fires ahead of the main mass. Later, when the fires had reached holocaust proportions, the park would allow the use of bulldozers to protect West Yellowstone and to prevent the North Fork fire from burning back into the Targhee. The lines the bulldozer etched didn't hold, however.

The North Fork fire turned out to be the largest, most expensive, and most attention-grabbing fire of the season. Within days it would be within eight miles of Old Faithful and prompt the first discussion of closing Yellowstone for the year. It would threaten Canyon Village twice; West Yellowstone, Montana; Roosevelt Lodge at Tower Junction;

and finally Mammoth Hot Springs. No matter what happened at Clover, Fan, Mink, Storm Creek, or Shoshone, the North Fork fire would dominate 1988. Its ignition by a man was secondary to the fuel and weather conditions that made it big. In a season when decisions about fighting fires and letting them burn were blurred, misconstrued, and misunderstood, the major issue was largely lost on all: Yellowstone's fire overwhelmed human capacities in the same way that floods, hurricanes, and volcanoes can.

Yet even after the Shoshone fire burned through Grant Village on July 25—its buildings were saved by the savvy firefighting of Incident Commander David Poncin and his team—Yellowstone's managers were still hopeful that they could bring the chaotic and complex situation under control. Barbee had called in an area command group to oversee the thirteen separate firefighting teams operating in and around Yellowstone. Thousands of firefighters were joining the effort that was soon to become the largest single firefight in history.

The national media also had arrived. The fires were shown live on network television and on the front page of newspapers across the nation. The Cable News Network (CNN), less than a decade old, was broadcasting hourly film of the flames and reports on the growing threats. Donald Hodel, who was now secretary of the interior, toured the fires on July 27 and tried to reassure the nation that what was happening was ultimately for the good. Appointed by President Reagan, Hodel was a devout Christian and a conservative who had served as the controversial secretary James Watt's assistant. His political views were in line with the congressmen of the surrounding states such as Senators Alan Simpson and Malcolm Wallop of Wyoming, who were angry that Yellowstone was not fighting the fires more aggressively.

At the same time William Penn Mott, Reagan's personal friend and Hodel's National Park Service director, was telling anyone who would listen that the fires were beneficial and that the park's natural fire policy was working well. Faced with this quandary, Hodel turned to the man who was in the same boat, Barbee, for advice. Politics was Barbee's game. Barbee told Hodel to announce that the park was not allowing the fires to burn. He should acknowledge the natural role they play in

Yellowstone's forests but point out the unusual conditions they were facing. Hodel took his advice and the message was mixed. Part of his story was based on Despain's basic lesson in fire ecology.

"We aren't going to waste our resources where fires aren't doing harm to the park," Hodel said. "There's a long-term beneficial effect from fire." But, he added, "It is our policy to fight wildfires in the national park."[6]

After returning to Washington, D.C., he was even more reassuring. "Yellowstone is not in danger. . . . We're not going to let Yellowstone be damaged by this," he said on ABC's *Good Morning America.*

The fire story had by now made the front page of hundreds of newspapers nationwide. Burning forests filled the evening news. NBC anchor Tom Brokaw owned a ranch north of the park and had a particular interest in the story. His western correspondent, Roger O'Neil, spent as much time on the scene as any network reporter. The network got the story precisely right, saying "firefighters reverse policy and use aggressive tactics at Yellowstone."[7]

The fires that had lit up television screens from coast to coast were burning through national forests and threatening communities north from Montana, east through Wyoming, west into Idaho, and south into the Tetons. Some started in the park, some started out. Lightning lit a few, and people lit others. But the distinctions were lost on most Americans. These were the Yellowstone fires, burning across the landscape they held dear. They were expecting men like Barbee and Sholly to protect it.

By July 31, with 115,000 acres burned in the park, the threat from the fires was beginning to diminish as the winds died down and they ran out of fuel. Barbee, Sholly, and the fire teams were catching their breath and awaiting an analysis by a team of the nation's top fire behavior experts. Their prognosis would steer the decisions for the critical months of August and September. However, the fires had already brought the nation's attention back to Yellowstone and to the natural forces that had spread beyond its borders.

CHAPTER 16

Burn, Baby, Burn

What we've found is there isn't much left to burn.

—Don Despain, August 2, 1988

B Y AUGUST 1 Don Despain's predictions about how large fires could get in Yellowstone had already been exceeded. The researcher was having the opportunity of a lifetime. Here was the kind of new data set a fire ecologist could only dream of.

Robert Barbee and the rest of the federal bureaucracy were ready to end the party if they could. But Despain knew, as he had known all year, that the size and scope of the fires would be dictated by nature, not men. Firefighters might be able to draw some lines and steer the blazes away from particular places. But weather and vegetation were the real managers of the Greater Yellowstone ecosystem, and no one knew Yellowstone's vegetation better than Despain.

When national fire officials organized a team of the top fire behaviorists in the country to analyze the Yellowstone situation, Despain was thus a critical addition. The team, which Barbee called the "fire gods," was headed by Richard Rothermel from the U.S. Forest Service's Fire Science Laboratory in Missoula, Montana. Rothermel had practically invented the science of fire behavior prediction, working in the 1960s with wind tunnels designed for aviation research. His mathematical model of how fire spread was state of the art. The generation of firefighters managing the fires in and around Yellowstone had all depended on it.

Within seventy-two hours the team had entered Despain's maps of the forest types, rangelands, and brushlands that covered the park onto their computers. They filled hard drives with the weather records from

203

the last twenty years, the topography, and Despain's fire history reports. The data were then run through Rothermel's fire spread model, which calculated all of the variables. Their final product was a multicolored map on which the best minds on fire behavior would base their assessment of the rest of the season.

The team's biologist, Jack Troyer, who only a year before had been analyzing timber sales on the Shoshone National Forest, was the Forest Service's face of ecosystem management in Yellowstone. He had been appointed the team leader of the Greater Yellowstone Coordinating Committee in May, which was made up of the supervisors of the six national forests and the two national park superintendents, and his job was to improve coordination in the Greater Yellowstone area (the Forest Service still considered the word "ecosystem" too politically sensitive to use). The fires had revealed some serious conflicts, including the decisions between Yellowstone and the Shoshone over accepting the Clover fire and the bulldozer dispute on the North Fork fire. An area command had been brought in to manage the firefighting effort. But Troyer organized a meeting for August 2 among forest supervisors and park leaders in West Yellowstone so they could all be working off the same page. The highlight of the meeting was to be the report of Rothermel's team.

In the old log railroad terminal of the Northern Pacific, the top managers and firefighters gathered in a room to hear the experts' findings. A few reporters were on the scene and some managers wanted to close the meeting. Eventually the mostly local reporters, including me, were allowed to sit on the floor. The land managers all knew their careers were on the line. So far they had been lucky; a lot of forest had burned but no homes or businesses. No one had been killed. But the worst month of the fire season wasn't July; it was always August.

Rothermel spoke first, explaining the limits of their ability to make predictions. But he had good news. Yellowstone's historical precipitation records showed that it almost always rained in August. One good rain would settle the fires down for good. Another expert talked about how wind and dry fuels had been the major factor pushing the fires in July. Only one major wind event—winds of more than forty miles per hour for more than two hours—or maybe two could be expected in August. The best news was the fuel. In front of the North Fork fire and the other large fires, large stands of young, green lodgepole pine created a natural barrier that would contain the flames. The prevailing winds would push the fire northeast, making it unlikely to threaten Old Faithful again, or West Yellowstone. In all, Rothermel said, they predicted that about 200,000 acres of Yellowstone and the surrounding forests would eventually burn.

Afterward, Despain spoke to reporters on the record. "They will probably run into fuels that won't carry the fire very well, and the fire will slow down considerably before the end of August if we don't have rain. If we do have rain, the fires will cover far short of what we've mapped out. We don't predict a whole lot more than we've already got."[1]

Rothermel's spread model, based on a fire history beginning long after 1910, predicted that the fastest fire would spread at about a quarter-mile per hour. The fire that had sent Sholly into a shelter in July had exceeded that rate. So did the burn through Grant Village and the North Fork fire, already the major beast of the summer. Even before the experts gave their presentation, gusting winds that evening had pumped up fires all across the southern end of the park and the Bridger-Teton National Forest, expanding the fires to 150,000 acres by dusk.

Four days later winds gusting to sixty miles per hour grew the fires again, and by August 12, 201,000 acres of the park had burned. Fire bosses, who had been skeptical about Rothermel's predictions in the first place, began squabbling with park officials about the strategies in place for containing the fires. Residents of West Yellowstone and Cooke City on the park's edges were getting anxious about the safety of their homes. On August 16 yet another windstorm carried the fire over the meadow where the Washburn expedition had held their mythic campfire discussion. The North Fork fire by now had jumped the Madison River and was spreading toward the heart of Yellowstone and east toward West Yellowstone. The myth of the fire gods was going the way of the campfire myth on which the glory of the Park Service was founded.

The previous two months of new data were also reshaping the way Don Despain and Bill Romme looked at the fire history they had gathered since 1984. They now recognized that the series of fires in the 1700s that they had identified must have been far larger than they earlier thought possible. The patches of older trees that separated some of the large burns were actually huge unburned areas like the mosaics of burning they had seen this year. Despain left Yellowstone the week of August 14 to present the results at the Ecological Society of America's meeting in Davis, California. There he and Romme told their colleagues that large fires had burned hundreds of thousands of acres of Yellowstone three hundred years before, in the 1700s. Their analysis was shaped by the events they were watching before their eyes, Romme said. Their exciting results were well received by their fellow ecologists, far better than the fire ecology message was selling to neighbors of Yellowstone National Park.

Jim Carrier of the *Denver Post* didn't question the science, but by the middle of August he was beginning to question the decisions he saw Barbee and other park officials making. Called "The Rocky Mountain Ranger," Carrier wrote a popular column that ran weekly in arguably the West's most influential newspaper. Two years earlier he spent the entire summer in the park writing a loving series of columns called "Letters from Yellowstone." In those columns it was obvious Carrier shared the views of the park's managers and scientists about the wisdom of allowing nature to take its course in the park. He knew the players and cherished the place like an old friend.

By mid-August his old friend had been turned into a black, burned-out wasteland. The special scenes he had come to love were gone forever. He had spent much of the last month breathing smoke and watching firefighters frantically fight to save places such as Grant Village, whose cedar shake roofs and wood construction surrounded by forest made it a firetrap.

Still, he was a professional, and he covered the fires with depth and fairness, presenting both the growing voices of criticism of the firefighters and community leaders, and the still mixed message of the Park Service about the beneficial effects of the fire.

For most of the nation, the story had once again slipped off the front page and out of network news. CNN reporters remained on the scene, but as the fire burned across Yellowstone's backcountry there wasn't much to report except typical stories about brave firefighters and the annual battle in the West. Yellowstone remained open and visitors often had the opportunity to drive near the fires, watching as firefighters went about their business.

In mid-August Carrier went back to Denver for a much needed break. But his R&R was to be stopped short on Saturday, August 20, the 102nd anniversary of Moses Harris's order to fight the first fire the government had seen in Yellowstone. More ominous, the day was the seventy-eighth anniversary of the Big Blowup—the day Ed Pulaski made his fateful run into the War Eagle Mine during the 1910 fires. Even though firefighters had seen more big fire already in 1988 than they had seen in one place since 1910, they were not prepared for what happened on the day they would forever remember as Black Saturday.

Bob Ekey, the *Billings Gazette* reporter who had interviewed Despain back in June, was one of the few reporters left in the park that day. He had stationed himself at Norris Junction, several miles ahead of where the North Fork fire had settled down in calm winds the night before. Midway through the morning the winds picked up to thirty to forty miles per hour, at times gusting to seventy miles an hour. "It just started howling," Ekey said.[2]

Trees were blowing down and flames climbed to two hundred feet high above the forest, driving the fire into a dead run. Rangers in patrol cars used loudspeakers to roust tourists from the path of the fire.[3] Trees snapped liked toothpicks in the heavy winds, now generated as much by the fires themselves as the weather. Ekey stood with a dozen fire officials stunned and amazed by the extent of the fury. "You could almost feel the fire first," Ekey recalled. "Then you would hear it like a freight train roaring toward you. Then you feel the heat." The fire burned past the crowd on the run and then the wind shifted, sending them running for their cars. Inside his small truck Ekey could still feel the heat of the fire like an oven.

It didn't take long for Carrier to get reports of the huge conflagration taking place on his beat four hundred miles away. When he and a photographer approached Yellowstone in a small plane they had chartered, the park was engulfed in a huge shroud of gray smoke punctuated with tall black columns that looked like mushroom clouds. "Coming from a distance there was a sense that a series of atomic bombs had gone off," he said.4

In less than eight hours the size of the fires had doubled, to 480,215 acres throughout the Yellowstone ecosystem. The Clover-Mist fire exploded over the park boundary into the Shoshone Forest and north toward Cooke City. It alone had grown 55,000 acres that day. Cooke City had other problems. The Storm Creek fire, which had smoldered for most of the summer, rose from the dead and made a ten-mile run that day, shocking fire experts because it ran south, against the prevailing wind. Two new fires were started south of Yellowstone by trees falling on power lines.

All of Yellowstone now appeared as one huge fire, and it was clear that nature, not humans, was in full control. After Black Saturday, all but the most stubborn fire suppression advocates had to acknowledge that all the technology, and all the expertise, and all the firefighters they could muster couldn't stop these fires. Smokey Bear's army of firefighters was humbled by Black Saturday and the fire behavior they saw in the days after it. Dick Panchero, part of the overhead team leading the fight on the North Fork fire, was typical of the seasoned firefighters who were awed by the fury they saw in Yellowstone. Even good fire lines on the lee side of a fire could not hold when north and south winds blew. It even burned into the wind. "This fire backs against the wind like no fire I've ever seen," he said. "That's because it's so dry." His colleague Stan Graham, a safety officer on the fire, spoke of the unusual spotting that would allow the fire to leap rivers and jump ahead of firefighters by one and one-half miles: "It will spot in back of you or it will spot in front of you."5

Even though the park's critics were saying the fire could have been stopped, most of the firefighters who fought in Yellowstone for more than two weeks realized they were powerless. Despite the earlier debates on the Clover-Mist and North Fork fires, the Huck fire and others that started on Black Saturday would never have been stopped and were as uncontrollable now as the others.

Barbee had spent the day herding tourists out of West Thumb in the south, consoling angry residents of West Yellowstone, and taking the long way back to Mammoth Hot Springs for a critical meeting with his staff. Ekey had reached him by telephone, and Barbee had revealed his plan to close the park. But he told the reporter to wait for his confirmation before going with the story.

The *Billings Gazette* editors had the page laid out with a headline saying Barbee had closed the park, Ekey said later. They were waiting for his call. Inside the meeting Barbee listened as rangers, scientists, and managers debated the issue. Everyone agreed that fire behavior had become so unpredictable that it was too dangerous to keep much of the park open. But closing Yellowstone meant declaring defeat. Senators Alan Simpson and Malcolm Wallop of Wyoming had asked him to keep the park open because closing would be even more devastating for the region's economy. The group convinced Barbee to keep at least the West Yellowstone entrance to the park open and the road to Old Faithful, the park's most important attraction. Other parts of the park would be opened as conditions dictated.

After Black Saturday, Barbee didn't want to talk about natural fire anymore. The message he wanted to send now was that Yellowstone administrators were throwing everything they could at the fires. "It was time for the brave firefighters story," Barbee said later. "We'll do the happy-face fire ecology story when it's over, I told people."[6] The national media were returning to the park in droves, and Barbee and other park officials were clearly frustrated that news stories made it seem like he was fiddling while the park burned.

"People keep saying why don't you put them out," he told reporters on August 22. "You don't take a 60,000- to 70,000-acre fire and just put it out." Then Barbee paraphrased what Moses Harris had written in 1886 and Elers Koch in 1935. "We could have had the entire United States Army in here and it wouldn't have made any difference."[7]

He would soon get the army and it would not make a difference. But in the meantime Carrier and Despain were about to make his life even harder.

DESPAIN WAS NOW BACK at his research in the park. For years he had set up test plots ahead of fires to gather data about fuel moisture, fuel loads, and other information to measure the effects of burning on the vegetation. The week after Black Saturday, Despain and ecologist Roy Renkin took Carrier and a photographer with them as they set up a test plot near Wolf Lake in the center of the park just ahead of the North Fork fire. Despain and Renkin worked all morning to get the plot set up. At noon they sat together inside the test area and ate their lunch.

Suddenly they began hearing trees torching in the distance as the fire moved toward them. Firebrands began raining on them and the plot. Lodgepole pines lit up as the fire climbed immediately from the ground into the crowns. Despain, usually calm, collected, and reserved, was now excited. For the first time he was watching one of his test plots burn. He was there. He couldn't help himself.

"Burn, baby, burn," he said.[8]

The phrase had been made popular by the Black Panthers in the 1960s when cities across the nation were burning in race riots. Despain's encouragement was nothing more than a scientist's exaltation. It was Despain's way of saying, "Eureka!"

Carrier accurately portrayed the moment and placed in it the context of his story on the beneficial effects of fire and fire ecology. But when it ran in the *Denver Post* on August 28, it ran with a huge picture of Don and the headline, "Burn, baby, burn." All of the cultural baggage of the phrase brought unconsciously to mind the idea of arson and chaos. Carrier defended the headline writers years later, saying it reflected the message that he delivered between the lines. Yellowstone officials had become arrogant in their natural management program: "I thought Don's attitude was typical of that arrogance," Carrier said. "'Burn, baby, burn' was a smack in the face to all of that."[9]

The reaction in 1988 when the story broke was immediate and national in scope. Wallop, referring to the headline, went on network news calling for the resignation of National Park Service Director William Penn Mott, who was still defending the natural fire policy. Wallop and Wyoming's other senator, Alan Simpson, both called Barbee and demanded he fire Despain.

Barbee wasn't very happy with Despain either, but he knew the researcher's attention was focused on science, not policy. With the nation's attention now on Yellowstone and attacks coming from all sides, Barbee needed to get control of the situation. He knew he couldn't control the fire. He also had little control over the huge firefighting army that had come to Yellowstone to put out the fires. It was no longer simply about keeping his job or Mott's or even about supporting Hodel, who had stood by Barbee when all of his Republican friends were attacking him.

At stake was the policy, the mission, of managing national parks as natural places instead of zoos or amusement parks. Get away from the hotels, ice cream stands, campgrounds, and roads and Yellowstone remained a wilderness, a reasonable illusion of what Nathaniel Langford and Gus Doane had seen when they arrived 118 years earlier. Preserving and, where possible, restoring the land's natural processes was at the core of Barbee's being. In August 1988 few places in the world were as wild as much of Yellowstone was. Yet no manager could claim to have done as much on-the-ground forest management as Barbee did in 1988. His tool wasn't logging, road building, or even stream restoration or species reintroduction. It was fire. Big fire. Natural fire. Or maybe, as Despain saw it, Barbee's role didn't matter much on the ground. But even Despain realized that a weakened Park Service might have to give in to absurd proposals like replanting the burnt forest or salvaging Yellowstone's timber. (Both ideas were seriously proposed in the fire's aftermath.) Barbee wasn't down yet, though, and no one could spin events better. He knew he had to start now.

Barbee muzzled Despain and hid him away from the press for the rest of the season. In his place John Varley, Yellowstone's head of research, became the voice and face of Yellowstone's fire policy. No one in the park, except for Barbee himself, was as gifted as Varley at handing out sound bites to television reporters.

Had Black Saturday been the last big day, Barbee and Varley's task would have been far easier. Cooke City's threat from the Clover-Mist fire subsided. But the North Fork fire's approach to West Yellowstone kept alive the specter of Yellowstone's fires burning an entire community of homes and businesses. And then the Storm Creek fire, resurrected on Black Saturday, came out of nowhere to threaten Cooke City again from the west. The fires were again daily events in national newspapers and on network television. CNN was sending dramatic video of giant flames on the hour.

Thirty-five years of Smokey Bear had hardwired the press and the American public to abhor forest fire. Despite the environmental awakening of the 1960s and the expanded recognition of the natural role fire plays in ecosystems, Barbee and Varley knew they couldn't make America think black is beautiful in Yellowstone. Now all they could hope for was to hold on to the respect the public had for the Park Service and its ranger corps. They knew they couldn't compete with Smokey Bear, but they didn't want to look like the hapless foil to Yogi Bear, Mr. Ranger.

When weather conditions turned more favorable, savvy firefighting did limit the damage. The North Fork fire stopped a mile from West Yellowstone, where Idaho potato farmers had wetted down a swath of forest with a sprinkler irrigation system. A well-timed backfire had turned the North Fork fire away from Canyon Village's ranger homes, in part because of last-minute fireproofing efforts. The lesson learned in Yellowstone, that clearing brush away from buildings and creating defensible space could save even the most flammable buildings, was all but lost to the public until more than a decade later.

By the end of August, the firefighting force had grown to nearly ten thousand, including soldiers from the army and marines. An army of reporters also returned as the summer of fire was reaching its crescendo. It was hard to believe that the fires could burn again as fiercely as they did on Black Saturday. But by September 6 nothing surprised Barbee or the fire command. The North Fork fire sat a half-mile from Old Faithful and even closer to Canyon Village. The Storm Creek fire had marched to Cooke City's doorstep. To add to their troubles, the huge winds that had threatened to burn one of the nation's most sacred landmarks were carrying the fires directly to Mammoth Hot Springs— the park's headquarters and the place it had all started ninety-eight years before, in 1886 when General Phil Sheridan sent in the cavalry.

Whatever happened, one thing was certain: it would all be live on national television.

CHAPTER 17

Moment of Truth

They keep telling me it's history, but I would rather see it as it was.

—Unnamed tourist interviewed on
NBC Nightly News, September 7, 1988

OLD FAITHFUL would turn out to be the people's firestorm. With dozens of journalists on the scene, satellite trucks beaming images, Americans were getting their first inside glimpse at the kind of fire behavior few firefighters had ever seen before 1988. The timing of the arrival of the fire added to the drama. At the very moment when the North Fork fire was cresting the western skyline, as Old Faithful was erupting, Tom Brokaw was beginning the *NBC Nightly News*.

"Old Faithful at Yellowstone, one of the most popular tourist attractions in our oldest national park, is under siege tonight," Brokaw began. "There are a lot of angry people who believe that the National Park Service is responsible and has let the fires burn too freely for too long."[1]

Then the picture moved from Brokaw in the studio to fiery scenes from around Yellowstone that day, quickly equaling Black Saturday for the fury and size of the conflagrations.

"This is what's left of Yellowstone tonight," Brokaw said. "No one argues that it will take decades to fix, but already the process has started." Then he cut to a live feed directly from the Old Faithful parking lot and correspondent Roger O'Neil.

"Tom, that North Fork fire has been making a strong march toward Old Faithful since noon, and it got considerably stronger in the last half hour," O'Neil reported. "We now have fifty to sixty mile an hour winds here, and the fire is less than two blocks from the inn. There is one way out—fire is on three sides."

For nearly everyone the historic Old Faithful Inn, the largest log structure in the world, became the symbol of victory or defeat. With four hundred buildings and $70 million worth of development surrounding the geyser, the National Park Service had a lot to lose. For the public, already angry that, as they understood it, Yellowstone had been allowed to burn, it would be the last straw.

"If the Old Faithful Inn . . . or any of those towns or any of the hundreds of firefighters and soldiers defending them were destroyed, then God help those of us who had been advocates of the park's natural burn policy," Dan Sholly later said.[2]

Ten days before, Lieutenant Colonel Richard Mackey of the U.S. Army led 120 soldiers to Old Faithful to clean up the flammable material surrounding the cabins, hotels, and stores. Their work was not as exciting as that of the firefighters on the line. But it would turn out to be far more critical when the firestorm arrived. They carried from the area several five-ton dump truck loads of trash and deadfall along with a giant slash-heap of branches and trees that had grown up next to the buildings.[3]

For seasonal ranger-naturalist Holly McKinney the whole scene was surrealistic. Despite the approaching fire she was ordered to work her regular shift dressed in traditional Park Service gray and green to explain Old Faithful to visitors, as if it were a regular day in paradise. She and her colleagues were directed to tell visitors to leave but not to force them to leave.

On September 5, Sholly and his team had developed an evacuation plan for the Old Faithful area. The first act was to be closing the road between Madison Junction and Old Faithful. Then, an orderly evacuation of guests at the Old Faithful Inn and other visitors would take place. All but nonessential staff also would be sent out. At 8 p.m. on September 6, West District Ranger Joe Evans said an evacuation was "not probable."[4] By 10 p.m., that had changed.

Evans announced at 10:30 p.m. that the inn would be evacuated and a "temporary closure" would take effect on September 7. All but nonessential employees would be gone by noon. Dennis Bungarz,

North Fork fire incident commander, said the fire was expected to reach Old Faithful on September 8. Experts predicted it would move quickly over the west ridge overlooking the area, then crawl down the eastern side, softly bumping the fire lines. The head of the blaze was expected to skirt the area to the south.

The original evacuation plans were thrown out the next morning. Park officials decided to close the inn for the season and keep around only employees needed for that task. When the fire came over the ridge it was not creeping down the other side. Instead, the entire western skyline was soon filled with two-hundred-foot-high flames.

Now it was time to get the visitors out without delay. It would be a dicey ballet. At the roadblocks rangers had been letting people in even as the inn was evacuated. Now they had to turn people away and get the remaining guests out before closing the road for good.

"I talked to so many visitors who had driven through walls of flames and they really didn't realize the amount of danger they were in because they were allowed in the national park," Holly McKinney said. As the critical moment arrived, the rangers responded. McKinney began running from car to car and stopping every person she saw.

"Get out of here now!" she shouted. "If I didn't have to be here right now, I'd leave."5

In the half hour before the road closed, all but about two hundred visitors left. Engine crews began watering down the buildings, and firefighters moved up the ridge to start a backfire. But they dropped the idea when it became apparent that a wind shift would trap them. Ranger Gary Youngblood had to pick up a man who had an epileptic fit. In the cabin area he found a man carrying a leather pouch and wearing an amulet around his neck and jeans with "some kind of spiritual painting around the leg," worshiping the flames. Youngblood told him to leave twice and then gave up. The fire worshipper was on his own.6

The most chaotic group was the reporters. Some were kept together by rangers and other public affairs staff. Television crews were sticking close to their satellite trucks in the large parking lot in back of the inn. Others would sneak away, saying they had to go to the bathroom, or would just walk off in the bedlam.

Jim Carrier was strolling through the cabins behind Snow Lodge and found one with a roof on fire. He used a fire extinguisher to put it out and received the thanks of Bungarz, who was patrolling the area in a car.

The *Denver Post* reporter had seen a lot of fire in the weeks before—more than nearly every firefighter in America. He and other reporters were admittedly a little cocky from their experiences. He walked toward what is known as the government area—houses and trailers in a grove of lodgepole pines on the western edge of the village. It was the front line of the fire, divided from the rest of the village by the main highway. From there he watched as firefighters sixty yards ahead manned the line. It was an incredible sight. The flames rose above them two hundred feet, yet because the wind direction was southeast, it appeared unthreatening.

Carrier chose the road as the safe spot, the place where he would deploy his fire shelter if needed. But he and I standing together realized we didn't have anyone around to tell us when to deploy. At 4:15 p.m., the roaring, smoky head of the fire suddenly switched directions and turned toward the development, the firefighters, Carrier, and me. Carrier and McKinney several hundreds yards apart each felt a blast of heat on their backs. The burning sensation was coming from the opposite direction of the fire.

"It was so hot behind me that I checked . . . to make sure that the fire had not jumped behind me," McKinney said. "It was not until later that I realized it was the plume effect—when the fire column grows tall it pulls oxygen into itself."[7]

Carrier knew we were in trouble. "Let's get out of here," he said. We ran toward the huge parking lot 150 yards away. Coals were pelting his back and I could see fist-sized firebrands by my head. We jumped a small stream and stumbled through the forest toward safety. The entire area turned black as night and the howling wind sounded like a jet engine as Carrier and I reached the road into the parking lot. With the wind blowing at eighty miles per hour, the parking lot hardly seemed safe. The oxygen returned to the forest we had just left and it ignited as if someone had lit a match to gasoline. The forest was engulfed in a wall of flame that tossed embers in our direction, swirling through the choking smoke like wind devils.

The parking lot was in chaos. The concession employees who'd been cheering the flames were running for cover. Without fireproof clothing, they and the other tourists and employees were trapped, and could have ignited. But rangers kept their heads and gathered all the people they could in and around the inn and Old Faithful and told them to lie down and cover themselves. Television crews and still photographers were scurrying around to capture the action. It was so dark at the peak of the firestorm that photography was nearly impossible. Both visitors and employees were crying and cowering in fear. Many journalists shared the panic and fear of the others who had never experienced anything like the fury of a firestorm.

But the firefighters, following the discipline needed to save their lives, reorganized in the parking lot and prepared to head back to the line when the storm passed. Jack Ward Thomas, the elk researcher with the U.S. Forest Service, had come to Yellowstone as a part of the team from the National Academy of Sciences examining the park's natural fire policy. He was bored with the endless meetings in Mammoth and wanted to see the fire firsthand. He promised Park Service officials he would stay out of the way of firefighters. When the firestorm hit he is not embarrassed to say he was scared to death. "I remember thinking I was at the wrong place at the wrong time," Thomas said.[8]

He laid flat on the ground near the inn as firebrands swirled over his head. "At that moment I realized that putting a fire like that out, if it wasn't a wild dream, it was probably a joke," Thomas said.[9]

A fireball shot a huge burning log a half mile over the village south of Observation Point, starting a new fire that grew quickly. Then the worst fears appeared to be coming true. Another spot fire started on the roof of the inn. An employee quickly stamped it out. The sprinkler system came to life. A warehouse caught fire and later exploded when an abandoned fuel truck near it ignited.

"I was thinking those people on the roof were basically dead," said Paul Strasser, a real estate agent from Sacramento, California. Then I saw the water streaming off the roof."[10]

Strasser was celebrating his thirty-fifth birthday that day. He and his wife Suzanne had regularly come to Old Faithful for years to observe and record the geyser eruptions throughout the basin. They had spent many happy days and nights in the inn and were sick that it might be destroyed. But when the smoke cleared, the inn and all the other major buildings remained. "Now I know how the people in London felt about seeing St. Paul's Cathedral after the bombings," Strasser said.[11]

Bungarz later acknowledged that had the fire's path moved a couple of degrees, his team probably could not have saved the inn. The firestorm would have thrown its full fury on the inn, the parking lot, and its occupants. Surprisingly no one was killed or even hurt. But the hundreds who lived through it and the millions who saw it on television shared a sense of awe.

"When you're facing a ball of fire rolling off a ridge like that, there ain't a whole hell of a lot you can do, except get out of the way," said Lieutenant Colonel Mackey. "I have never experienced anything like that before."[12]

Up at Mammoth Hot Springs Robert Barbee and Sholly were breathing a sign of relief. The lines held at Cooke City and Canyon Village, and only twenty-eight buildings, mostly obsolete cabins, were burned at Old Faithful. They too felt like they had survived the blitzkrieg.

But the ordeal for them was far from over. Another 200,000 acres had burned that day, even more than on Black Saturday. In Wyoming a dozen trailers, a store, and seven cabins burned, the first private property lost in any of the various Yellowstone fires. And now the fires had converged into one big fire that was quickly surrounding Mammoth Hot Springs and the park's headquarters. On September 10 the winds were forecast to blow even harder than they had on Black Saturday. Barbee finally declared defeat. He closed the park and urged employees to evacuate their homes. There was no doubt about the message now.

As his son loaded the car with belongings, John Varley watered down the roof of the historic housing on the site of old Fort Sheridan. Now the park's chief spokesman for its natural fire management policy found himself in the same awful spot that residents in Cooke City, Silver Gate, and West Yellowstone had been in shortly before. He faced losing his home and most of his belongings to the fires he knew would provide significant ecological benefits to the park. But there was little talk about a forest rebirth during these tense days of early September. "Your attitude changes when you're on your own roof," he said.[13]

Despain prepared his family and home as well. But he kept his sense of humor through the darkest moments. When the North Fork fire burned through the remains of the Lava fire, which had long been extinguished, Despain couldn't help but remind Barbee of one of his few early decisions to fight a fire. "I said, 'See Bob, because we put Lava out, Mother Nature had to bring a fire all the way from Old Faithful,'" Despain quipped.[14]

At 2 a.m. on September 9, the winds kicked up at Mammoth and held at thirty miles per hour for most of the day. Several hours later the glow of fire appeared on the eastern hills overlooking the valley. The fire had not dropped throughout the entire night. Now it was burning through the same area where Moses Harris's soldiers had begun the nation's firefighting effort. This time there was a lot more than buckets and shovels and a few dozen soldiers though. Dozens of fire engine crews had driven all night from eastern Wyoming to beef up the defense of park headquarters. Employees and guests were evacuated from Mammoth in the morning, leaving a skeleton crew of park staff and a horde of reporters and firefighters left to wait for the firestorm. President Reagan was so disturbed by the television reports from Old Faithful that he sent a Cabinet team—including Hodel—to the park to investigate. Barbee had to leave the headquarters in the hands of Sholly so he could meet Hodel and others in West Yellowstone. His trip through the flaming forest, with his wife, Carol, at his side, took hours as rangers were forced to cut and move trees that had burned and fallen on the roadway of the closed park.

Back at Mammoth, Despain sat on the hill above the old hotel and watched the fire approach. The wind was so strong it could knock him over, he remembered. Sholly was directing the evacuation and preparing for what appeared to be a rerun of threats to Old Faithful, Cooke City, and Canyon Village. In the early afternoon there was still no sign of a letup. The wind was sending burning firebrands north, spreading spot fires from the south off of Bunsen Peak and forcing firefighters to scurry in an effort to prevent the now dry meadows from flaring. At 3 p.m., the humidity dropped just as it had before at Canyon Village, Cooke City, West Yellowstone, Old Faithful, and Tower Junction when other firestorms arrived. An orange glow rose above the hills as flames reflected off the smoke. It was only a matter of time before the flames could crest the ridge and the firestorm would fill Mammoth Hot Springs.

But something was different this time. Even as the winds rose to as high as eighty miles per hour, the flames never came. Although the humidity dropped, it started the afternoon of September 10 at forty-four percent instead of the two and four percent it had been on Black Saturday. It never dropped into single digits. Heavy winds blew humid air and even a misty drizzle into the fires.

Snow fell on September 11, and a pattern of cool, moist fall weather ended the active fire season in the park. The fires smoldered until November, but the debate over how they were fought burned on for years to come.

Twenty-five thousand firefighters passed through the fires that season and no one died until the fires were nearly gone. Pilot Don Kykendall died on September 11 when his plane crashed while carrying firefighters in Jackson Hole, Wyoming. Firefighter Ed Hutton was killed on October 11 when a snag, a single standing burnt tree, fell on him.

As the smoke cleared, the agencies determined that 1.2 million acres had burned in Yellowstone and the surrounding national forests. Up to 2 million tons of particulates, 4.4 million tons of carbon monoxide, 129 tons of nitrogen oxide, and 106 tons of hydrocarbons were released into the air and dropped in the form of air pollution as far away as the East Coast and Amarillo, Texas. Remarkably little commercial timber—170 million board feet, enough to build 11,000 homes—burned since most of the area was wilderness. Records showed that the wood was valued at about $12 million but would have cost more than $21 million to harvest. Overall the fires cost $140 million, fourteen times Yellowstone's annual budget.

A SERIES OF REVIEW TEAMS of fire professionals examined the summer's major fires. The early fires likely could have been brought under control, they concluded. The Clover fire, one of the largest, was the most controversial because reviewers argued that the fire could have been controlled had firefighters been on it before July 14. They were saying that had Barbee and Sholly decided to fight the Clover fire the day Sholly saved the Calfee Creek cabin, and followed their own fire plan, they might have stopped one of the season's largest fires, one that had destroyed homes in Wyoming.

Hodel and Secretary of Agriculture Richard E. Lyng appointed a separate Fire Management Policy Review Team to take a big-picture view of the fires. It concluded that the objectives of prescribed natural fire were sound but that the policies needed to be refined to ensure that the fires burn "under pre-determined conditions."[15] The panel was the first of a long line of reviewers continuing into 2004 critical of national forests and parks for having outdated, inadequate fire plans. It also urged fuel reduction around buildings and the creation of firebreaks near developments. Overall the Hodel-Lyng panel and other policymakers recommended that natural and prescribed fires shouldn't be allowed in drought years.

The immediate effects of the fires and the policy reviews stretched far beyond Yellowstone; they essentially stopped prescribed burning throughout the nation until each park or forest brought its plan up to date. That delayed burning on thousands of acres in Florida, the South, and California, where nearly all managers supported it. Overall, it restored the atmosphere long in place in the Forest Service that penalized a manager who allowed a fire to escape. "What the politicians forced us into was that the head guy had to personally guarantee that a fire wouldn't get out of hand," John Varley said.[16]

Surprisingly, despite the shifting policies, Barbee survived and even thrived in the wake of the fires. The media, who had brought so much scorn on both him and the let-burn policy in the middle of the summer, later began reporting "the happy-face fire ecology story." Led by magazines such as *National Geographic* and *Audubon*, writers began telling a familiar story in the context of an old Egyptian myth about a large brilliantly colored bird, the phoenix, that rose from the ashes of its own funeral pyre. Yellowstone's lodgepole pine forest was being reborn, the reports said. It was a pretty good, easy way to tell how fires opened up the lodgepole cones so they could spread seeds on the open soil and grow.

Park officials, however, hated the rebirth story as much as the let-burn stories of August. "In our culture, death is evil," wrote Barbee and Paul Schullery, then a park historian who interpreted the fires and their aftermath along with many of the park's managers and experts. "In the rhetoric of rebirth, Yellowstone has been killed by fires that must, by implication, have been evil too."[17]

The fact is to most of the public the fires had been evil. No matter their ecological implications or the federal government's ability to stop them, the fires destroyed memories, scenes, and places in time cherished by millions of Americans. No matter what Park Service officials said, the fires destroyed a sense of innocence not only in the general public but in the environmental movement as well. Many environmentalists clung to the overall idea that nature knows best. There subsequently came to be a growing recognition that in a world where even the global environment, perhaps even the climate, has been reshaped by humans, a "reasonable illusion" of natural was the best we can hope for.

"As I skied alongside the Madison River, it occurred to me that Yellowstone's values hadn't changed for me," Jim Carrier wrote in November 1988 after the fires finally went out. "Peace, wilderness, endurance, change. The path I skied looked like it did two years ago when I first spent time here. Across the silent river, the woods were burned, the scene black and white. It was still Yellowstone. But I felt a loss. The Yellowstone fires seared away any notion that man could leave nature alone and still run a park around her—a park full of people, a park surrounded by summer homes, tourist businesses, and commercial forests."[18]

Environmental historian William Cronon teased out this idea in the 1990s with a remarkable essay, "The Trouble with Wilderness; or, Getting Back to the Wrong Nature."[19] Wilderness, Cronon wrote, "is quite profoundly a human creation—indeed, the creation of very particular human cultures at particular moments in history. It is not a pristine sanctuary where the last remnant of an untouched, endangered, but still transcendent nature can, for at least a little while longer be encountered without the contaminating taint of civilization. Instead, it is the product of that civilization, and could hardly be contaminated by the very stuff of which it is made."[20]

Curt Meine, an ecologist and writer, had just finished his biography of Aldo Leopold when he drove through Yellowstone in early spring of 1989. He too was initially sobered by what he saw. But when he looked inside the text he had written, the lessons Leopold had learned about fire and humans, he could see that the Yellowstone fires were a transforming event.

"I watched the reactions of people who had grown up in the environmental era," Meine said in a 2004 interview. "They had limited ability to understand the levels of landscape change because neither the pro-environmental forces nor the anti-environmental voices had taken the time to educate themselves how landscapes maintain their own health."[21]

All the spin in the world couldn't make people love fire any more than they could love a tornado, a flood, a hurricane, or a volcano eruption. But they could learn to place it in the realistic concept of their lives on earth. The Yellowstone fires were, for many, the beginning of this lesson at the end of the twentieth century. They reframed the context in which ecosystem or landscape management was debated. Now it was no longer viewed as simply a way to keep human beings as much as possible from disturbing wilderness or wildlife habitat. The fundamental dividing line between preservation and use in the environmental paradigm, in place since the days of Muir and Pinchot and Hetch Hetchy, was broken. Man and nature, civilization and wilderness, could not be separated neatly.

Still, determining what parts of nature humans can control remained an enigmatic challenge and was hardly better understood after 1988 than it had been in 1910 or 1886.

CHAPTER 18

From Old Faithful to Los Alamos

> Everyone thinks that Aldo Leopold was the first one to have
> this idea: "To save every cog and wheel is the first precaution
> of intelligent tinkering." But this idea appears in the ancient
> religious texts, the Bhagavad Gita, the Bible. You can find it in
> the story of Noah's Ark. Life is precious.
>
> —Jack Ward Thomas, *E, The Environmental*
> *Magazine*, April 1994

THE OLD FAITHFUL FIRESTORM would seem like a camp-fire compared to the heat elk biologist Jack Ward Thomas was to attract in the years following the Yellowstone fires. In less than a decade Thomas, as director of the U.S. Forest Service, would reshape the agency that Pinchot created and turn the lessons of Yellowstone into law. For his efforts he would be savagely attacked by partisans from both industry and the environmental community. When he was done, only natural laws and human nature would remain unchanged.

Thomas's arrival on the scene came as the debate over the Yellow-stone fires still had not cooled. Those fires had amplified the rediscov-ery of General Sheridan's concept of a "Greater Yellowstone" and its expansion into the philosophy of landscape or ecosystem management.

By 1988, Thomas was recognized as a leader among the two thou-sand researchers employed by the U.S. Forest Service. The curmud-geonly but nearly always polite and witty Texan rose to such heights in the unlikely path Aldo Leopold had blazed in wildlife management. Born in the Depression in a Texas small town, Thomas graduated from Texas A&M in the 1950s and went to work for the Texas Parks and

Wildlife Department after a stint in the Air Force. There he learned, he said, that managing wildlife "was as much about managing people as critters."[1] He earned a master's degree in wildlife biology and a Ph.D. in forestry and land use planning, and in 1966 he joined the Forest Service as a research biologist. He had worked at a Forest Service experimental station in Massachusetts for some years when, in 1974, he was able to follow his dream to La Grande, Oregon, to head a team of researchers at the Pacific Northwest Forest and Range Experimental Station branch there. He came to Oregon as the Forest Service was becoming more sensitive to the effects of its road building and logging on wildlife. The work of Thomas and other wildlife researchers grew in prominence, especially as environmentalists began challenging concessions and timber sales based on their impacts on wildlife. Researchers helped the agency adjust its practices to reduce impact on wildlife without stopping logging, grazing, and other activities.

In 1989, Thomas was asked by then Forest Service Chief Dale Robertson to head an interagency committee to develop a strategy to protect the northern spotted owl, a creature of the remaining old-growth forests of the Pacific Northwest. The Reagan administration had dramatically increased the harvest of the few remaining old-growth forests of the region, and environmentalists were seeking to stop logging by listing the bird as an endangered species. "Ecosystem management" was still not in the Forest Service's vocabulary. But in Yellowstone, for example, after the devastating fires of 1988, forest supervisors could now see that development of a landscape management plan that crossed jurisdictions could help them address large-scale impacts on the land and wildlife. After all, the fires knew no boundaries, and what happened in the parks, whether it be fire, grizzly bear management, or wolf reintroduction, could limit their options or affect their users. The wisdom of such thinking was becoming more apparent although the word "ecosystem" still sent chills through the bones of loggers, ranchers, and the congressmen who represented them. To them it meant more limits on what they did.

Thomas and his team of sixteen scientists faced a huge challenge. They and everyone else involved, except perhaps some of the thousands of loggers whose jobs were on the line, knew that protecting the owl would force a dramatic reduction in the level of logging over 24 million acres of land in Oregon, Washington, and northern California. They would need a conservation strategy for the bird and the forest that could stand up to the greatest scientific scrutiny and strongest political attack. The ideas behind the strategy were the same as those that underscored the plans for a Greater Yellowstone: Think big, keep wild places wild, and develop corridors to link the habitat. In the end their plan called for 6 million acres of reserves across the three states and strict management between the reserves to preserve enough forest canopy to allow owls to disperse among them. The plan would reduce logging by twenty-five percent on national forests and by thirty to forty percent on lands overseen by the Bureau of Land Management.[2]

When the strategy was announced on April 4, 1990, all hell broke loose. Loggers and their families snaked into Portland, Oregon, by the thousands in logging trucks and chartered buses on April 11 to protest the plan. Mothers cried as television cameras rolled. Northwest senators and officials of the George H. W. Bush administration all decried the plan that, once implemented, they claimed, would shut down timber mills across the region and force up to 100,000 people to lose their jobs. U.S. Senator Bob Packwood of Oregon, long considered a moderate Republican, dismissed the science and even the goal of the committee. "Folks, the owl is not the issue," Packwood said. "If the natural predator of the owl swept in tonight and ate all of the little devils, this issue would not go away. Their goal is no jobs."[3] Thomas himself was privately called arrogant by Northwest senators long used to being themselves in control of timber policy. He was the man on the hot seat, brought before the House Agriculture Committee and grilled for hours by ranking Republican Edward Madigan of Illinois.

"Madigan never asked me to sit down," Thomas said later. "I was at parade rest. He treated us like bugs on a pin."[4] Ecosystem management was proving to carry a high political cost. Still, the plan predicted, spotted owl numbers would continue to drop for years before stabilizing.

Back in Yellowstone, Jack Troyer, the Forest Service's Greater Yellowstone coordinator, and his new partner, Sandra Key, from the

National Park Service, were coordinating the writing of the agencies' Greater Yellowstone Blueprint, a document that they then planned to use to set policy for all of the land managers in the Greater Yellowstone Ecosystem, a term they were beginning to accept. The effort did not carry the same kind of potential economic displacement that the "Thomas Committee's" owl plan had. But it was no less threatening to the ranchers, loggers, miners, and oil and gas explorers around Yellowstone. By recognizing the values of grizzly bears and other wildlife and seeking to limit new roads and other development into wild country, the document, now called the "Yellowstone Vision," seemed aimed directly at their operations in surrounding national forests. In response these user groups helped develop a new movement to take the place of the Sagebrush Rebellion that helped sweep Ronald Reagan into the presidency. This loosely knit mix of ranchers, miners, and mill workers was called the Wise Use Movement, and it tapped directly into the anger many small town westerners shared about the changes they saw in the resource industries on which they depended. They joined organizations such as People for the West and turned out by the hundreds to hearings on the blueprint, now called the "Yellowstone Vision Document." The fires, and the growing battle lines forming over the vision document, also swelled the membership of the Greater Yellowstone Coalition, which supported the document's direction. As the forests turned green with fireweed and seedlings, the fires and the debate over the let-burn policy disappeared from the public consciousness except for the annual covey of rebirth stories during fire season. But the battle over the vision document, wolves, mining, and other issues replaced it.

In 1992, at the behest of Alan Simpson and other western senators, the Bush administration watered down the vision document to be no more than a list of recommended coordinating actions. Environmentalists held Bush's action on the vision document as proof that George Bush had not been the "environmental president" he had promised he would be when he ran in 1988. Now he faced Arkansas governor Bill Clinton in a race for reelection. In the critical states of Oregon and Washington, the battle over the Thomas Plan, spotted owls, and timber jobs was raging. Clinton waded in and made a dramatic promise to wood-working labor leaders. If elected, he would convene a summit among industry, labor, government, environmentalists, and scientists to resolve the issue once and for all.

Meanwhile, Thomas's boss, Forest Service chief Dale Robertson, was following the lead of the Thomas Committee and spreading its ideas to the entire 191 million acres of national forest. Robertson said he would begin to implement a strategy of ecosystem management across the entire Forest Service. "By ecosystem management we mean an ecological approach will be used to achieve the multiple use management of the national forests. It means we will blend the needs of people and environmental values in such a way that the national forests represent diverse, healthy, productive and sustainable ecosystems."[5]

Clinton was elected, and on April 2, 1993, as advertised, he held a Northwest Forest Summit. Thomas's drawling charm and straight talk made him the star of the conference that was heavily covered in the national media. He told the panel a basic truth about ecology that impressed the wonkish Clinton: "The ecosystem is not only more complex than we think; it is more complex than we can think." By the end of the day Thomas had a new job, leading a Forest Ecosystem Management Assessment Team. Clinton gave them ninety days to develop a plan that would meet the requirements of a federal judge who had halted all timber sales in the region. They came up with a plan that would allow 1.2 billion board feet of timber to be cut annually, a far cry from the peak of 9 billion board feet cut in the 1980s. Once again it was known as the "Jack Ward Thomas plan."

As the plan moved through Congress, Clinton himself decided he wanted Thomas as chief of the Forest Service. It would be a stunning move. Thomas would be the first biologist to lead the agency long dominated by foresters and engineers. However, a far more personal issue kept Thomas initially from accepting. His wife, Margaret, had been diagnosed with colon cancer, and since the cancer had already spread to other organs, doctors did not expect her to live beyond eighteen months.[6] Thomas said he couldn't take the job because of Margaret's cancer. When Thomas told his wife of the conversation, she was not pleased that he had not consulted her about his decision. "What will you say when in later years," Thomas quoted her as asking, "you ask yourself if you could have made a difference and we didn't even try?"7

Thomas took the job then and spent his first four months traveling between Washington, D.C., and the West Coast, attempting to broker the deals that would finalize the forest plan and end a crisis that had lasted since soon after the Yellowstone fires went out. In December 1993, two months before Thomas's wife finally succumbed to cancer, U.S. District Judge William Dwyer of Seattle ruled in favor of the Forest Service in the long-standing lawsuit over the spotted owl. Thomas's ecosystem management–based forest plan was now the law of the land. One man's journey from Old Faithful had taken him to the pinnacles of natural resources power in America. Thomas implemented Aldo Leopold's ideas in the agency Pinchot's young man had left. The process that began with Sheridan's Greater Yellowstone movement more than a century before was now complete. Managers of the more than 600 million acres of public land protected because of the army's success at fire fighting in Yellowstone would now look across the boundaries of the lands they controlled to the biological and geological boundaries set by the migrations of fish, wildlife, and even plants. Land management in America was forever changed. And the changes were spreading around the world.

Despite this leadership, the job as head of the Forest Service brought Thomas vicious attacks for his support of limited logging and salvage programs. When he allowed the timber giant Weyerhaeuser and other timber companies to cut timber in spotted owl habitat, environmental writer Jeffrey St. Clair declared: "This concession to corporate America from the father of ecosystem management is the ecological equivalent of infanticide."8

But fire once again crowded its way back on to the national agenda. On July 6, 1994, a fire on Storm King Mountain on the outskirts of Glenwood Springs, Colorado, blew up when winds whipped dry Gambel oak to a frenzy, killing fourteen firefighters. Many of the young men and women killed fleeing the enveloping flames were members of the agency's elite crews of hotshots and smokejumpers. Thomas arrived the next day and immediately began consoling the survivors. He wasn't looking for someone to blame. His mind was drifting back to Old Faithful: "Those memories came back to me when I was at Storm King," Thomas said, "how quick that must have happened and when things went sour how little time anyone had to do anything."9

In the wake of the Yellowstone fires the pendulum had shifted back to a preference for suppression over less aggressive tactics that allowed fire back on the land. Fires were getting bigger and more deadly across the land. Firefighters were giving themselves permission to take more risks. They were returning to their roots, breaking the rules if necessary to battle the fires that were threatening an ever-growing western population moving deeper and deeper into the flammable landscape. Soon after the Storm King deaths Thomas held a meeting with the agency's top firefighting officials at the Wild Land Fire Lessons Learned Center in Marana, Arizona. He told them they would either follow all of the agency's safety rules or quit fighting fires. One veteran fire manager rose up in the back of the room and sneered that such a limit would mean they couldn't realistically fight fires. "I told him he was done fighting fires because I was going to take away his red card," Thomas said.10 Without a red card, a firefighter can't legally fight a fire. The audience was stunned into silence. Then, one man started clapping. Others joined in, and Thomas received a standing ovation.

From that point on fire bosses began routinely to pull firefighters off fires strictly for safety reasons. In some high-elevation forests, managers used the safety policy to allow fires to spread across the landscape, a decision they could never have justified if they said they were letting it burn. For David Alexander, Payette National Forest supervisor in McCall, Idaho, for example, the pressure to throw everything he could on fires there was intense. Fires were burning near-million-dollar lakeside homes around Payette Lake that were owned by many of the most powerful people in Idaho. Fresh in his mind was the memory of McCall smokejumper Jim Thrash, who had died on Storm King. Alexander was going to do what he thought was right. He told firefighters to secure the southern edge of the fires—now moving away from McCall and civilization—to protect human lives and then to protect isolated structures. But no firefighters were placed in the direct path of the conflagration, not even to save cabins and second homes.

Alexander and his fire experts had the collective experience of the

1988 Yellowstone fires behind them. Many of the crew leaders had been Yellowstone firefighters then and they shared the view of Dee Sessions, a safety officer on one of the fires: "You could dump millions and millions of dollars on this fire and it's still going to do what it's going to do. These are just like the Yellowstone fires. They control their own destiny."[11]

Slowly managers gained back their willingness to use prescribed burning, especially in the low-elevation ponderosa pine forests that spread from New Mexico and Arizona north to Montana. The issue of excess fuel, undergrowth that carries fires into the crowns of trees, first discussed by John Wesley Powell, promoted by advocates of light burning such as Thomas Barlow Walker, and proven scientifically by Harold (Harry the Torch) Biswell, was rediscovered by a new generation of fire ecologists such as Wallace Covington at Northern Arizona University and Leon Neuenschwander, professor emeritus at the University of Idaho. They convinced most of the fire establishment that a century of suppression, added to overgrazing of the fine grasses and the selected cutting of the oldest, most valuable ponderosa pines, had left millions of acres of low-elevation forests in the West susceptible to uncharacteristically large fires. The answer was either thinning out thickets of younger trees that grew up because of suppression, or using fire, either prescribed or wildfire, to do the thinning.[12]

The scientists triggered a debate once again between the timber industry and environmentalists over forest management. The timber industry advocated active management—using the tools of logging and the expertise of foresters to thin out forests the way it had done successfully on many of its private forestlands. Environmentalists were distrustful of the industry's intentions and skeptical about renewing logging they had all but stopped on most public lands. They preferred prescribed burning. The debate obscured the potential for ecosystem management to offer both wildlife and watershed protection as well as lumber and fiber from forests. Both sides spun the science the way it best supported their own position. Industry spread the benefits of thinning into all kinds of forest types, no matter the frequency of fire or the burning patterns. Despain, Bill Romme, and a multitude of scientists had demonstrated that fire suppression does not increase the flammability of high-elevation forests. Environmentalists were often quick to ignore the benefits of thinning for ecosystems, urging its use only near communities.

Thomas left the Forest Service in 1996 and was succeeded by another biologist, Michael Dombeck. When Dombeck left at the end of the Clinton administration in 2000 he was succeeded by another biologist, Dale Bosworth. The die had been cast.

Meanwhile, big fires continued regularly after 1988 as the drought in the West hung on. The 2000 fire season once again brought the West's fire debate to center stage nationally. The first fire of the season was started intentionally by National Park Service employees at the Bandelier National Monument near Santa Fe, New Mexico. Prescribed fire had finally become acceptable again, even popular due in part to its promotion by Secretary of the Interior Bruce Babbitt. Spring was the popular season for prescribed burning because generally conditions were dry enough to start and sustain a fire but not so dry that the fire would get out of control.

In Los Alamos, New Mexico, only a few miles away from Bandelier, conditions were unusually hot and dry. But in the ten-thousand-foot-high mountains to the south in Bandelier, the slow melting of the snow pack had prevented park officials from burning throughout March and April. The first week in May was considered the end of the burning window, and on the evening of May 4, firefighters torched grasses and brush on Cerro Grande Mountain, in the northern part of the monument. Their goal was to reestablish an alpine meadow from the encroaching forest. The next morning the fire slipped out of control of the park's firefighters and burned into the Santa Fe National Forest, and it was declared a wildfire. Three days later high winds pushed the 1,900-acre fire into the outskirts of Los Alamos National Laboratory and the town of Los Alamos, where the first atomic bomb was developed and nuclear research continued. Eventually it burned more than six hundred buildings and 47,000 acres and left three hundred families homeless. Superintendent Roy Weaver, a thirty-three-year Park Service veteran, followed Barbee's lead and took full responsibility for the fire. But unlike Barbee, he was placed on administrative leave. The review blamed him and others for poor planning and judgment, a step beyond what reviewers had said about Barbee's 1988 decisions in Yellowstone. Weaver challenged the report as political, an effort to find a scapegoat to protect the prescribed burning program so important to Secretary of the Interior Babbitt.

"I don't want to deny our responsibility for igniting the prescribed fire," Weaver said. "But we did it with a plan that seemed valid and workable. Things happened that we couldn't or didn't anticipate. And that we couldn't control."[13]

Weaver chose to retire, but not before receiving a letter of support from Barbee. He too had finally retired after a six-year stint as Park Service regional director in Alaska.

Cerro Grande, as the Los Alamos fire was called, was just the first of a wildfire season that included large fires in Arizona, California, Colorado, Montana, Idaho, Nevada, Oregon, South Dakota, Utah, Washington, and Wyoming. More than 8 million acres burned nationally, even more than the 7 million acres that burned in 1988. In the Northern Rockies it was the worst fire season since 1910.

Congress acted quickly, authorizing in October 2000 a $1.6 billion package to cover the costs of fighting existing fires, increasing the cache of equipment and people to fight future fires and money for thinning and prescribed burning programs. The immediate result was a huge growth of the fire suppression establishment. Now fire bosses had everything they ever wanted. In 2001, a mild fire season, they used the new resources to meet the fears of westerners, jumping even on fires in wilderness areas. Smokey Bear and pork-barrel politics continued to crowd out science.

Fire bosses used the same tactics in 2002, but even though they were able to snuff out more than ninety-eight percent of the fires reported, huge conflagrations in Colorado and Arizona burned hundreds of homes and threatened dozens of communities. In 2003 California suffered through its worst fire season in thirty years as 750,000 acres and 3,700 homes were burned, killing twenty-four people.

In 2003, Congress approved President George W. Bush's Healthy

Forests Initiative, which increased funding for thinning programs West-wide. But even this ambitious program was expected to make only a dent into the millions of acres of forests that were identified as unusually flammable.

Randal O'Toole has studied the Forest Service the way Despain has examined Yellowstone's vegetation. Using only economics as his tool, the Oregon-based economist helped bring the changes Jack Ward Thomas made to the agency. He showed that the agency was cutting more timber and building more roads than the forest ecosystems could sustain because of its perverse incentive systems. Managers were rewarded when they cut more timber or built more roads even if they lost money, destroyed wildlife habitat, or silted up rivers and streams.

After the 2000 fire season prompted Congress to give the agency $1.6 billion for firefighting, O'Toole saw a new, major shift in the incentive systems. Even though Congress removed Pinchot's 1908 blank-check provision for fire funding in 1978, the years of big fires in the 1990s had brought it back in practice. Each year after the fire season, the Forest Service would simply go to Congress for additional firefighting funds during the big fire years. Now firefighting and presuppression funds and money for prescribed burning and thinning are driving the Forest Service's budget the same way the subsidized road and logging programs did in the 1980s. The spending is necessary, agency officials say, to protect communities near national forests. But O'Toole has found that West-wide only 7 million acres have a high to moderate risk of having wildfires that threaten structures. Of that ninety percent are private land and only eight percent are federal.

IN THE 119 YEARS since Moses Harris's men unsuccessfully tried to put out the first fire they fought in Yellowstone, the federal government had not yet managed to develop a way for Americans to live with wild-land fire. The series of bureaucracies developed in response to fire—the Forest Service, the Bureau of Land Management, and the National Interagency Fire Center—believed itself that it had made the West more dangerous, not less, in the 95 years since 1910. Scientific management—the control of resources by foresters and other professionals shielded from commercialism—had obscured the role of fire in the ecosystem. Ecosystem management was recognizing fire's natural place. But the managers who were following in Thomas's footsteps were finding the concept of ecosystem management no easier to sell to the public than the ecological benefits of the Old Faithful firestorm.

Forest fire and the army's response in Yellowstone had helped create the conservation movement and the modern environmental movement in America. They set in motion a response to fire and nature that would dominate the approach to land management and environmental protection for a century. They had given the National Academy of Sciences the impetus for recommending federal protection of millions of acres of public land. They had justified the creation of huge bureaucracies for managing those lands. They also led to the preservation of parks around the world. Understanding fire helped lead scientists such as Aldo Leopold recognize the workings of ecosystems. Others, such as his son Starker and Jack Ward Thomas, were to wrestle with the limits of human control over fire. From the establishment of campgrounds to the creation of Smokey Bear, our policy toward fire steered the relationship Americans would have with the wildlands that fire had left in their collective hands. But just as a firestorm creates its own weather, forest fires have continued to spawn the conditions necessary for their own continuance. Just like floods, hurricanes, volcanoes, and other natural phenomena, forest fires present humans with cataclysmic forces that are disruptive and painful. We have measured our human progress in part by our ability to control these forces. But our humanity may be found in our ability to live with them.

IN 1993 IN THE MIDWEST, floodwaters from the muddy Mississippi and its tributaries inundated dozens of communities and thousands of acres of farmland. Since 1927, the Army Corps of Engineers has spent more than $25 billion on an elaborate system of locks, levees, dams, and dikes to bring the Mississippi and its tributaries under control. The system was designed to prevent flooding on the scale of the worst flood that had taken place in the previous hundred years, a level of prediction similar to that of fire experts in Yellowstone.

In 1993, however, the combination of runoff and rains raised the rivers higher than ever in the recorded history of the river. The Corps of Engineers levee and dike system may even have made the flooding worse. Since then the Corps has attempted to turn the Mississippi back to a more natural flooding state, in which the surrounding wetlands are used to soak up the rising waters, releasing them slowly and safely. Still, people continue to live in floodplains and face the day when the flood waters return to reach them.

The same is true with fire. Living in a forest or rangeland means living with fire, not stopping it. We can collectively or individually decide where and when we want to take the risks of confronting wildfire. But we don't have the choice of deciding whether to live with the changes it brings. Just as Jack Ward Thomas learned that wildlife management was more about managing people than critters, ecosystem management and fire management may eventually be accepted as mostly about managing people and our willingness to accept change.

Epilogue

> We call all the troops, get them together and do a lot of things.
> When the weather changes, we succeed. So how much do we
> really do?
>
> —Don G. Despain, 2003

I T WAS JUNE 2004 as Don Despain walked through an isolated stretch of sagebrush country in Yellowstone's northern range. He had brought dozens of reporters, cameramen, photographers, sound men, and producers to tour this open expanse of ground that had been burned in 1988. To the untrained observer the ground looked like thousands of miles of sagebrush range throughout the desert West. But to Despain's eyes the soils, grasses, shrubs, and fire scars were like a mathematical formula. They were a story problem he had solved in the years following the fire that defined his career as an ecologist.

"This was all covered in sagebrush with a thick green carpet underneath," he explained, taking himself back to the days before 1988. "It's an area with good soil, thick grass, and little exposed dirt."[1]

Underneath each sagebrush, he said, lies organic material: accumulated twigs, dead grass, and the like. When the North Fork fire burned into the area on September 9, 1988, this material burned even hotter than the surrounding grass. When Despain arrived in 1989 he found "black holes" where the sagebrush had burned, a vivid contrast to the green carpet of grasses already growing back. A closer look reveals the stump of earlier sagebrush plants burned in the blaze, even sixteen years later.

"These were the only places that seeds could get started," he explained, pointing to a former black hole. "The only place sagebrush came back is in those black holes."[2]

He had walked through this same spot and explained the same mystery to journalists in every major fire season since 1988. It was the first stop on what had become to Despain what a reunion tour was to an aging rock band. His audience came to hear the story of Yellowstone's rebirth, Despain's version of his greatest hits. It was yet another summer in the Rockies. Fires were burning out of control somewhere in the West. Television cameras were once again bringing the all too familiar images of conflagration into America's living rooms.

As always the news reports were dominated by reports from the front. They showed yellow-shirted firefighters marching up steep mountains to dig fire lines. Air tankers dropped retardant on raging crown fires. Fearful homeowners evacuated or stood and did what they could to fight impending disaster themselves.

Since 1988, Despain and Yellowstone had become a regular part of the annual journalistic Kabuki show on wildfire. The news programs show flames and the martial images in one segment, then in another return viewers to Yellowstone, where nature is the story. The National Park Service now sends the journalists to other scientists. Despain was transferred to the U.S. Geological Survey—the agency created by John Wesley Powell—in the 1990s during one of the federal government's restructuring programs. But veteran reporters and those who comb the Internet looking for research on Yellowstone's fire ecology are drawn back to Despain, whose work still dominates the field.

Despain doesn't look like a scientific superstar. He doesn't have the ego or the ambition to take center stage. He prefers to argue with himself in a grove of Douglas-fir about his observations than to be the front man for fire ecology. He avoids personal discussions of his life and trials. But he has told the story of Yellowstone's fire cycles to millions of people because, on that subject, he shows the same enthusiasm he had when he watched his plot burn in August 1988.

Despain stopped walking and asked his audience if they noticed any difference. Only steps away from the first area was range with far more sagebrush and less grass. There is a lot of exposed ground. A reporter's first guess was that overgrazing by elk might have encouraged the sagebrush at the expense of grass. Wrong, said Despain.

"The soil right here isn't as good," Despain explained. Without a thick carpet of grass, the sagebrush seeds find many places to grow in the exposed dirt. Differences in soil, not fire or elk, were the determining factor in how these two pieces of range look and are structured. Through one example, he was challenging not only the critics of Yellowstone's natural fire policy, but also critics of its natural regulation policy on which the fire policy is based.

In one area you can predict with precision where each sagebrush will grow, not just in the next few years but after the next fire and on into the next centuries. In the other range nature's random chaos also restores its own continuity. After fifteen years the area looks much as it did before the fire, Despain said. Before white settlers came to this area, it burned every twenty-five to thirty years, he went on. In a lot of ways fire is superficial. The underlying ecosystem has adapted to it. Anything that would be damaged by fire died out a long time ago.

Although Yellowstone's ecosystem had adapted to fire over millions of years of evolution with it, its human inhabitants are only beginning to get used to fire. The sudden changes forced upon those who love Yellowstone were too much for almost anyone to take, save for Despain and a few other fire ecologists. Since 1988, Despain has experienced a comeback nearly as spectacular as the unique ecosystem he studies. But the fire program that was based on his research has not recovered. Even as the role of fire has become generally accepted by most federal land managers, Yellowstone's leaders from Barbee on have been far more careful about when they would allow a fire to burn in the park.

The most obvious case occurred in 2002 when lightning started a fire in the remote backcountry east of Yellowstone's Grand Canyon only a few miles south of where the Clover-Mist fire burned in 1988. Because the prevailing winds were from west to east and huge swaths of past fires limited the potential for its growth, the fire seemed to ideally fit the natural fire policy. But huge fires were burning in Colorado and Arizona, prompting the same political outcry from western politicians that Yellowstone's fires did in 1988. Computer modeling showed that in the worst case the Broad fire, as it was named, might burn to towns thirty miles away in Wyoming or maybe even back to Canyon Village. The Park Service called in a top fire management team, three hundred firefighters, and twelve helicopters, and spent $3.5 million to fight the blaze. It still burned 9,140 acres.

Phil Perkins, Yellowstone's fire management officer, said, "This area does need to burn."[3]

Despain would not make that value judgment. Fire doesn't *need* to burn in Yellowstone, it just does. The ecosystem has dozens, maybe hundreds, or even thousands of different factors that control its destiny. A sagebrush or lodgepole pine growing in a particular spot might be shaped by the precipitation, the nitrogen available, the sunlight, the soil. Inches away conditions can be dramatically different. Or in one day when a fire was burning nearby the wind might last a couple hours and burn through thousands of acres. A slight change in humidity might protect a grove of trees on a north slope. "Just like mathematically you can have more than three dimensions ecologically," Despain said.[4]

Fire continues to dominate management on the public lands it helped to create. The effort and desire to control fire is like every act humans take to protect both the human community and the larger life community that Aldo Leopold identified in his land ethic. Though many debate the role of humans in the larger life community, almost no one suggests we play no role in the fate of the plants and animals with whom we share the earth. The challenge for land managers and for the entire human community is to decide when to take a particular action and when to step aside.

Since before Sheridan rode the stage to Helena, Americans have come west aiming to subdue nature to their will or carry home gold or silver. Men and women worked collectively and individually to rein rivers into canals, turn deserts into gardens, extract minerals from the hills, and remake forests in the image of the engineered groves of Europe. Nature would take the place of fate. Where the soils were rich and the land near water, entrepreneurs and farmers created agricultural Edens. Where gold, silver, copper, and quicksilver were rich and easy to remove, mining communities grew. Forests were cut and grown again as humans replaced the cycle of fire for more than a century.

Some places, such as Yellowstone and millions of acres of wilderness and other national parks, were set aside to preserve their natural values and the sense of the place that pioneers saw when they arrived. Other places remain protected by the barrenness of the soil, their remoteness, or limits set by nature such as steepness, flooding, or harsh climate. Ecosystem management, to the extent that it has become accepted by governing institutions, added new limits on where and when humans can develop. Those limits attributed to nature ultimately are tied to human values for wildlife, wildness, or clean water, or simply to reducing the costs of management.

Despain recalls a time when he and wildlife biologist Doug Houston came upon an antelope while walking through Yellowstone's northern range. When the antelope saw the two men, he didn't bolt as they expected.

"He attacked the bush because he couldn't decide whether to run," Despain said. "Houston called it displacement activity."

This well-known animal behavior pattern occurs when an animal is torn between two conflicting stimuli. In the case of the antelope it was fear and aggression. To Despain, most of the firefighting across public lands is just displacement activity. Our fear of fire coupled with our desire to control forces us to take action. But the quiet ecologist who grew up raising crops on a Wyoming farm looks beyond fire at the issue of what humans do in the name of managing ecosystems. He stops at another piece of rangeland that looks the same as the others. Here, though, park officials had dumped asphalt from road construction years ago. Yet it takes a keen eye to find the tar and gravel blocks now covered by sagebrush and grasses.

When wolves were reintroduced into Yellowstone in 1995, it was considered one of the great environmental success stories of the twentieth century. The wolves had been eliminated by park officials in the 1930s and most biologists believed restoring wolves would reduce the elk herds that critics said were overgrazing the rangeland. Unlike the fire policy, reintroducing wolves took active management steps to accomplish, which in the eyes of many people have paid off. Elk numbers have dropped significantly and aspen, once thought limited by elk, is returning throughout the northern range. Despain isn't so sure wolves are the reason aspen is returning. He's more apt to credit fire.

More significantly, despite his place in the scientific and cultural debate, Despain is neutral on wolf reintroduction. For him it was a matter of human values, not ecological need.

Fire historian Stephen Pyne said the Big Blowup in 1910 became the founding saga of the nation's wildfire-fighting establishment. He waxes poetically and accurately about how the heroism of Ed Pulaski and others became the "Creation saga"[5] for generations of firefighters. The author of the best book about those fires woefully regrets that a new song has not been written to reflect the complex realities of a modern fire culture that includes controlled burning, thinning, and even the practice of letting fires burn, now labeled more pleasingly as fire use.

Pyne rejected the 1988 Yellowstone fires as fodder for such a new narrative. His problem, he said, is that Yellowstone's managers had not prepared the public for the possibility of such large fires. Its natural fire plan predicted far smaller blazes. It didn't follow the plan's own triggers for fighting fire when it allowed the Clover fire to burn after threatening the Calfee Creek cabin. Yellowstone's managers, Pyne said, violated "the social compact."[6] He accepts what remains a persistent myth within the firefighting community itself: Yellowstone's fires could have been stopped or significantly limited had park officials begun suppression immediately. None of the reviews—save perhaps the Clover review—suggest that 1988 in Yellowstone could have been anything but a season of fire of historic proportions, however. Author Micah Morrison, who wrote the most detailed look at the 1988 fires, said the early fires—Red, Shoshone, Fan, and possibly Clover—likely could have been stopped. But those fires that started after July 14—including the largest, the North Fork fire—could not have been stopped.[7] Morrison, a writer for the conservative magazine *The American Spectator*, went into his investigation skeptical of the natural fire policy and still came to those conclusions.

Pyne's strongest aversion to the Yellowstone story is that it reinforced the public's opposition to prescribed burning and suggested that the rebirth story that emerged implied an absolutism—fire is good— equally as simplistic as the "fire is evil" thesis that underscored the suppression policies started by the army in Yellowstone in 1886.[8] On that point Pyne's argument is strongest. For fire is neither good nor bad. It just is. In fact, the suite of natural disasters—floods, hurricanes, drought, or even insect infestations—come unladen with values. Humans insert values in our responses, almost inevitably defensive. Or when we see the opportunity, we react proactively to prevent those forces we believe we have the power to control. When we recognize we can't control the unleashed power of natural forces, such as a tsunami that spreads death and destruction across southern Asia, we consider strategies to stay out of the way. These are basic survival tactics that are not limited to humans. However, we make these choices based on the experiences of each one of us and our larger community.

Yellowstone's fires were the first in a series of giant conflagrations that burned across the West. In 1989, 40,000 acres burned in the Lowman area of the Boise National Forest in three days. In 1990 the Paint fire in southern California burned 648 structures and caused $248 million in damage. The East Bay fire in 1991 burned only 1,600 acres in Oakland, but it killed twenty-five people and injured 150 others, destroyed 3,354 homes, and caused $1.5 billion in damage. In 1992, 150,000 acres burned again in the Boise National Forest's Foothills fire. In 1993, a firestorm raced through southern California near Los Angeles burning 200,000 acres, destroying more than 1,100 structures, killing three people, and costing $1 billion to suppress. The years 2000, 2002, and 2003 were all among the biggest fire seasons since 1910. Part of the problem is that the dominant view of the twentieth century, that we could control fire, led people to build in areas that are inherently unsafe and difficult to protect. Instead of taking the soft path of placing developments in more appropriate areas we have chosen the hard path of trying to defend homes and communities in the natural line of fire. However, something else was going on that was far larger than Yellowstone or the decisions Barbee and others made.

Many blame excess flammable material filling up the woods after decades of fire suppression. But Despain's research clearly showed that in the lodgepole forests that dominate Yellowstone, fire is tied first to weather, climate, and wind. He also has strong evidence that the park's Douglas-fir forests had all but stopped reproducing and were no longer loading up on fuel, for decades before effective fire suppression began. John Burns, the former Targhee National Forest supervisor who was the first to call for fighting fires in Greater Yellowstone in 1988, says the strongest evidence that suppression isn't the culprit is the 1910 fires themselves. No one had been fighting fires on those forests before they burned.

Scientists who have analyzed charcoal deposits in Yellowstone found that the frequency of forest fires in the park is correlated to the level of drought during July for the last 17,000 years.[9] But Despain said the changing climate conditions of the present might make looking back an unreliable predictor of the future. The increase of carbon dioxide in the atmosphere is now accepted by a majority of scientists as the cause of changing climate conditions worldwide. The Forest Service and the Pacific Northwest Climate Impacts Group at the University of Washington said in 2004 that the area burned by wildfires in eleven western states could double by the end of the century if summer climate warms by slightly more than a degree and a half. Montana, Wyoming, and New Mexico are especially sensitive to temperature changes, and fire seasons there may shift more dramatically due to global warming than in states such as California and Nevada, the researchers said.[10] In Montana, the area burned by fires could increase five times over the acres burned from 1970 to 2000.

The effects of global warming on Yellowstone and other places challenges the prevailing view of wilderness advocates before 1988: If we just leave nature alone, it will retain or return to its glory. The evidence that humans have caused these changes forces us to respond as Leopold urged—to protect all of our communities, both human and natural. But the story of our approach to forest fires must give us pause. Will our efforts to reverse our own impacts save the world or be just another round of displacement activity? What will be the unintended consequences of action or inaction?

In 2003, more than 20,000 acres burned in Yellowstone, the most since 1988. Firefighters jumped on twenty-three of the twenty-four fires that started, and only the East fire, near the east entrance, escaped control. Teams of firefighters were brought in to keep it under control too.

But for the first time since 1988, managers were confident enough to steer the fires rather than try to put them out when they were not threatening Fishing Bridge or Lake Yellowstone Hotel. Once again huge columns of smoke rose high into the atmosphere as the fire sucked in the oxygen to drive it through the fuel it needed to stay alive. When the rains came, the fires went out. The firefighters went home, just as they had in 1988.

DESPAIN USUALLY ENDS his walk near Norris Geyser basin, in the blowdown area where the Yellowstone fires burned the hottest, turning blown-down pines into ashes, cooking the soil several inches deep. Here the Park Service still has a sign that explains to visitors the great burn on Black Saturday. It tells them that they can expect to see a meadow for years to come because of the forces of that day. Instead, already a thick forest of 15-foot-high lodgepoles, well spaced and uncrowded, rise naturally from the ash. Despain smiles when he sees the sign. "I told them then I didn't agree."[11] Drive west from Yellowstone through the Targhee National Forest where the clear-cuts that could be seen from space also have come back with much of the same vigor as the burned stands in Yellowstone. Environmentalists suggested in national advertisements that the Targhee was ruined for the ages. Burns, the Targhee's former forest supervisor, shows the same smile as Despain when he remembers their attacks.

The two men have diametrically opposed views of the role of human beings and nature in Yellowstone. Despite the major changes their policies left on the land, Greater Yellowstone lives on, largely intact though with scars and new threats to its integrity, including a growing human population and climate change.

Even though the campfire myth, the creation myth, has been debunked, the power of Yellowstone as a measure of our faith in wild places remains. It is proof that despite all of our sins against the earth and Yellowstone itself, paradise is not lost. The fires of Yellowstone continue to help us to examine our choices about taking action and letting go and finding our proper place in the life community with which we share the earth.

Notes

Chapter 1: The General

1. Sheridan, P. H. *Personal Memoirs of P. H. Sheridan*. New York: Charles L. Webster Co., 1888, vol. 2, 349.

2. Hutton, P. A. *Phil Sheridan and His Army*. Lincoln: University of Nebraska Press, 1985.

3. Hutton, *Phil Sheridan*, 355.

4. Sheridan, *Personal Memoirs*, vol. 1, 5.

5. Ibid., 1–9 to 13.

6. Ibid., 9.

7. Ibid., 156.

8. Ibid., 303.

9. Catton, B. *Grant Takes Command*. Edison, NJ: Castle Books, 2000, 90.

10. Ibid., 216.

11. Ibid., 347.

12. Morris, R., Jr. *Sheridan: The Life and Wars of General Phil Sheridan*. New York: Crown Publishers, 1992, 213.

13. Brown, D. *Bury My Heart at Wounded Knee*. New York: Henry Holt, 1970, 170.

14. Russell, O. *Journal of a Trapper or Nine Years Residence among the Rocky Mountains between the Years of 1834 and 1843*. http://www.xmission. com/~drudy/mtman/html/russell.html. 2004. A general description of the country, climate, rivers, lakes, mountains, etc. and a view of life led by a hunter in those regions. Boise, Idaho: Syms-York, 1914.

15. Arrival of General Sheridan. *Helena Daily Herald*, May 17, 1870, 3.

16. Haines, A. *The Yellowstone Story*, Vol. 1. Yellowstone National Park: Yellowstone Library and Museum Association and University of Colorado Press, 1977, 164.

17. Thoreau, H. D. *Walking*. American Transcendentalism Web. 2004. http://www.vcu.edu/engweb/transcendentalism/authors/thoreau/walkingtext.html.

18. Emerson, R. W. *Essays Second Series (1844) Nature*. American Transcendentalism Web. 2004 http://www.vcu.edu/engweb/transcendentalism/authors/emerson/essays/nature1844.html.

19. Chittenden, H. M. *The Yellowstone National Park*. Norman: University of Oklahoma Press, 1964, 78.

20. Ibid., 79.

21. Sheridan, *Personal Memoirs*, 304.

22. Bonney, O. H., and L. Bonney. *Battle Drums and Geysers*. Chicago: The Swallow Press, 1970, 201.

Chapter 2: Jay Cooke, Nathaniel Langford, and the Northern Pacific

1. Mather, R. E. Henry Plummer Revisited. Originally published in *Wild West Magazine*. The History Net.com. http://www.thehistorynet.com/we/blhenryplummer/index2.html.

2. Trumbore, B. "Jay Cooke: Part 1." http://www.buyandhold.com/bh/en/education/history/2000/jay_cooke1.html.

3. Howe, H. Ottawa County, Ohio History, Part 3. 1898 http://ftp.rootsweb.com/pub/usgenweb/oh/ottawa/history/part3.txt 2004.

4. Draffan, G., and D. Jensen. *Railroads and Clearcuts*. Sandpoint, ID: Keokee Co. Publishing, 1995, 11.

Chapter 3: The Creation Myth

1. Houston, D. "Wildfires in Northern Yellowstone National Park." *Ecology* 54(5), Late Summer 1973, 1114.

2. Nash, R. *Wilderness and the American Mind*. New Haven: Yale University Press, 1973, 110.

3. Schullery, P., and L. Whittlesey. "Yellowstone's Creation Myth." *Montana: The Magazine of Western History*. Spring 2003, 4.

4. Baird, D., and L. Baird. "A Campfire Vision: Establishing the Idaho Primitive Area." *Journal of the West* July 26, 1987, 50.

5. McPhee, J. *Encounters with the Archdruid*. New York: Farrar, Straus & Giroux, 1989.

6. Chittenden, H. M. *The Yellowstone National Park*. Norman: University of Oklahoma Press, 1964.

7. Ibid., 5–6.

8. Langford, N. P. *The Discovery of Yellowstone National Park*. Lincoln: University of Nebraska Press, 1972, 117–118.

9. Haines, A. L. *Yellowstone National Park: Its Exploration and Establishment, Part II*. Washington, D.C.: U.S. Department of the Interior, National Park Service, 1974. http://www.cr.nps.gov/history/online_books/haines1/iee2d.htm.

10. Hampton, H. D. *How the U.S. Cavalry Saved Our National Parks*. Bloomington: Indiana University Press, 1971, 25.

11. Ibid.

12. Lubetkin, J. "The Forgotten Yellowstone Surveying Expeditions of 1871." *Montana: The Magazine of Western History*. Winter 2002, 32–47.

13. Haines, A. L. *Yellowstone National Park: Its Exploration and Establishment, Part III*. Washington, D.C.: U.S. Department of the Interior, National Park Service, 1974. http://www.cr.nps.gov/history/ online_books/haines1/iee3d. htm.

14. Ibid.

Chapter 4: Yellowstone's Preservation Imperiled

1. Haines, A. L. *Yellowstone National Park: Its Exploration and Establishment, Part II*. Washington, D.C.: U.S. Department of the Interior, National Park Service, 1974. http://www.cr.nps.gov/history/online_books/haines1/iee2d. htm.

2. Langford, N. P. Report of the Superintendent of The Yellowstone National Park 1872, 4. http://www.yellowstone-online.com/history/langford/ langford2.html.

3. Ibid.

4. Trumbore, B. "Jay Cooke: Part 3." http://www.buyandhold.com/bh/en /education/history/2000/jay_cooke3.html.

5. Cook, J. *The Border and the Buffalo*. Chicago: R.R. Donnelley and Sons, 1938, 164.

6. Arthun, D., and J. L. Holechek. "The North American Bison." *Rangelands* June 1982, 32.

7. Robbins, J. "Historians Revisit Slaughter on the Plains." *New York Times*. Nov. 16, 1999.

8. Hutton, P. A. *Phil Sheridan and His Army*. Lincoln: University of Nebraska Press, 1985, 246.

9. Reiger, J. F. *American Sportsmen and the Origins of Conservation* 3rd Edition. Corvallis: Oregon State University Press, 2001, 99.

10. Grinnell, G. B. "Report of a Reconnaissance from Carroll, Montana, to Yellowstone National Park and Return," by William Ludlow, U.S. Govt. Print. Off. Washington, D.C. *Zoology* 1876, 640–655.

11. Jacoby, K. *Crimes Against Nature: Squatters, Poachers, Thieves, and the Hidden History of American Conservation*. Berkeley: University of California Press, 2001, 88.

12. Ibid., 86.

13. Hutton, *Phil Sheridan,* 354.

14. Ibid.

15. Ibid., 355.

16. Ibid.

17. Ibid.

18. Hampton, H. D. *How the U.S. Cavalry Saved Our National Parks*. Bloomington: Indiana University Press, 1971, 55.

19. Hutton, P. A. "Phil Sheridan's Crusade for Yellowstone." *American History Illustrated* Oct. 1985, 12.

20. Hampton, *How the U.S. Cavalry Saved Our National Parks*, 61.

21. Ibid., 12.

22. Ibid., 62.

Chapter 5: The Cavalry Rides to Preservation's Rescue

1. Hampton, H. D. *How the U.S. Cavalry Saved Our National Parks*. Bloomington: Indiana University Press, 1971, 63.

2. Wainright, Capt. R. P. P. History of the 1st U.S. Cavalry. Excerpts from *The First Regiment of Cavalry*. http://www.usregulars.com/UScavalry/1us_cav. html.

3. Home of Heros.com. Moses Harris, Congressional Medal of Honor Citation, 1896. http://www.homeofheroes.com/moh/citations_1862_cwh/harris_moses.html.

4. Ibid.

5. Ibid.

6. Hampton, *How the U.S. Cavalry Saved Our National Parks*, 66.

7. Jacoby, K. *Crimes Against Nature: Squatters, Poachers, Thieves, and the Hidden History of American Conservation*. Berkeley: University of California Press, 2001, 118.

8. Hampton, *How the U.S. Cavalry Saved Our National Parks*, 66.

9. Ibid.

10. Pyne, S. J. *Tending Fire*. Island Press, Washington, D.C. 2004, 44.

11. Whitlock, C., S. H. Millspaugh, and P. Bartlein. "Variations in Fire Frequency and Climate over the Past 17,000 Years in Central Yellowstone National Park." *Geology* March 2000, 211–214.

12. Harris, M. Superintendent's Report Yellowstone National Park, Yellowstone National Park Archives, 1886.

13. Harris, M. Superintendent's Report Yellowstone National Park, Yellowstone National Park Archives, 1889.

14. Sargent, C. S. "The Army and the Forests." *Garden and Forest* Sept. 10, 1890, 1.

15. Hampton, *How the U.S. Calvary Saved Our National Parks*, 118.

16. Ibid., 120.

17. Ibid., 121.

18. Ibid.

19. Ibid.

20. Ibid.

21. Ibid.

22. Weber, D. "Fighting Fire with Firepower: Firefighting in Yellowstone National Park 1872–1918." *Yellowstone Science* Summer 2000, 3.

23. Ibid.

24. Muir, J. *The Eight Wilderness Discovery Books*. Seattle: The Mountaineers, 1992, 604.

25. Pinchot, G. *Breaking New Ground*. Seattle: University of Washington Press, 1947, 89. Reissued by Washington, D.C.: Island Press, 1998.

26. Pyne, S. J. *Year of the Fires*. New York: Viking, 2001, 11.

27. Pinchot, *Breaking New Ground*, 89.

28. Muir, *The Eight Wilderness Discovery Books*, 601.

Chapter 6: The Gospel of Fire

1. Pinchot, G. *Breaking New Ground*. Seattle: University of Washington Press, 1947, 103. Reissued by Washington, D.C.: Island Press, 1998.

2. Ibid.

3. Cohen, M. *The Pathless Way: John Muir and the American Wilderness*. Madison: University of Wisconsin Press, 1984, 294.

4. Ibid., 10.

5. Muir, J. *The Eight Wilderness Discovery Books*. Seattle: The Mountaineers, 1992, 191.

6. Miller, C. *Gifford Pinchot and the Making of Modern Environmentalism*. Washington, D.C.: Island Press, 2001, 137.

7. Marsh, G. P. *Man and Nature; or, Physical Geography as Modified by Human Action*. Cambridge, MA: Belknap Press of Harvard University, 1965, 465.

8. Muir, *The Eight Wilderness Discovery Books*, 959.

9. Pinchot, G. "Relations of Forests and Forest Fires." *National Geographic Magazine*, Volume 10, 393–403 (October 1899). http://www.idahoforests.org/fires5.htm.

10. Ibid.

11. Ibid.

12. Muir, *The Eight Wilderness Discovery Books*, 599.

13. Miller, *Gifford Pinchot*, 10.

14. Cutright, P. R. *Theodore Roosevelt The Naturalist*. New York: Harper Brothers, 1956, 116.

15. Bonnicksen, T. M. "Wildfires Should Motivate a New Century of Forest Restoration." *National Policy Analysis*, No. 434, September 2002. http://www.nationalcenter.org/NPA434.html.

16. Cutright, *Theodore Roosevelt*, 170.

17. Koch, E. *Forty Years a Forester*. Missoula, MT: Mountain Press, 1998, 42.

18. Leiberg, J. B. Forest Conditions in the Absaroka Division of the Yellowstone Forest Reserve, Montana, and the Livingston, and Big Timber Quadrangles. U.S. Govt. Print. Off. Geological Survey, 1904, 27.

19. Ibid.

20. Pinchot, G. *The Fight for Conservation*. New York: Doubleday, Page and Co., 1910. http://www.gutenberg.net/1/1/2/3/11238/11238-h/11238-h.htm.

21. Ibid.

Chapter 7: Fire and Rain

1. deBuys, W. *Seeing Things Whole: The Essential John Wesley Powell*. Washington, D.C.: Island Press, 2001, 289.

2. Worster, D. *A River Running West: The Life of John Wesley Powell*. New York: Oxford University Press, 2001, 487.

3. Laskin, D. *Braving the Elements: The Stormy History of American Weather*. New York: Doubleday, 1996, 105–106.

4. Nelson, R. *Public Lands and Private Rights*. Lanham, MD: Rowman & Littlefield, 1995, 18.

5. Fiege, M. *Irrigated Eden: The Making of an Agricultural Landscape in the American West*. Seattle: University of Washington Press, 1999.

6. deBuys, *Seeing Things Whole*, 290.

7. Ibid., 291.

8. Ibid., 292.

9. Sargent, C. S. "Major Powell's Destructive Theories." *Garden and Forest Magazine*. Aug. 13, 1890, 389.

10. Pyne, S. J. *Year of the Fires*. New York: Viking, 2001, 10.

11. Pinchot, G. *Breaking New Ground*. Seattle: University of Washington Press, 1947.

Chapter 8: The Big Blowup

1. Pyne, S. "The Big Blowup." *High Country News*, April 23, 2001. http://www.hcn.org/servlets/hcn.Article?article_id=10428#.

2. Weigle, W. G. "Coeur d'Alene Forest Fire of 1910." *Idaho Historical Society, 18th Biennial Report*. Boise: Idaho Historical Society, 1942, 25–34.

3. Koch, E. *History of the 1910 Fires in Idaho and Western Montana*. U.S. Forest Service, 1942, 2.

4. Pyne, S. J. *Year of the Fires*. New York: Viking Press, 2001, 22.

5. Cohen, S., and D. Miller. *The Big Burn, the Northwest's Forest Fire of 1910*. Missoula, MT: Pictorial Histories Publishing Company, 1978. http://search.tpl.lib.wa.us/unsettling/unsettled.asp?load=Forest+Fire+of+1910&f=disaster/firesfor.10.

6. Pyne, *Year of the Fires*, 116.

7. Brown, W. S. "Fire Prevention and Pre-Suppression." In *History of the Modoc National Forest*. U.S. Forest Service, 1945. http://www.fs.fed.us/r5/modoc/about/history-1945/8b-fire-prevention.shtml.

8. Cohen and Miller, *The Big Burn.*

9. Koch, *History of the 1910 Fires,* 3.

10. Pyne, *Year of the Fires,* 165.

11. Koch, *History of the 1910 Fires,* 3.

12. The Commission on Physical Sciences, Mathematics, and Applications. *The Effects on the Atmosphere of a Major Nuclear Exchange.* Washington, D.C.: National Academies Press, 98.

13. Pulaski, E. Statement in "Coeur d'Alene Forest Fire of 1910," *Idaho Historical Society, 18th Biennial Report.* Boise: Idaho Historical Society, 1942, 25–34.

14. Ibid.

15. Ibid.

16. Ibid.

17. Ibid.

18. Pyne, *Year of the Fires,* 165.

19. Ibid., 166.

20. Pulaski, E. Statement in "Coeur d'Alene Forest Fire of 1910."

Chapter 9: The End of the Trail

1. Koch, E. *History of the 1910 Fires in Idaho and Western Montana.* U.S. Forest Service, 1942, 11.

2. Koch. E. *Forty Years a Forester.* Missoula, MT: Mountain Press, 1998, 93.

3. Ibid., 91.

4. Pyne, S. J. *Year of the Fires.* New York, Viking Press, 2001, 196.

5. Ibid.

6. Ibid.

7. Ibid.

8. Greeley, W. B. *Forests and Men.* Garden City, NY: Doubleday, 1951, 24.

9. Greeley, W. B. "Piute [Paiute] Forestry or the Fallacy of Light Burning." *Timberman,* March 1920, 38–39.

10. Ibid.

11. Clements, F. E. *The Life History of Lodgepole Forests.* U.S. Forest Service Paper No. 79, Washington, D.C., 1910.

12. Peterson, J. "Clash of the Titans." *Evergreen Magazine.* Winter 1994–1995. http://www.idahoforests.org/fires4.htm.

13. Ibid

14. Ibid.

15. Ibid.

16. Ibid.

17. Ibid.

18. Silcox, F. "A Challenge." *Service Bulletin,* Vol. XXI, no. 23, Dec. 13, 1937. http://www.lib.duke.edu/forest/usfscoll/people/Silcox/A_Challenge.pdf.

19. Pyne, S. J. *Fire in America.* Seattle: University of Washington, 1982, 323.

20. Ibid.

21. Miller, C. *Gifford Pinchot and the Making of Modern Environmentalism.* Washington, D.C.: Island Press, 2001, 318.

22. Koch. E. *Forty Years a Forester.* Missoula, MT: Mountain Press, 1998, 189.

23. Ibid., 190.

24. Ibid., 190.

25. Ibid., 191.

26. Ibid., 191.

27. Ibid., 192.

28. Ibid., 194.

29. Ibid., 194.

30. Pyne, *Fire in America,* 279.

31. Ibid., 283.

32. Koch, *Forty Years a Forester,* 196.

Chapter 10: Green Fire

1. Leopold, A. *A Sand County Almanac.* New York: Oxford University Press, 1966, 130.

2. Meine, C. *Aldo Leopold, His Life and Work.* Madison: University of Wisconsin Press, 1988, 99.

3. Lorbiecki, M. *Aldo Leopold: A Fierce Green Fire.* New York: Oxford University Press, 1996, 56.

4. Callicott, J. B., and S. L. Flader. *The River of the Mother of God and Other Essays by Aldo Leopold.* Madison: University of Wisconsin Press, 1991, 69.

5. Callicott and Flader, *The River of the Mother of God,* 115.

6. Ibid., 116.

7. Ibid., 119.

8. Miller, C. *Gifford Pinchot and the Making of Modern Environmentalism.* Washington, D.C.: Island Press, 2001, 339.

9. Ibid., 240.

10. Bradley, N. L. *Good for the Soil, Good for the Soul. The Legacy Lives On.* Washington, D.C.: The Wilderness Society, 1998, 4.

11. Callicott and Flader, *The River of the Mother of God,* 195.

12. Ibid., 182.

13. Ibid.

14. Ibid., 220.

15. Bradley, *Good for the Soil,* 6.

16. Callicott and Flader, *The River of the Mother of God*, 255.

17. Ibid., 298.

18. Ibid.

19. Lorbiecki, *Aldo Leopold,* 178.

20. Ibid.

Chapter 11: The Face of Conservation

1. Miller, C. *Gifford Pinchot and the Making of Modern Environmentalism*. Washington, D.C.: Island Press, 2001, 359.

2. Meine, C. Interview with author. March 13, 2005.

3. Lawter, W. C., Jr. *Smokey Bear 20252: A Biography*. Alexandria, VA: Lindsay Smith Publishers, 31.

4. Ibid., 39.

5. Armstrong, M. *Where There's Smoke, There's Smokey!: A Critical Analysis of 50 Years of Smokey Bear Advertising*. Master's dissertation, University of New Mexico, 2004, 10.

6. U.S. Forest Service. Wildland Fire Statistics. Washington, D.C.: U.S. Department of Agriculture, Forest Service, 1998. http://www.sdi.gov/Curtis/tab 7x17.html.

7. Little, C. E. "Smokey's Revenge." *American Forests*. May/June 1993, 58.

8. Armstrong, *Where There's Smoke*, 17.

Chapter 12: The Natural Revolution

1. Despain, D. Interview with author. January 2003.

2. Barbee, R. Telephone interview with author. July 31, 2004.

3. Rydell, C. H. L. *Aldo Starker Leopold: Wildlife Biologist and Public Policy Maker*. Master's thesis, Montana State University, Bozeman, MT, 1993, 13.

4. Ibid., 18.

5. Ibid., 89.

6. Ibid., 90.

7. Pyne, S. J. *Fire in America*. Seattle: University of Washington Press, 1982, 111.

8. Rydell, *Aldo Starker Leopold,* 91.

9. Ibid., 91.

10. Ibid., 92.

11. DeVoto, B. "Let's Close the National Parks." *Harper's Magazine*. October 1953, 51.

12. Ibid., 52.

13. Chase, A. *Playing God in Yellowstone*. Boston: Atlantic Monthly Press, 1986, 28.

14. Leopold, A. S., S. A. Cain, C. M. Cottam, I. N. Gabrielson, and T. L. Kimball. "Wildlife Management in the National Parks: The Leopold Report."

National Park Service, March 4, 1963. http://www.cr.nps.gov/history/online_books/leopold/leopold4.htm.

15. Ibid., http://www.cr.nps.gov/history/online_books/leopold/leopold4.htm.

16. Ibid., http://www.cr.nps.gov/history/online_books/leopold/leopold6.htm.

17. Barbee, interview with author, 2004.

18. Ibid.

19. National Park Service, "Administrative Policies for Natural Areas, 1968." *America's National Park System.* National Park Service, 1968. http://www.cr.nps.gov/history/online_books/anps/anps_6j.htm.

20. Barbee, interview.

21. Meagher, M. Interview with author, August 3, 2004.

22. National Park Service, 1968. http://www.cr.nps.gov/history/online_books/anps/anps_6j.htm.

23. Sellers, R. E., and D. G. Despain. "Fire Management in Yellowstone National Park." *Proceedings, Tall Timbers Fire Ecology Conference and Intermountain Fire Research Council and Land Management Symposium.* Tallahassee, FL: Tall Timbers Research Station, 1976, 108.

24. Schullery, P. Interview with author, June 24, 2004.

25. Barbee, interview.

26. Rydell, *Aldo Starker Leopold,* 311.

27. Ibid., 312.

Chapter 13: Greater Yellowstone Rediscovered

1. Craighead, F. C. *Track of the Grizzly.* San Francisco: Sierra Club Books, 1979, 261.

2. Reese, R. *Greater Yellowstone: The National Park and Adjacent Wildlands.* Helena, MT: American and World Geographic Publishing, 1991, 4.

3. Maughan, R. Interview with author, 2004.

3. Chase, A. *Playing God in Yellowstone.* Boston: Atlantic Monthly Press, 1986, 364.

4. Hutton, P. A. "Phil Sheridan's Crusade for Yellowstone." *American History Illustrated* 19(10), 1985, 12.

5. Koon, C. "Fremont Opposes Park Buffer." *Idaho Falls Post Register.* October 15, 1985, 1.

6. Freemuth, J. *Islands Under Siege: National Parks and the Politics of External Threats.* Lawrence: University Press of Kansas, 1991, 30–31.

7. Barker, R. "Reports Scrutinize Yellowstone Area." *Idaho Falls Post Register.* May 29, 1987, 1.

8. Barker, R. "Grand Experiment or Benign Neglect?" *Idaho Falls Post Register.* July 13, 1986, 1.

9. Chase, *Playing God in Yellowstone,* 318.

10. Mott, W. P. Remarks to Greater Yellowstone Coalition. May 30, 1987. Bozeman, MT.

Chapter 14: Calm before the Storm

1. Barker, R. "National Park Managers Exhorted to Take Risks." *Idaho Falls Post Register.* June 2, 1988, 1.
2. Ibid.
3. Barker, R. "Yellowstone: Nature Renews Itself with a Vengeance." *Idaho Falls Post Register.* October 17, 1988, C2.
4. Burns, J., to R. Barbee. July 12, 1988. Targhee National Forest files.
5. Kingwill, F. Interview with author, 1988.
6. Romme, W. H., and D. G. Despain. "Historical Perspective on the Yellowstone Fires of 1988." *Bioscience* 39(10), 1989, 695–699.

Chapter 15: The Fires of Summer

1. Sholly, D. R., and S. M. Newman. *Guardians of Yellowstone.* New York: William Morrow & Co., 1991, 210.
2. Morrison, M. *Fire in Paradise.* New York: HarperCollins, 1993, 13.
3. Barbee, R. Interview with author, 2003.
4. Barker, R. "Fires in Wyoming Grow." *Idaho Falls Post Register.* July 17, 1988, 1.
5. Lewis, E. *The View from Greater Yellowstone. Greater Yellowstone Report.* Greater Yellowstone Coalition. Summer 1988, 3. Bozeman, MT.
6. Barker, R. "Yellowstone: Nature Renews Itself with a Vengeance." *Idaho Falls Post Register.* October 17, 1988, C4.
7. Morrison, *Fire in Paradise,* 93.

Chapter 16: Burn, Baby, Burn

1. Rothermel, R. Interview with author, 1988.
2. Ekey, B. Interview with author, February 2003.
3. Ekey, B. "Yellowstone on Fire." *Billings Gazette,* Billings, MT, 1989, 19.
4. Carrier, J. Interview with author, 2003.
5. Barker, R. "New Team Takes over Park Fire." *Idaho Falls Post Register.* September 1, 1988, 1.
6. Barbee, R. Interview with author, 2003.
7. Associated Press. "Yellowstone Fires Grow." *Livingston Enterprise,* Livingston, MT. August 23, 1988, 1.
8. Carrier, J. "Burn, Baby, Burn." *Denver Post.* August 28, 1988, 13A.
9. Carrier, J. Interview with author, 2003.

Chapter 17: Moment of Truth

1. NBC News staff. *NBC Nightly News* transcript. September 7, 1988.

2. Sholly, D., and S. Newman. *Guardians of Yellowstone*. New York: William Morrow & Co., 1991, 230.

3. Wilkinson, T. "The Siege at Old Faithful." *Jackson Hole News*. September 14, 1988, 11.

4. Evans, J. Interview with author, 1988.

5. McKinney, H. Interview with author, 2004.

6. Youngblood, G. Interview with author, 2003.

7. McKinney, H. Interview with author, 2004.

8. Thomas, J. W. Telephone interview with author, 2003.

9. Ibid.

10. Strasser, P. Interviews with author, 1988, 2003.

11. Ibid.

12. Wilkinson, T. "The Siege of Old Faithful." *Jackson Hole News*. September 14, 1988, 11.

13. Varley, J. Interview with author, 1988.

14. Despain, D. Interview with author, 2004.

15. Fire Management Policy Review Team. *Report on Fire Management Policy. Departments of Agriculture and Interior.* December 14, 1988, i.

16. Varley, J. Interview with author, January 2003.

17. Barbee, R., and P. Schullery. "Yellowstone: The Smoke Clears." *National Parks*, March–April, 1989.

18. Carrier, J. "Old Soldiers Relive War, Mourn Lost Ideal." *Denver Post*. November 20, 1988, 1.

19. Cronon, W. "The Trouble with Wilderness; or, Getting Back to the Wrong Nature." In *Uncommon Ground: Rethinking the Human Place in Nature*, edited by W. Cronon. New York: W.W. Norton, 1996, 69.

20. Ibid., 69.

21. Meine, C. Telephone interviews with author, 2004–2005.

Chapter 18: From Old Faithful to Los Alamos

1. Thomas, J. W. Interview with author, 2003.

2. Durbin, K., *Tree Huggers: Victory, Defeat and Renewal in the Northwest Ancient Forest Campaign*. Seattle: The Mountaineers, 1996, 117.

3. Ibid., 120.

4. Ibid., 121.

5. Barker, R. *Saving All the Parts*. Washington, D.C.: Island Press, 1993, 241.

6. Thomas, J. W., and H. K. Steen. *The Journals of a Forest Service Chief*. Forest History Society. Seattle: The University of Washington Press, 2004, 54.

7. Ibid., 55.

8. St. Clair, J. "Meditations in Green." *Wild Forest Review*. January/February 1994. Portland, OR: Save the West, 6.

9. Thomas, J. W. Interview with author, 2003.

10. Ibid.

11. Sessions, D. Interview with author, 1994.

12. Covington, W. W. 1994. "Post-Settlement Changes in Natural Fire Regimes and Forest Structure: Ecological Restoration of Old-Growth Ponderosa Pine Forests." *Journal of Sustainable Forestry* 2, 153–181.

13. Easthouse, K. "Scapegoat." *Forest Magazine*. May/June 2001. http://www.fseee.org/forestmag/0103eastscape.shtml.

Epilogue

1. Despain, D. Interview with author, 2004.

2. Ibid., 1994.

3. Ring, R. "A Losing Battle." *High Country News*. May 26, 2003, 11.

4. Despain, D. Interview with author, 2004.

5. Pyne, S. *Firechasing*. Tucson: University of Arizona Press, 2003, 147.

6. Pyne, S. *Tending Fire*. Uncorrected proof. Washington, D.C.: Island Press, 2004, 81.

7. Morrison, M. *Fire in Paradise*. New York: HarperCollins Publishers, 1993, 216.

8. Pyne, *Tending Fire*, 81.

9. Whitlock, C., S. H. Millspaugh, and P. Bartlein. "Variations in Fire Frequency and Climate over the Past 17,000 Years in Central Yellowstone National Park." *Geology*, March 2000, 211–214.

10. McKenzie, D., P. Mote, D. Peterson, Z. Gedalof. "Climatic Change, Wildfire, and Conservation." *Conservation Biology*, August 2004.

11. Despain, D. Interview with author, 2004.

Acknowledgments

Scorched Earth began as I recovered from the traumatic shock of covering the Yellowstone fires in 1988.

I already had planned a sabbatical from my regular job in 2003 as environmental reporter with the *Idaho Statesman*, thanks to a visiting fellowship offered to me by the Andrus Center for Public Policy and funded by the Hewlett Foundation. The center, led by former Idaho governor and interior secretary Cecil Andrus, had collaborated in 2000 with the *Idaho Statesman* to put on a successful conference, The Fires Next Time, which addressed many of the controversial issues surrounding western fire policy.

It was Rob Robertson, my literary agent, who convinced me to expand my research, to go beyond the stories, debates, and focus of the 1988 fires. He nudged and prodded me to look back at the beginning of Yellowstone, at the early acts and decisions that set the stage for 1988.

The more I studied, the more I realized some of the best stories, some of the more important decisions, came long before 1988. I began to follow the paths of historian Paul Andrew Hutton, who rediscovered in the 1980s the critical role General Phil Sheridan played in Yellowstone's early days; of Duane Hampton, who demonstrated how the U.S. Army saved the national parks; of John Reiger, the biographer of George Bird Grinnell; and of course, of Yellowstone's finest, Aubrey Haines and Paul Schullery.

Then there was Stephen Pyne. The fact is that Pyne dominates the fire field so well one cannot help but walk in his footsteps. I first met Pyne when he was the keynote speaker for the fire conference in 2000. There he told us of the 1910 fire saga and expressed his discontent that a new story had not come along to replace the one based on Ed Pulaski and his tool. He urged someone to come forward and write that story.

Pyne's call became my goal. I would make the Yellowstone story the new fire story, I said to myself and anyone who would listen. But the

263

more I studied, the more I realized the story wasn't about the modern fire saga. Fire and Yellowstone had played a far larger role in the development of the conservation and environmental movements than I believe most people realized. This led me into new recognition of Gifford Pinchot's critical place in the modern environmental movement provided by Char Miller, the rediscovery of Powell's views on fire provided by Pyne and William deBuys, the wonderful story of Elers Koch, and the multidimensional picture of Aldo Leopold captured by Curt Meine, and others. Carol Henrietta Leigh Rydell's master's thesis (Montana State University) on Aldo Starker Leopold, which showed how he transformed his father's ideas into public policy, filled in an important part of history that was critical to my story.

I must thank Don Despain, Jack Ward Thomas, and Robert Barbee for the time and patience they shared as they helped walk me through their own stories of 1988 and beyond. Bob and his wife, Carol, graciously put me up in their home as we talked through the old war stories we shared from 1988. Don and I had walked through Yellowstone's forests several times before we took a day in June 2004 that became the basis for the epilogue. Marsha Karle and Cheryl Matthews, who carried the heavy burden of fielding journalists' requests and translating Yellowstone's policies and wonders to the world, have done so much for me over the years that I can never repay them. Joan Anzelmo and Amy Vanderbilt, who led the same effort in 1988, also have continued to demonstrate the highest level of government service in their park service roles. John Varley and Mary Meagher gave me critical bits of information. Paul Schullery offered several hours of his time to listen to the thesis of the book, provided valuable insights, and pointed me to Rydell's work. Lee Whittlesey and others at the Yellowstone archives helped me go through the records. When they were closed, Hal Rothman generously shared copies of several key reports on the army in Yellowstone. Judy Austin helped me find sources on the Corrine to Helena trail.

Three journalists, Bob Ekey, Todd Wilkinson, and Scott McMillion, were tough competitors who shared their stories that ended up in places in the book. Cathy Koon and Robert Bower of the *Idaho Falls Post Register* also aided my research. Jim Carrier saved my life at Old Faithful that fateful day in September 1988 when he told me to run.

John Freemuth, the senior fellow at the Andrus Center and a student of professor Philip Foss at Colorado State University, has guided me in my advanced education of political science and public policy. He listened and critiqued as I was developing the story line of this book. We also co-wrote a white paper on fire for the Andrus Center with Marc Johnson that helped shape my thoughts about modern fire issues. My colleague Dan Popkey at the *Idaho Statesman* generously agreed to read my manuscript before I submitted it to my editors. Char Miller, author of *Gifford Pinchot and the Making of Modern Environmentalism*, also read my manuscript and offered excellent advice for changes. Julianne L. Newton read the chapter on Aldo Leopold, and Ron Cogswell read the Civil War chapters. Both readers' comments made the book better. I also want to thank Kent Shifferd, professor emeritus of history and peace studies at Northland College, for igniting my interest in environmental history.

Several editors deserve canonization for putting up with me over the years. Bill Hathaway, my editor at the *Post Register* in 1988, tried to make me stay a quarter-mile away from the fires and tried to make me come home. Jerry Brady made it possible for me to develop the *Post Register*'s first Web site, which was long the home of my early Internet account of the fires. Carolyn Washburn, executive editor of the *Idaho Statesman*, allowed me to take six months off in 2002 and 2003 to do the initial primary research for this book. She also encouraged my continuing role with the *Idaho Statesman* and the Andrus Center in sponsoring conferences, including a second fire conference in 2004.

Clareene Wherry at the Andrus Center was a collaborator and editor who kept me on task but free to conduct research during my sabbatical. Jonathan Cobb's enthusiastic support as my Island Press editor gave me faith when I needed it. His collaboration made the book far better than when he first saw it.

But no one deserves more credit for the success of this book than my wife, Tina, and my children, Daniel, David, and Nichole. Tina suffered long through my absences during the 1988 fires. When I once again decided to write a book, mostly on my family's time, she sacrificed again, picking up the added load in the household and patiently listening as I thought out loud what I was going to write. I can never give her back all I have taken.

Index

About the Author

As a reporter first for the *Idaho Falls Post Register* and now for the *Idaho Statesman*, Rocky Barker has covered fires across the West for many years and has written about environmental issues ranging from mining in Wisconsin, acid rain in Canada, and rain forest protection in Hawaii, to fish and wildlife conservation in Russia's Far East and in Africa. He is a contributor to National Public Radio's *Living on Earth* program and syndicated as a columnist in more than seventy newspapers by Writers on the Range, a service of *High Country News* that he cofounded.

Barker is the author of *Saving All the Parts: Reconciling Economics and the Endangered Species Act* (Island Press, 1993), a finalist for the Sigurd F. Olson Nature Writing Award. He has contributed chapters to *Living in the Runaway West* (2000), *The Next West* (1997), and *Writers on the Range* (1998), and has coauthored, with Ken Retallic, *Flyfisher's Guide to Idaho* and *Wingshooter's Guide to Idaho* (1996). The National Wildlife Federation awarded him its National Conservation Achievement Award in 1999.